MW00399665

RELIGION ON
THE BATTLEFIELD

RELIGION ON
THE BATTLEFIELD

RON E. HASSNER

CORNELL UNIVERSITY PRESS
Ithaca and London

First published 2016 by Cornell University Press

Printed in the United States of America

Library of Congress Cataloging-in-Publication Data

Names: Hassner, Ron E. (Ron Eduard), author.
Title: Religion on the battlefield / Ron E. Hassner.
Description: Ithaca : Cornell University Press, 2016. |
    Includes bibliographical references and index.
Identifiers: LCCN 2015045361 | ISBN 9780801451072
    (cloth : alk. paper)
Subjects: LCSH: War—Religious aspects. | Soldiers—
    Religious life.
Classification: LCC BL65.W2 H38 2016 | DDC 201/
    .7273—dc23
LC record available at http://lccn.loc.gov/2015045361

Cornell University Press strives to use environmentally responsible suppliers and materials to the fullest extent possible in the publishing of its books. Such materials include vegetable-based, low-VOC inks and acid-free papers that are recycled, totally chlorine-free, or partly composed of nonwood fibers. For further information, visit our website at www.cornellpress.cornell.edu.

Cloth printing   10 9 8 7 6 5 4 3 2 1

For Laura

CONTENTS

1. Why? Religion as a Cause of War   1

2. When? Sacred Time and War   29

3. Where? Sacred Space and War   52

4. Who? Sacred Leaders and War   87

5. How? Sacred Rituals and War   110

6. Religion on the Battlefield in Iraq,
   2003–2009   135

Acknowledgments   161

Notes   165

Index   217

RELIGION ON
THE BATTLEFIELD

CHAPTER 1

Why?

Religion as a Cause of War

How does religion shape the modern battlefield? In the following pages, I argue that religion acts as a force multiplier, both enabling and constraining military operations. This is true not only for insurgents and terrorists motivated by radical religious ideas but also for professional soldiers, including contemporary U.S. soldiers, who have to contend with religion as a constant feature of their landscape. Like other environmental factors, such as topography or climate, religion relentlessly affects the calculus of war. And, as with these other factors, combatants have learned to adapt and even exploit the attributes of religion to their advantage. In the last century, religion has influenced the timing of attacks, the selection of targets for assault, the zeal with which units execute their mission, and the ability of individual soldiers to face the challenges of war. Religious ideas have not provided the reasons why conventional militaries fight—but religious practices have influenced their ability to do so effectively. The religion of our soldiers has served to motivate or inhibit combat. The religion of our opponents has created opportunities for exploitation and temptations for overexploitation, prompting backlash.

This is not a book about fanatic insurgents or Islamic suicide bombers. Unlike recent scholars of religion and war, I am not interested in how extreme religious ideas propel individuals into battle. My interests lie in everyday religious practices: the prayers, rituals, fasts, and feasts of the common religious practitioners who make up the bulk of the adversaries, bystanders, and observers in twentieth-century wars. To show that religious practices have influenced battlefield decision making, even in the absence of fundamentalism and radicalism, I draw most of the examples in this book from major wars between Western militaries. We do not need to fall back on ethnic or sectarian conflicts, wars of religion or wars for religious ends, to show that religion influences war. Instead, I focus on hard cases—modern, rational, and bureaucratized military organizations conducting conventional warfare—to show that, even under conditions that favor rational combat, religion has to be taken into account.

My goal in this introductory chapter is fourfold. First, I briefly review the existing literature on religion and war. I show that it has privileged the question of motivation—the "why" question about religion as a cause of war—at the expense of a wide range of alternative questions we might ask about religion and the shape of war, questions such as "when," "where," "who," and "how." It is questions such as these that I begin to address in this book. Second, I outline my approach to religion, which centers on practices relating to the sacred. In the third section, I exemplify this practice-centered approach by exploring the puzzling pattern of combat deaths among British chaplains in World War I. In the fourth section, I turn to the lessons that scholars and practitioners of international security might draw from this volume. I explore the four primary effects that a particular religious setting can have on a military organization or its target. Two of these effects, which I call *motivation* and *exploitation*, are force multipliers; the other two, *inhibition* and *provocation*, are force dividers. I illustrate several of these effects at work in a brief study of the Allied bombing of the Monte Cassino Abbey in World War II.

The ensuing chapters in this book explore the two force-multiplying and two force-dividing effects of religion in four religious-issue areas—sacred time, sacred space, sacred authority, and sacred rituals—corresponding to the questions "when," "where," "who," and "how," respectively. In the concluding chapter, I turn to the recent counterinsurgency campaign in Iraq to show that religious practices play their force-multiplying role, with yet greater force, in that more familiar setting.

Scholars of international relations conceive of religion as a deviant and irrational set of ideas that propel radical nonstate actors into conflict. To use the language of social constructivists, scholars have emphasized the constitutive effects of religion at the expense of its regulative effects.[1] The alternative, I suggest, is to envision religion as a common and pervasive background condition that shapes not just the mind-set of combatants but also their actions. This is true for secular as well as religious combatants, be they nonstate violent actors or conventional military forces. Studying religion and violence cannot just mean studying other people's religion and other people's violence. It must also include studying the day-to-day religion of our soldiers and its effects on combat operations.

What Do We Know about Religion and War?

The study of religion and war—once a minor preoccupation of political scientists—boomed in the 1990s and skyrocketed at the start of the new millennium.[2] The number of books under this subject heading in the Library of Congress catalog has expanded from two or three books per year in the late twentieth century to an average of fourteen books per year since 9/11. More books have been published on Islam and war since 2001 than in all of human history prior to 2001.[3] Further, over 80 percent of articles published on religion in international relations journals appeared after this watershed moment. The prominent journal *International Security* now publishes three times as many articles with references to religion as it did in the 1970s or 1980s.[4]

This sudden surge of interest is attributable to world events, starting with the Yugoslav civil war and culminating with U.S. incursions into Afghanistan and Iraq. But it can also be traced, in no small part, to the popularity of Samuel Huntington's work on religion, to this day the most widely cited academic source on the topic.[5] This historical and academic setting helps explain the preoccupation of analysts with understanding the causes, as opposed to the characteristics, of religious conflict and with locating those causes in religious ideas rather than in religious practices.

Since the end of the Cold War, political scientists have relied on religion to answer one pressing question about war: Why? The answer, provided by Huntington and his followers, is that clashing religious identities provide an inevitable source of conflict. Huntington cared little about the roots of these religious identities. For example, he dedicates less than one page of *The Clash of Civilizations* to highlighting some of the differences between Christianity ("separate realms of God and Caesar") and Islam ("a religion of the sword"), reducing both religions to a simplistic version of their formal beliefs.[6] This attitude helped to reinforce the scholarly disinterest in informal religious ideas, practices, symbols, or social structures, seen as irrelevant to the study of international conflict. I fell into this conceptual trap myself in much of my prior work, which emphasized how ideas about sacred space cause conflict rather than exploring how the wide range of religious practices surrounding sacred space can both motivate and constrain violence.[7]

In its emphasis on formal theologies, the new scholarship on clashes of religion mirrors the only other research tradition on religion and international relations: the study of ethics of war. Like their Huntingtonian counterparts, scholars of just war theory and religious pacifism explore how lofty religious ideas, captured in sacred scriptures and medieval scholasticism, reflect on war. They too have little interest in how these abstract religious ideas affect what religious practitioners actually believe, let alone do. It is startling to see in some of the most influential analyses of Jewish, Christian, and Muslims laws of war how much emphasis is placed on the ancient origins of idealized principles and how little emphasis is placed on their actual impact on contemporary conflict. These scholars offer many examples of how religious ideas could constrain war but offer no evidence that soldiers are, in fact, constrained by religious ideas about justice and war.[8]

Indeed, Huntington's proposal that differences in religious identity suffice to explain conflict led many scholars to forgo the study of religious ideas altogether. In these often rationalist analyses, religion is seen as a proxy or cover for some other set of interests or strategies.[9] For if religion is little more than an identity tag, and all groups separated by religious difference—regardless of kind or scope—are locked in perpetual conflict, what use is there in studying the effects of particular religious ideas, let alone religious practices, at any length? The "why" question of religion as a cause of war can be reduced to a proposition about religious identities: states tagged "Muslim" are more likely to wage war against states tagged "not Muslim," and the same holds for the relations between "Confucian states" and "Shinto states."[10]

This research trajectory has yielded contradictory and ultimately disappointing findings. Whereas most scholars have refuted Huntington's claims, others have confirmed them.[11] Whereas some have found that differences in religious identity between groups are a key contributor to civil wars, other prominent scholars have rejected the ethnic or religious root of these conflicts.[12] Scholars have also been unable to reach an agreement on whether religious conflicts are deadlier than nonreligious conflicts.[13] Some claim that Muslim actors are disproportionately involved in civil wars; others provide evidence to the contrary.[14]

Why have studies of religion as a cause of war yielded such incongruous findings? The problem, in part, has to do with the fixation on religious identity as a stand-in for religion. Most of the state and nonstate actors that participate in conflict have no obvious religious identities. Scholars have felt the need to assign crisp identities to the participants in conflict but have been unable to agree on which indicators to use, let alone how to quantify these. Some scholars have relied on the religious identity of the majority of

individual members, others have sought clues to religious identity in founding documents and laws, and yet others have used the religious affiliation
of leaders as a proxy.[15] Each option presents significant drawbacks (consider how differently the United States would be coded in each case), but
none comes close to capturing "religiosity," arguably the most intuitive way
of conceiving of religious identity. These myriad ways of operationalizing
religion have also had the unfortunate effect of reinforcing a circular logic:
once scholars have assigned crude religious identity tags to all international
actors, they can code all conflicts that involved actors with disparate religious
identities as "religious conflicts," making it even easier to claim that religion
is a prominent cause of war.[16]

Another possible reason for the limited success of this path of inquiry is
that religion is simply not a prominent cause of war. Contrary to widespread
impressions outside academia, most scholars of international conflict have
sought the causes of modern wars elsewhere. Indeed, religion may never
have provided a primary reason for conflict, not even during the Crusades
or the so-called wars of religion.[17] Several terrorist organizations and some
insurgent groups brandish religious symbols and proclaim religious grievances and goals, sincerely or otherwise. But the majority of violent actors in
the international arena are driven to war in a quest for security, territory, and
resources, as the international relations literature has established very clearly.
Religion influences and shapes war, as I show throughout this book, but states
and would-be-state actors have far more concrete priorities in mind when
they launch costly conflicts.

The fixation on religion as a cause of conflict continues unabated, thanks
in large part to the events of 9/11. Huntington had already singled out
Islam as the most war-prone of all "civilizations." Al Qaeda's attacks on the
United States evinced a preoccupation with Islam that manifested in both
academia and the popular media. The *New York Times*, for example, tripled
its references to Islam after 9/11 and usually mentioned it in the context of
extremism, terrorism, and insurgency. The journal *International Security* now
publishes more articles on Islam than on Judaism, Christianity, Hinduism,
and Buddhism combined.[18] The statements and actions of Muslim insurgents
and terrorists seem to provide the hard evidence needed to back up the claim
that religion is a core cause of nonstate violence.

I do not wish to weigh in for or against that claim in this book; I merely
wish to point out that the emphasis on conflicts involving radical Islamic
nonstate actors has come at the expense of exploring the wide range of other
conflicts involving other religious actors, radical and moderate, Muslim and
non-Muslim. These cases far outnumber, in quantity and scope, the subset

of cases involving Muslim extremists. The fixation with radical Islam has also had the disadvantage of shifting the scholarly emphasis onto a particular subset of religious ideas: extremist ideas about martyrdom, suicide bombing, and terrorism that propel individuals to take violent action. These ideas are influential in certain settings, but they are unrepresentative of the wide range of ideas across world religions that motivate and constrain the use of force. Because all religious ideas combined represent a very small slice of the discourses, symbols, rituals, and experiences that religion offers its practitioners, an undue emphasis on radical religious ideas paints a truly distorting picture of religion on the battlefield.

In sum, the research on religion and conflict suffers from four blind spots. First, the focus on religion as a cause of war risks obscuring how religion can shape the meaning, nature, and outcomes of wars. Second, it overemphasizes religious identities as the primary drivers of conflict. Third, it has rooted these identities in formal religious ideas, gleaned from sacred texts, as opposed to religious practices. And, fourth, the contemporary association of a particular brand of Islam with a temporary trend in global terrorism has led to an overemphasis on particular extremist religious ideas. This, in turn, has placed the religion of insurgents and terrorists in the spotlight at the expense of the religion of professional military forces.

These four biases are interrelated. Because few religious ideas, let alone religious practices, provoke conflict, an interest in religion as a cause of war has meant a focus on an idiosyncratic subset of religious ideas. Because these extreme ideas are held primarily by Islamic insurgents and terrorists, analysts have shied away from exploring how religious practices affect states, Muslim or otherwise. Because the religious practices of soldiers and militaries do not motivate their participation in conflict, scholars have missed the impact of religion on other aspects of war, including the nature of fighting after the war has begun.

Objectives

In this book, I seek to correct for these biases in four ways. First, on the religious side of the equation, I expand the conceptualization of religion beyond theology or belief. By conceiving of religion as a lived system of symbols and practices, I account for informal as well as formal beliefs, religious ideas, rituals, social structures, and discourses. The religious ideas inside the heads of actors are important, but what these actors actually do with these ideas should matter no less. It does not require tremendous familiarity with religion to know that, just as with political ideas and identities, there are often tremendous gaps separating the formal principles, how individuals interpret those principles, and how they implement those principles in practice. Certainly, religious ideas and religious identities matter: they can provide motivation for certain wars and provide overarching meaning for other wars. Our studies of the effects of religious ideas and identities are far from complete, but they are not the focus of this volume. The study of religious ideas as constitutive of conflict ought to be supplemented with a study of religious practices as regulative of conflict. This volume explores how religion affects combat, even in the absence of motivating religious ideas and identity cleavages.

For example, U.S. military operations in Afghanistan and Iraq were not motivated by religious principles. By no stretch of the imagination were these wars of religion, wars because of religion, or wars launched to achieve religious goals. Nonetheless, the prevalence of religious beliefs and practices among U.S. troops, Muslim insurgents, local noncombatants, and regional observers shaped and constrained U.S. decision making on the battlefield. U.S. troops have had to contend with the effects of the Muslim calendar on insurgent attacks; recognize the vulnerability of community rituals to sectarian violence; and consider the costs of initiating operations during dates of religious sensitivity to a broad Muslim audience, both inside and outside these two countries. U.S. troops have also striven to protect churches and mosques from assault while risking condemnation for desecrating holy sites in which insurgents have sought refuge. Throughout, military chaplains, Islamist clerics, and local religious leaders have played a key role in the conflict, acting as mediators, motivators, and interpreters of religious principles relevant to the conduct of war. Rather than directly compelling U.S. involvement in Afghanistan or Iraq, religion has indirectly influenced U.S. planning and performance by shaping the interests of U.S. troops, their opponents, and third parties.

Second, rather than focusing exclusively on religion as a cause of war, I explore how religion shapes the nature of war. In doing so, I join a small but growing cohort of scholars that has investigated the effects of religion on the duration, intensity, and resolution of conflicts.[19] This multifaceted view of religion reveals a series of intricate relationships between religion and war that does not end when conflict begins. Most scholars of religion and conflict have focused on "why" questions of religion and war, which constrain religion to the realm of ideas. A shift to studying religious practices opens up "where," "when," "who," and "how" questions for analysis.

Seen in this light, answers to the "why" question that has dominated the literature so far are merely a special case of a broader and more ambitious research agenda on religion and conflict. In many ways, the gradual move of scholarship towards these nuanced questions resembles the maturation of the literature on gender and war.[20] Just as that literature has moved from a stereotypical conceptualization of masculinity and violence to sophisticated studies of gendered discourse, roles, symbols, and practices, so the literature on religion and war must distance itself from crude claims about "wars of religion" and take on more subtle questions involving the full range of religious practices and the entire spectrum of international and civil conflicts.

Third, I show that, once we recognize the multiple ways in which religion can shape war, we can begin to notice that it plays this role in all wars, not just in conflicts that cross religious boundaries. Religion can influence ostensibly secular conflicts as well as conflicts among groups adhering to the same belief system. By the same token, religion can prove conducive to compromise and peacemaking in conflicts regardless of the religious or secular nature of the combatants. Moreover, religion can prove of significance in a war not only because of how it affects the parties in conflict but because of how it affects its targets and third-party observers.

The fourth way I contribute to this scholarship is to show that, by unraveling the role of religion, broadly understood, across different stages of war and across various types of conflict, we can begin to unpack the relationship between Islam and war. If Islam is unique, this is due to the contemporary association of a particular brand of Islam with a temporary trend in global terrorism. Deemphasizing Islam allows us to expand the range of actors under our scrutiny from insurgents and terrorists to states and professional military forces. The result is a universe of cases that makes up in relevance, significance, and quantity for what it may lack in superficial drama. Scholars of war have been studying a very narrow slice of the religion-and-conflict nexus, leaving out modern, interstate, conventional wars in which religion plays a sometimes small and at other times a substantial role. Students of geography and war do not study just conflicts along earthquake fault lines. Students of psychology and war do not study just lunatic leaders. As students of religion and war, we should not limit our analyses to fanatics and suicide bombers.

What Is Religion?

Most international relations scholars writing on religion and conflict have dodged the thorny theoretical problem of defining religion and have, instead, opted for easily identifiable and operationalizeable religious indicators as the cornerstones of their analyses. A recent wave of scholarship in religion and international relations, however, has followed in the footsteps of critical theorists to challenge the validity of the concept of religion altogether.[21] This work has sought to unmask religion as an ideological force that is deeply implicated in power structures. Post-colonial scholars allege that the concept of religion is a Western invention that has been manipulated for the purpose of colonial projects and Christian missionary work. If Eastern religions such as Hinduism, Buddhism, and Confucianism are the inventions of colonial officials, missionaries, and orientalists, then the concept of religion has no universal validity and no scholarly merit.[22]

I depart from this viewpoint and adopt an interpretivist view of religion that places the experiences and self-understandings of religious practitioners at the center of the analysis. My definition of religion leans on recent work by Martin Riesebrodt, a sociologist who seeks to salvage the study of religion from its post-modern critics and reestablish its empirical foundations.[23] Riesebrodt defines religion as a system of practices, related to superhuman powers, that seeks to ward off misfortune, provide blessing, and obtain salvation.[24] He notes that all societies distinguish charismatically gifted individuals, recognize sacred times, and demarcate sacred places. These sacred sources allow participants to prevent crises by commemorating and expressing gratitude for past favors and by asking for future favors.[25] Religion consists of the practices that surround the sacred, along with the rules, rituals, and penalties that attach to them.

The emphasis of this theory of religion is not on metaphysics, ethics, or worldviews, not on the purity of doctrine, theological tradition or elite discourses; rather, this theory focuses on the concrete reality of religion, the practices of worship as understood by common participants in that worship.[26] It is an interpretivist approach that is rooted in the internal perspective of the religious actor. Unlike the critical theorist and the rationalist who prescribe what religion ought to mean or aim to unmask what it *really* means, this approach starts with the self-representation of the practitioner.[27] In this perspective, scholars are free to employ the concept of religion because that is what the subjects of their analysis are doing. As another sociologist of religion, Ivan Strenski, notes:

> In ordinary usage, and even for those who people our law offices, judicial courtrooms, legislative houses, public and parochial schools and such, there is no problem about identifying or listing the "religions," or for that matter even giving a formal definition of religion. . . . The particular wisdom of ordinary usage lies in its reflecting a deep feature of the world in which we live. Thus, just as "everyone knows" what religion is, so do we all know what "art," "politics," "language,"

"nation," "race," sex," "privacy," "economics"—all the commonplaces of our culture—are. Part of what it is to live at our time and in our place is that we all assume insuperable authority to discourse on what these things are.[28]

This is not to say that social scientists should ignore the Western bias that may be inherent in the term, fail to explore its contingent meanings over time, or neglect the many meanings that such a loaded term seeks to invoke or obscure. Scholars should do just that, offer their own definition of the term, or suggest an alternative. And then they ought to move on to focus on the primary task: the analysis of social reality. For the term religion, as Ludwig Wittgenstein would have put it, is not "language that has gone on holiday."[29] It is not merely an archaic turn of phrase of peculiar origins and problematic ethical implications. It is also a commonplace term used by practitioners today to convey clear and specific meanings.

Embracing Riesebrodt's intuitive definition offers multiple advantages. In addition to my own preference for interpretative epistemology, this approach transcends religious boundaries, embracing Eastern as well as Western traditions. It is broad enough to include both formal and informal ("magical" or "superstitious") practices.[30] Moreover, it is well suited for an analysis of religion on the battlefield, a setting in which humans seem to rely heavily on divine guidance and support. Religion, Riesebrodt writes, is "especially concerned with warding off and overcoming crisis situations. Religion not only makes it possible for the inexplicable to be explained; it also maintains people's ability to act in situations in which they run up against their own limits."[31]

This approach has the added advantage of pragmatic utility.[32] Political scientists take a similarly matter-of-fact approach to studying other socially constructed or historically contingent concepts of Western origin. *Religion* is no more problematic a term than *sovereignty, nationalism,* or *the state,* concepts that scholars use regularly to communicate with their audiences and with one another. Even if religion is a modern European invention, a claim that Riesebrodt refutes persuasively, it has long since come to function as a useful shorthand.[33]

To bring the argument full circle: The word religion, like the concept it represents, is a matter of practice. It is not just an idea of interesting pedigree and troublesome biases but a term that people do, in fact, use regardless of whether scholars approve of their doing so.

Finally, this approach is distinct in emphasizing religious practices rather than religious ideas. Naturally, ideas and practices are connected at the hip.

They give rise to one another and shape one another in turn, thus becoming difficult to disentangle. Ideas and practices are best thought of as two sides of one coin: the cerebral and experiential aspects of religion versus its physical and corporeal facets. In privileging religious practices, I do not mean to imply that these are unaccompanied by appropriate ideas; rather, these practices are the primary cause of the effects that I am trying to explain. In all these cases, religious ideas are present, but they play a secondary or mediating role.[34]

Sacred scriptures, sacred symbols, and sacred experiences are all examples of religious practices. In this volume, I focus not on these but on four other instantiations of religion. In the next four chapters, I explore, in order, how sacred time, sacred space, sacred authority, and sacred rituals have influenced modern combat.

The Strange Case of the Chaplains in the Trenches

So far in this chapter, I have argued for a study of religion and war that emphasizes religious practices. I have advocated shifting attention away from religion as a cause of war and onto religion as shaping the conduct of war, and I have proposed that scholars analyze modern, professional, and Western armed forces and not just radical nonstate actors. What might such an approach look like? The following miniature case study offers an example, chosen not because of its military significance but because it exemplifies what I mean by religious practice. It concerns the odd pattern of fatalities among British chaplains during World War I.

Of the roughly 5,000 British chaplains who served in World War I, 97 died "in action."[35] In exploring the circumstances of their deaths more closely, I found that twenty-one of these chaplains died in the front lines during battle.[36] Others died in the rear while conducting funerals and church services, for example, or under circumstances unknown. Of these twenty-one chaplains, eleven were Catholic, five were Anglican, and the rest ministered to smaller denominations (Wesleyans, Congregationalists, etc.).

The two-to-one death ratio of Catholic to Anglican chaplains among British chaplains is surprising considering that Anglican chaplains outnumbered their Catholic counterparts at a ratio of three to one, at least, during the Great War.[37] Proportionately speaking, how did the deaths of Catholic chaplains during battle come to outnumber sixfold those of their Anglican counterparts?

The circumstances of World War I sharpen this puzzle, not only because it is the first war for which precise chaplain allotments, casualty figures, and names are available but also because, unlike prior U.S. or British conflicts, religious denominations and their chaplains were evenly distributed across the front. Thus, it is not the case—as in the U.S. Civil War, for example— that Catholic chaplains faced a greater risk of death because they were attached primarily to Catholic units, nor is it the case that Catholic units were discriminately placed in the most hazardous battle fronts.[38] Moreover, World War I is the last conflict in which chaplains participated with no precise instructions as to how and where they were to perform their duties; individual chaplains had some leeway in choosing how much risk to assume in battle, a freedom they would be deprived of in subsequent wars.

Such ad hoc guidelines as did exist for World War I chaplains discouraged their presence in the front lines. One week prior to the Battle of the Somme, for example, the commander general of the Fourth Army, Lieutenant-General Henry Rawlinson, ordered that "chaplains should, under no circumstances, advance with their Regiments or Brigade, or . . . take up positions other than with a Medical Unit."[39] Commanders felt that chaplains could best serve by ministering to the wounded at the advanced dressing stations found 2–3 miles behind the lines rather than at the front, where the wounded were widely dispersed and where chaplains might get in the way of the fighting.[40] The puzzle, then, is why Catholic chaplains ignored such orders at a far higher rate than their Anglican counterparts.

There is no reason to believe that Catholic chaplains were more coura-geous or patriotic than Anglican chaplains or that Catholic chaplains were more dedicated to their men.[41] In terms of overall casualties, fatalities, or med-als awarded, Anglican chaplains proportionately matched or even exceeded their counterparts; further, many Anglican chaplains committed acts of great courage.[42] What set apart the Catholic chaplains was not their willingness to die but their choice of location in battle among the advancing units. Why did Catholic chaplains elect to be at the battlefront rather than to minister to the wounded in the rear?

The answer to this question, I argue, has little to do with religious ideas and much to do with religious practices. The primary duty that set apart Catholic chaplains from their counterparts was the administration of last rites: final absolution, extreme unction, and the *viaticum* (a final holy com-munion) had to be administered to Catholic soldiers just prior to their death. Whereas Anglican chaplains could perform their duties—comforting the wounded or burying the dead—behind battle lines, Catholic padres had to be in the thick of battle to perform their most important religious services.[43] As Cardinal Michael Logue, senior Catholic leader of Ireland, explained in an October 1914 speech that advocated sending chaplains into the line,

"What we want is that chaplains be permitted to go to the Front—not merely to go to the French hospitals, but to go to the firing line, so that when the poor fellow drops he may have a priest beside him to give him the last consolations of religion."[44]

The number of chaplains who died in the front lines of battle—21 out of a total of 5,170—is far too low to offer statistically robust evidence for this

FIGURE 1.1 Father John Gwynne giving the Last Sacrament to a dying German soldier just before he himself was killed on Hill 70 at Battle of Loos, France, October 1915.
From "The War Illustrated Album, deLuxe," London, 1916.

hypothesis.[45] Nor can one gather evidence for this phenomenon from prior wars due to the inconsistent participation of chaplains in these wars and the absence of systematic records on their fatality rates.[46] Yet details about the deaths of World War I chaplains offer some confirmation that the requirements of religious practice drove British Catholic chaplains into the front lines. The dramatic martyrological style of some of these accounts need not place in doubt the religious rituals observed by witnesses. Father W. J. Finn was the first chaplain who fell in the Great War, on the beaches of Gallipoli: "Although lead was splattering all round him like hailstones, he administered consolation to the wounded and dying, who, alas, were so thickly strewn around . . . and as he was in the act of giving consolation to [a] stricken man, this heroic Chaplain was struck dead by a merciless bullet."[47] Father William Doyle, the third British chaplain to die during a World War I battle, "went forward and back over the battlefield with bullets whining about him, seeking out the dying and kneeling in the mud beside them to give Absolution, watched by his men with reverence and a kind of awe until a shell burst near him and he was killed."[48] Similar descriptions attest to the precise manner of death of other Catholic padres (see figure 1.1).[49]

I have dedicated several pages to the case of British chaplains in the trenches, not because it typifies the behavior of religious authority figures in other wars, let alone because it determined the outcome of even a single engagement during World War I. Rather, this case is instructive because it runs counter to everything we have come to believe about the role of religion in war. It was religious practices—and not theologies or extremist beliefs—that produced this outcome. These Catholic practices were consonant with Catholic beliefs, just as they were consistent with Catholic doctrine and scripture. Nonetheless, what mattered was not so much what the Catholic padres believed in their minds about religion but the actions they took because of religion. This all occurred against the backdrop of a modern Western war that pitted Christian-majority armies against one another. It was not a war because of religion, about religion, or for religion, yet religious practices exerted a peculiar effect on some of its participants. As I argue in this book, such is the case with all participants in all wars.

Religion as a Force Multiplier

So far in this chapter, I have focused on analytic and definitional issues, setting my approach to the study of religion apart from prevalent scholarship on religion and international relations. What can scholars and practitioners of international security hope to learn from this analysis? I argue that religious practices can act as force multipliers or force dividers. Religion can be manipulated at the margins, but this impact can also be compared to the strategic effects of other tactical and environmental variables, such as lunar cycles, tides, and weather patterns. These religious practices can affect both individual practitioners of religion, such as soldiers or commanders, and larger groups of religious practitioners, such as entire military units.

At times, religious practices affect outcomes directly by shaping the physical environment in which soldiers operate, influencing the appearance, structure, and components of that environment. Religious practices influence what soldiers wear or eat, the weapons they carry, or the places and times at which they congregate. At other times, ideas mediate between practices and outcomes; practices shape what individuals and groups think, feel, or experience, and this, in turn, influences soldiers' morale, their effectiveness in battle, or their ability to recover from combat.

In borderline cases, shrewd leaders can initiate these effects; influential chaplains and aggressive religious propaganda may sway soldiers, even in a professional fighting force. Most of the time, however, religious factors are beyond the control of commanders. Their best option is to manage the foreseeable effects of religion. For example, if commanders have some freedom to decide when or where to fight, they can align these choices with advantageous religious conditions, just as they would seek expedient meteorological or topographical conditions for combat. Military operations must go on, regardless of the religious environment, and the effects are not always easily preventable, although their impact can be mitigated by means of training and discipline.

To explore how and why religious practices affect war, I return to the definition of religion used in this volume: religion is a system of practices through which participants seek to ward off misfortune, acquire blessing, and obtain salvation. These can include prayers, ablutions, feasts, fasts, honors, and status symbols, or prohibitions on particular actions, speech, clothing, or attitudes. Transgressions, such as eating sacred foods at secular times, omitting gestures of approach when entering a sacred space, or disregarding the rulings of a prominent cleric, for example, constitute acts of desecration, sacrilege, or blasphemy that provoke divine wrath. Because these practices are shared by a religious community and because divine sanctions are said to be directed at the entire community and not just the individual worshipper, compliance and desecration are also accompanied by social sanctions. Sacrilege thus incurs two kinds of penalties: divine penalties, such as the denial of salvation, and social penalties.

Some of these religious categories share a kinship with parallel cultural and political phenomena. The primary organizing concepts in this volume—sacred time, sacred space, sacred authority and sacred ritual—are not unlike national, ethnic, or civil-religious time, space, authority, and ritual. The difference is one of degree. Religious sources enjoy a higher salience, appeal to a wider audience, and tend to be circumscribed by crisper rules. This clarifies and amplifies the rewards and penalties for appropriate behavior or sacrilege. The desecration of a Christmas has greater repercussions than the violation of a Fourth of July; the boundaries and the rules governing appropriate behavior are more easily identified, their breach provokes a more visceral response, and it does so among a broader, potentially international audience. Consequently, religious practices on the battlefield can carry graver consequences than parallel practices from the realms of ethnicity or nationalism.[50]

Sanctioned and prohibited practices may not have the explicit purpose of regulating or motivating combat, but they are nonetheless salient at times of conflict. In times of war, as in times of peace, combatants who share religious affiliation wish to partake in ceremonies that honor holy days and wish to avoid desecrating holy days by abstaining from prohibited behavior; they seek to honor the ordinances governing access to and behavior within sacred sites and strive to respect the rules regarding the rights and obligations of religious leaders. At the same time, the symbolic significance of the sacred can shape the meaning of action in the presence of sacred time, space, authority, and ritual, thus influencing how combatants understand their actions. Religion thus encourages or discourages participation in conflict, and it constrains what participants are and are not willing to do in the course of conflict. Even when the sacred does not provide the impetus for disputes and instead merely serves as backdrop for conflict, it can encourage or discourage the use of force.

Where religious practices limit the use of force, I call the setting a "constraining religious environment." For example, if regard for the sacred requires combatants to forgo sleep, consume intoxicants, abstain from work or from bearing arms, fast, isolate themselves, or congregate at inopportune moments, then these demands may heighten their vulnerability. Similarly, sacred practices associated with quietism, pacifism, or harmony may inspire reluctance in actors contemplating combat. A constraining religious environment of this sort can have two kinds of effects. Insofar as it affects one's own troops, its impact is *inhibition*. This is a force-dividing impact. In contrast, insofar as the constraint affects one's opponents, it creates vulnerabilities that can be exploited. This *exploitation* effect is a force multiplier from the initiators' point of view.

Conversely, in an "enabling religious environment," religious practices facilitate the use of force. Holy days that commemorate triumphal martyrdom or celebrate religious victories, as well as holy places that honor martial deities, will influence the fervor with which combatants pick up arms and fight. Similarly, sacred sites that provide physical protection or tactical advantage, or religious leaders who provide comfort and encouragement, can have a *motivation* effect on troops and act as a force multiplier. Yet the same enabling religious environment can result in a force-dividing impact if it affects one's opponents. Such will be the case when initiators have gone so far in exploiting the religious vulnerabilities of their opponents as to provoke outrage in their targets or in third parties. This *provocation* effect is a force divider, from the initiators' point of view.

As table 1.1 shows, constraining and enabling religious environments produces four kinds of outcomes, depending on whether they affect one's own

Table 1.1   Religion as a force multiplier

		RELIGIOUS ENVIRONMENT	
		CONSTRAINING	ENABLING
Target	Self	A. Inhibition *Force divider*	B. Motivation *Force multiplier*
	Other	C. Exploitation *Force multiplier*	D. Provocation *Force divider*

forces or one's opponent's forces. Two of these effects, inhibition and provocation, are force dividers. The other two, motivation and exploitation, are force multipliers. This explanatory framework is complicated by the coexistence of sacred phenomena that exert multiple effects. Indeed, even one and the same sacred phenomenon can elicit more than one response in the same actor or community.

To summarize, religion acts as a force multiplier when it affords opportunities for exploiting the religious practices of one's opponents or when it can be used to motivate one's own units. Religion acts as a force divider when it constrains one's own units or when the overexploiting of an opponent's religious practices leads to backlash.

When are these conditions likely to arise? This is the wrong question. Religion, like other environmental factors, is always "there." There are no battlefields from which sacred time, space, authority, or ritual are absent. The better question is: When are these conditions most likely to be of consequence? First, religious practices are most likely to affect combat when the religious factors present on the battlefield are salient. The greater the

ability of a sacred time, place, leader, or ritual to provide salvation to participants, the more likely participants are to account for it in their decision making. It follows that decision makers cannot be expected to benefit from the
force-multiplying effects of religion—or to ward against its force-dividing
effects—unless they are able to gather intelligence about the relative salience
of religious practices present in the battlefield, a topic to which I turn in the
final chapter of this book. The primary requirements for collecting "religious intelligence" are the realization that the religious practices of bystanders and the religious practices of one's own soldiers matter no less than the
practices of rivals and a sensitivity to the significance of formal and informal,
localized, and idiosyncratic practices. Such information cannot be gleaned
from ancient texts or historical analyses; it requires an intimate familiarity
with religious practices as they manifest on the ground in real time.

Second, military training can mitigate some of the force-dividing effects
of religion. Consequently, gathering religious intelligence is a worthwhile
enterprise regardless of the many obstacles it poses, particularly when that
intelligence pertains to one's own troops. A disciplined army can prepare
to counter the inhibition effects that accompany religious practices or can
even curtail the practices themselves by imposing regulations that curb religious expression; it can also restrain its exploitation of an opponent's vulnerabilities so as not to unleash provocation. Indeed, under limited conditions,
commanders can harness the preexisting motivating force of religion to
affect the morale of their troops by encouraging specific small-group rituals or by judiciously employing chaplains on the battlefield. In contrast, an
undisciplined army will invite opponents to exploit its religious vulnerabilities, particularly when those practices impact military effectiveness. For
example, religious restrictions on food, work, or sleep; impediments against
accessing particular parts of the battlefield; and constraints on mobilization
during particular time periods expose combatants by curtailing their ability to efficiently project force. These possibilities are explored at length in
ensuing chapters.

Finally, insofar as decision makers have some control over which religious
factors are at play, they will want to ensure that the impacts of motivation
and exploitation are asymmetrical—that only one's own troops are subject to
the enabling effects of the sacred and only the opponents' units are subject
to the constraining effects of the sacred. Contra Huntington, this is as likely
to occur in wars between denominations of the same religion (say, Sunni
versus Shi'a or Catholic versus Protestant) as it is in wars across civilizational divides. Conversely, armies are least likely to engage in exploitation in
wars of occupation that involve a "hearts and minds" component, lest they

alienate local populations who share the religious identity of their rivals. In such conflicts, occupiers must contend with a double standard and an asymmetry of perceptions; locals may forgive religious transgressions committed by co-religionists but will respond with outrage when similar actions are performed by religious outsiders. Even military operations that were not intended to include a religious dimension may be perceived as transgressive and religiously loaded by observers and third parties. Toward the end of this book, I show this logic at work in an analysis of the U.S. counterinsurgency efforts in Iraq.

The following chapters explore the four effects of religion in each of the four issue areas: sacred time, sacred space, sacred authority, and sacred ritual. Each of these manifestations of the sacred produces, to some extent, all four effects. Empirically speaking, however, some effects have proven more influential in the interstate conflicts that I explore in this book (see table 1.2).

Table 1.2   Religious practices in modern interstate war

PUZZLE	PHENOMENON	PRIMARY EFFECTS	PRIMARY ACTORS	NET RESULT
When	Sacred time	Exploitation, provocation	Individual, unit, command	Mixed
Where	Sacred space	Inhibition	Command	Divider
Who	Sacred leaders	Motivation	Individual, unit	Multiplier
How	Sacred rituals	Motivation	Individual, unit	Multiplier

The primary effects of sacred time, for example, have been exploitation and provocation; armies have relied on the religious practices of their opponents to launch surprise attacks in the hopes of catching their enemies off guard, but this has prompted backlash on occasion. Because these are two understudied effects, with conflicting implications for both the initiators and the targets, I dedicate the first empirical chapter of this volume to sacred time.

The primary effect of sacred space, in contrast, has been inhibition. As I show in chapter 3, militaries have constrained their attacks lest they harm their opponents' sacred sites. In chapter 4, in turn, I argue that sacred actors have mostly had a motivation effect on troops; they have done little to inhibit combatants' use of force, nor have combatants exploited the dependence of their opponents on religious leaders. Finally, the sacred rituals examined in chapter 5 primarily motivate participants in war; however, this participation can have a perverse effect on the religiosity of soldiers, because some soldiers recoil from religion due to the experience of war.

Two additional patterns become immediately apparent. First, whether religion eased or hindered the use of force in twentieth-century interstate wars depended in large part on the ability of combatants to control the presence of religion on the battlefield. Because soldiers and commanders could choose whether to involve religious leaders and rituals in the course of war, it stands to reason that they did so with the expectation that these would act as force multipliers. As regards sacred time, decision makers enjoyed less leeway, with mixed results. When they were able to control the timing of combat in relation to holy days, commanders did so to advantage their forces; however, this freedom was not always available to them. Further, commanders had far less flexibility regarding the presence of holy sites on the battlefield. They skirted sacred places when they could or suffered their constraining effects when they could not.

Second, the grassroots effects of religious practices—meaning the effects at the individual and unit levels—tended to act as force multipliers. Had that not been the case, commanders would have curtailed their expression. The force-dividing effects of religion, in contrast, worked their effects at the command level. As a rule, they constrained decision makers, not their troops.

I show in chapter 6 that these patterns are amplified and augmented in conflicts involving nonstate actors that are motivated by religious ideas and identities. In such conflicts, each religious phenomenon exerts a wider range of effects on a broader set of actors; moreover, it does so with greater vehemence, making its net effect on the use of force difficult to foresee.

The Bombing of Monte Cassino

The deliberations surrounding the bombing of the Abbey of Monte Cassino in February 1944 illustrate nicely how a single sacred feature—in this case, a sacred place—can have multiple effects on the conduct of war. The Abbey did not cause the conflict; Allied forces and their German opponents did not fight for, or because of, the sacred structure. Its presence was incidental to their fighting; the Abbey happened to be located at a key position on the main German defensive line. Nevertheless, because the building had religious value for participants and observers worldwide, its presence affected military decision making.

The presence of the Abbey had three primary effects. It had an inhibiting effect on the German troops, who, despite the tactical advantages offered by the fortress-like structure, refrained from occupying it or even using it as an observation post. It also constrained their Allied opponents, who, although convinced that the Germans had occupied it, refrained from destroying the

Abbey over the course of two months of deliberations and multiple failed assaults. Finally, once the difficult decision to bomb the Abbey was made, German leaders were able to exploit the destruction for propaganda purposes, provoking international outrage over the destruction of a religious and cultural treasure.

The Abbey of Monte Cassino is the oldest monastery in the Western world. It was established in 529 C.E. by Saint Benedict, founder of the Benedictine Order, who died and was buried at the Abbey. The structure is located halfway between Naples and Rome, atop 1600 feet of solid rock, flanked by jagged mountains. It occupied a key position in the center of the Gustav Line, a series of high-ground positions stretching the width of Italy that was designed to prevent the Allies from reaching Rome. The Abbey thus controlled the main route connecting Naples, where the Allies had landed in September 1943, to the Italian capital. It was, in the words of General Harold Alexander, "one of the strongest natural defensive positions in the whole of Europe."[51]

The German commander-in-chief in Italy, Field Marshall Albert Kesselring, ordered German troops to stay away from the Abbey, explaining, "The Roman Catholic Church was simply promised that the Abbey of Monte Cassino would not be occupied by German troops."[52] Kesselring gave his personal assurance to the abbot, Gregorio Diamare, that the building would not be used for military purposes, and he communicated this decision to the Vatican as well as to the incredulous Allies. German soldiers, aided by monks, drew a circle of 1000 feet from the walls of the monastery, establishing an exclusion zone that soldiers were forbidden from entering. The monks monitored the exclusion zone and reported violations to the Vatican, which issued formal complaints to the German embassy from time to time. Although German soldiers entered the exclusion zone on occasion, they never entered the Abbey itself.[53]

As shells continued to pour down on Allied soldiers from the vicinity of the Abbey and as their casualties mounted, Allied commanders came to see the structure as the primary obstacle to their advance on Rome. They were hampered not only by orders to spare the Abbey itself but also by their inability to target German positions around the Abbey for fear of accidentally hitting the building.[54] Major General Howard Kippenberger, the leader of the New Zealand forces, stated, "it was impossible to ask troops to storm a hill surmounted by an intact building such as this."[55] Major-General Francis Tuker, commander of the Indian Division that was tasked with making the assault on Monastery Hill, told his commander, Lieutenant General Bernard Freyberg, that "nothing would induce me to attack this feature [Monte

Cassino] directly unless the garrison was reduced to helpless lunacy by sheer unending pounding for days and nights. . . ."[56] Freyberg relayed to General Mark Clark that the destruction of the monastery was a military necessity and "it was unfair to assign to any military commander the mission of taking the hill and at the same time not grant permission to bomb the monastery." He told the U.S. chief of staff, General Alfred Gruenther, "I want it bombed. The other targets are unimportant, but this one is vital."[57] Freyberg reiterated this claim more forcefully in the days before the attack, warning Clark that "he did not believe that it would be sound to give an order to capture Monastery Hill and at the same time deny the commander the right to remove an important obstacle to the success of this mission." Ominously, he added, "Any higher commander who refused to authorize the bombing would have to be prepared to take the responsibility for a failure of the attack."[58]

The view that the integrity of the Abbey was a liability was shared by commanders, troops, and the U.S. media alike. This point is worth emphasizing because the Allies eventually failed to exploit the destruction of the Abbey to achieve a breakthrough, leading some to question the strategic value of the building after the fact. At the time, however, the leadership's desire to protect the sacred space encountered fierce opposition. The January intelligence report of the 34th Division, for example, stated, "[E]nemy artillery was provided with exceptional observation on the high ground all along the line, and particularly by the use as an observation post of the Abbey de Monte Cassino, from which the entire valley to the east [was] clearly visible. Orders preventing our firing on this historical monument increased enormously the value of this point to the enemy."[59] Intelligence gathered prior to the bombing of the Abbey concluded that "in the past few days this monastery has accounted for the lives of upwards of 2,000 American boys who felt the same as we do about church property and who paid for it because the Germans do not understand anything human when total war is concerned. . . ."[60] Cyrus L. Sulzberger, writing for the New York Times, ran a dispatch with the byline "Courtesy to Vatican Handicaps Advance as Enemy Is Said to Use Religious Sites for Artillery Observation." The abstention from shelling the Abbey, Sulzberger concluded, "hampered our advances greatly." The Des Moines Register protested, "Catholic boys are dying because we are leaving [the Abbey] alone."[61]

Despite these pleas, the Allied command refused to issue the order to bomb the Abbey. General Harold Alexander informed General Clark in early November 1943 of the "urgent importance of preservation from bombing" of the Abbey. Clark responded with a promise: "Every effort will continue to be made to avoid damaging the Abbey in spite of the fact that it

occupies commanding terrain which might well serve as an excellent observation post for the enemy."[62] In late December that same year, the U.S. War
Department relayed an explicit request from the Vatican to General Dwight
Eisenhower regarding the Abbey. Eisenhower responded by formalizing the
Allied policy toward historic and religious buildings. His statement struck a
careful balance between moral and pragmatic reasoning and made it all too
clear that pragmatism alone would not carry the day:

> If we have to choose between destroying a famous building and sac-
> rificing our own men, then our men's lives count infinitely more and
> the buildings must go. But the choice is not always so clear-cut as that.
> In many cases the monuments can be spared without any detriment to
> operational needs. Nothing can stand against the argument of military
> necessity. That is an accepted principle. But the phrase "military neces-
> sity" is sometimes used where it would be more truthful to speak of
> military convenience or even of personal convenience. I do not want
> it to cloak slackness or indifference.[63]

Eisenhower's policy led Clark to dismiss various appeals for a bombing
from officers in the field during the winter of 1943–1944.[64] By February 1944, however, the Allied situation in Cassino had turned desperate. Several attempts to cross the Rapido River at the foot of the Abbey
had failed. The casualties from these operations exceeded 10,000 troops,
ranking among the most painful defeats the Allies would experience in
the European theater. The Allies were particularly distressed because a
breakthrough at Cassino could have provided the desperately needed relief
for Allied troops that had landed and stalled at Anzio in late January.[65]
Even Eisenhower was convinced that the Germans were exploiting the
Allied reluctance to take action against the Abbey. In a subsequent statement about the protection of the cultural heritage of Europe, Eisenhower
recalled that "at Cassino . . . the enemy relied on our emotional attach-
ments to shield his defense."[66]

After months of deliberations, General Alexander finally issued the order
to bomb the Abbey on February 15, 1944. Pilots with religious scruples were
invited to recuse themselves from participating in the operation, but none
accepted the invitation.[67] Amid the cheers of Allied soldiers, 250 bombers
dropped 600 tons of high explosive on the Abbey, followed by shelling from
howitzers, reducing the beautiful thousand-year-old Abbey to rubble (see
figure 1.2).[68]

The bombing sent shockwaves through Europe. The U.S. envoy to the
Vatican tried, in vain, to present "unquestionable evidence" that the Germans

FIGURE 1.2 Monuments Man Lt. Col. Ernest T. Dewald makes his way up to the ruins of Monte Cassino Abbey to document the extent of the damage.
NARA

had exploited the Abbey but was told by the Vatican secretary of state, Luigi Maglione, that the bombing was "a colossal blunder . . . a piece of gross stupidity."[69] The Vatican would reference the destruction of the Abbey time and again in its subsequent appeals to Franklin D. Roosevelt against the bombing of Rome.[70] The Germans were just as quick to capitalize on the event. Photographers from the German Propaganda Office in Rome had taken photos of the Abbey prior to the attack so that "in case it was destroyed, they could use the pictures to show the barbarity of the Anglo-Americans."[71] At the insistence of German Propaganda Minister Joseph Goebbels, the abbot was brought to a transmitting station to broadcast his condemnation of Allied behavior. Moreover, at the request of German Foreign Minister Joachim von Ribbentrop, he was pressured into signing a written statement testifying to the Germans' respect for the monastery and its inhabitants. This statement, in the abbot's handwriting, was reproduced and plastered around Rome. German diplomats abroad were instructed to exploit the abbot's testimony to the best of their abilities.[72] A diarist recorded, "All Rome is thickly placarded today with posters showing photographs of the ruins of Monte Cassino with monks and refugee civilians, and reproductions of handwritten signed statements by the Abbot and his administrator. This is certainly a trump card in the German propaganda game."[73] The outcry was so great as to lead some in the diplomatic corps to speculate that the German army had somehow tricked the Allies into bombing the Abbey to reap the propaganda rewards.[74]

In summary, the religious value of the Monte Cassino Abbey had a constraining effect on both the German and Allied forces, as well as a subsequent provocative effect on Christian observers. These effects did not influence the bottom line: the Abbey was bombed. Nonetheless, they shaped the timing of the attack and the content of the deliberations that preceded it, with tangible effects on the ability of Allied forces to forge their way to Rome. The inhibiting effect worked at the command level, not at the individual or unit level; Allied officers and soldiers, Catholic and non-Catholic alike, supported the bombing with enthusiasm.[75] It was senior Allied decision makers who hesitated to destroy the Abbey, realizing the harm that such an act would cause to relations with the Vatican, European perceptions of Allied intentions, and support for the war on the home front. Despite the prevailing perception that the Abbey was the prime obstacle to a successful assault, Allied officers in Cassino had to spend two months, with mounting losses, trying to persuade their superiors that military necessity trumped the religious value of the Abbey. The outrage provoked by the bombing, in turn, undermined efforts to persuade Italians to cease fighting and to greet the Allies as welcome liberators. As I discuss in chapter 3, efforts to undo the reputational damage from Cassino by safeguarding religious and cultural sites would have an enduring effect on Allied targeting policy throughout the liberation of Europe.

Ironically, the bombing of Monte Cassino proved to be of limited utility. The Allies were slow to follow up on the bombing with an attack on Monastery Hill, and German paratroopers were quick to take up positions in the Abbey ruins. This was a tactical blunder that commanders could not have predicted prior to the bombing. They were confident that the sparing of the Abbey and the ban on shelling German installations in its vicinity came at a significant daily toll in fatalities, yet they were constrained from acting on that intuition. The man who gave the order to bomb the Abbey of Monte Cassino, General Harold Alexander, encapsulated this dilemma in his recollections after the war. The Allies had spared the Abbey, he wrote in his memoirs, "to our detriment." Even if the Germans were not inside the Abbey itself, "this huge and massive building offered the defenders considerable protection from hostile fire, merely by their sheltering under its walls."[76] He also confessed to a friend, however, that "giving the order to bomb the abbey had been the most difficult decision he had ever had to make, but that he had finally decided that men's lives must come before stones however holy."[77]

Case Selection and Methodological Considerations

My goal in this volume is to shift the lens away from a preoccupation with religious ideas as causes of war and onto the study of religious practices as inhibiting and motivating factors in the conduct of war. These are heretofore unexplored aspects of religion and war. Consequently, my goal is not to test the conditions under which the sacred acts as force multiplier or divider, nor is it my intention to quantify how significant these factors have been in contemporary wars. Rather, I intend to illustrate the variety of underappreciated pathways through which religion has affected military decision making. I do so by identifying explanatory typologies and salient causal mechanisms. I illustrate each of these typologies and mechanisms with empirical evidence that acts as a plausibility probe in the hopes of stimulating the development of hypotheses and further research.[78] My methodology mixes qualitative analysis, which forms the bulk of the evidence, with occasional quantitative evidence whenever such evidence seems appropriate for describing large-scale trends.

The cases that I have chosen to exemplify these processes at work are hard cases in the sense that they are instances in which the current literature on religion and conflict would not expect religion to have any effect on combat at all. If Huntington is to be believed, we should expect religion to play a role on the battlefield in conflicts that cross large religious divides, in which religious identities are at their most salient. If Osama bin Laden is to be believed, we should expect religion to play a role in insurgencies and terror operations, in which the religious identities of participants are at their most salient. My goal in the following chapters is to show that religion played just as interesting a role in the great interstate wars of the twentieth century. The rational post-enlightenment military organizations that prosecuted these wars shared many of the religious practices that we associate with the wars of religion or with radical nonstate actors today, albeit in attenuated form.

Most of the examples offered in the next four chapters are drawn from recent interstate wars in the West. As a consequence, and in contrast with much of the literature on religion and violence, my emphasis is on the effects of Christian practices on war making. I draw occasional examples from Judaism and Islam but make only rare references to non-Western religions.

I also eschew cases in which religious identities and ideas played a dominant role to demonstrate that, even in their absence, religious practices can affect war making. Occasionally, I make mention of the U.S. Civil War and the Arab-Israeli Wars, conflicts that had implicit religious dimensions but lacked overt religious causes. Although we should expect religion to have had significant effects in conflicts such as the Spanish Civil War, the Iran-Iraq War, the Indo-Pakistani Wars, and the civil war in the former Yugoslavia, I have excluded these conflicts from my analysis to separate novel questions about religion and the *conduct* of war (the "when," "where," "who," and "how" questions) from familiar questions about religion and the *cause* of war (the "why" question). In chapter 6, I explore the recent war in Iraq, a case in which Western armies faced nonstate violent actors very much motivated by religion, to show that the phenomena I point to in the first five chapters apply with greater force when religious practices are overlaid with religious identities and motivations.

A few methodological caveats are in order. Because my epistemology is interpretivist, I take the reports of participants, in combat and religious practice, as the starting point of my analysis. Yet my epistemology is also positivist and materialist; I assume that these statements refer to a concrete reality and have material effects on reality. But because my focus is on practice, rather than belief, I make no assumptions one way or another about whether participants "truly" believe.

Like ethnic and nationalist practices, religious practices can be manipulated, albeit less so than religious ideas. In this volume, however, I am less interested in the strategic distortion of religion by shrewd leaders; I focus instead on the fundamental effects that preexisting religious practices exert on combat. I document how astute decision makers have used the extant practices of soldiers, their own and their opponents', to their advantage. They have done so less by modifying the content of practices—a challenging task for any lay leader—and more by adapting military decision making to fit the existing religious landscape present, timing an attack with a religious holiday or diverting combat away from a sacred site, for example. In addition, I show that religious practices often constrained combat in ways that inconvenienced decision makers yet lay beyond their abilities to influence. The use of religion in this volume is thus instrumental but also highly constrained. My focus is not on religion as a pliable military tool but on religion as a series of challenges and opportunities that commanders must contend with.

The literature on religious ideas and identities has privileged religious ideas held by individuals and small groups as a source of combat motivation. As a result, this scholarship has emphasized the force-multiplying effects of religious radicalism. In the following chapters, I document that the effects of religious practices can vary in their mechanisms and the actors involved; consequently, they can act as force multipliers, force dividers, or both. Some manifestations of the sacred motivate combat, others inhibit it, and still others provide opportunities for exploitation or spark provocation. Most sacred phenomena prompt more than one of these effects and involve multiple actors at the same time.

CHAPTER 2

When?

Sacred Time and War

Sacred time has affected modern conflicts, from both world wars, the Vietnam War, and the 1973 Arab-Israeli war to the ongoing insurgency in Iraq. At times, initiators of conflict have timed their surprise attacks to coincide with significant dates in the religious calendars of their opponents in the hope of securing a tactical or strategic advantage. At other times, holy days have influenced the ability or willingness of combatants to fight effectively.

I begin this chapter by offering an investigation into the notion of sacred time based on work by Mircea Eliade, a sociologist of religion. I define sacred time, examine the religious functions that sacred time provides for believers, and discuss the challenges of estimating the relative importance of particular sacred days. The more significant a holy day is to a particular community, the more confident war initiators can be of its effects on combat involving members of that community.

When will decision makers exploit sacred time in planning an offensive? In the second section of this chapter, I argue that the practices associated with sacred time can advantage or disadvantage the party that has chosen to conduct combat on a sacred day. To calculate whether the benefits of attacking on a sacred day outweigh the costs, leaders must assess the relative impact of constraining and enabling sacred time on sets of actors: their own troops, their opponents, and relevant third parties.

One's own troops may refuse to fight if they perceive a dissonance between the significance of a sacred day and their participation in combat (inhibition). Conversely, a leader who times an attack to coincide with a sacred day can expect the religious setting to provide justification for the attack and foster support among combatants if the religious symbolism of the date amplifies or reinforces the rationale behind the conflict (motivation). Regarding opponents, initiators of conflict will benefit from timing their attack on an opponent's sacred day when the target's religious practices hamper mobilization or combat on that date; I refer to this as the exploitation effect of sacred time. Finally, timing an attack to coincide with a sacred date can prove costly if a sacrilegious attack inadvertently provokes a vehement response from the target and its supporters (provocation).

Therefore, leaders will time their attacks to coincide with sacred dates if the force multipliers, motivation and exploitation, outweigh the force dividers, inhibition and provocation. This is most likely to occur under three conditions: when conflict occurs across religious divides, when the sacred day is unambiguous in significance and meaning, and when rituals connected to that day are likely to undermine an opponents' military effectiveness.

In the third section, I illustrate these deliberations by means of case studies that most clearly illustrate the range of different effects caused by war initiation on holy days. In an effort to draw attention away from the current preoccupation with religiously motivated insurgencies and bygone wars of religion, I draw evidence primarily from twentieth-century examples of conventional war between professional Western military forces. Most of the examples thus focus on Jewish, Christian, and Muslim sacred time, with far less attention dedicated to non-Western religions. On occasion, I draw on particularly salient nineteenth-century cases, as well as contemporary insurgencies and terror campaigns that highlight specific attributes or dilemmas linked to launching an attack on a sacred date.

In the fourth section, I address the problem of spurious correlation. Because most dates in the calendar can be identified as holding religious significance for the followers of some religious movement or other when viewed in hindsight, might not the concurrence of combat and sacred time be coincidental? One way of addressing this challenge is to closely examine statements made by conflict initiators. I explore testimonies from the 1973 Arab-Israeli War to show that the Egyptian decision makers were mindful and explicit about the religious significance of Yom Kippur, the date on which they chose to launch their attack.[1]

What Is Sacred Time?

A paradox underlies the concept of sacred time: if believers consider all time and space to be a divine creation, then all time and space should be equally sacred. Nonetheless, members of all religious movements recognize that time, like space, is not homogeneous. The gods have designated certain periods as being more "important," "lucky," "strong," or "pure" than others. Believers perceive these times as possessing unique value and power.[2] This, in and of itself, is a good reason for students of international conflict to take an interest in the phenomenon of sacred time; as far as believers are concerned, sacred time can imbue agents with extraordinary power, both on and off the battle-field. Sacred time is a force multiplier.

This particular notion of sacred time, meant to designate specific periods in the calendar that are deemed holy, can be contrasted with a more diffuse notion of sacred time as pervading and organizing all of creation. In the fol-lowing pages, I use the term *sacred time* interchangeably with *holy days* to refer to periods, usually days, weeks, or months, in which a religious movement commemorates key events in its past or fulfills religious obligations.[3] This category includes religious feasts, fasts, festivals, times of mourning, com-memorations, periods of rest, times of pilgrimage, and holidays.

Sacred time can recur at varying intervals in the religious calendar. Some movements mark the most sacred moments of the day by observing daily prayers and rituals at prescribed times, as do Muslims during their five daily prayers. Most religious movements set aside one day of the week as particu-larly sacred, be it Friday among Muslims and Baha'i, Saturday among Jews, and Sunday among Christians. *Uposatha*, the Buddhist day of reflection, occurs approximately once a week among Theravada Buddhists and six times a month among Mayahana Buddhists. Other groups emphasize monthly, seasonal, or yearly rituals.

Believers rely on rituals, practices, and prohibitions to maintain the dis-tinction between sacred and secular time, and to emphasize the unique status of sacred time. These practices can include feasts or fasts; abstention from work, speech, washing, or sex; required rites, prayers, or ceremonies; and the permission or requirement that actions prohibited during secular times of the year be committed. Transgressing on these distinctions, by eating sacred foods at secular times or secular food at sacred times, for example, constitutes a desecration of sacred time. The rules guarding against this kind of sacrilege offer one way of identifying sacred time; sacred time is distinguished by virtue of practices that are mandated at particular times of the year and that often cannot take place at other times of the year.

Figure 2.1 Door Gunner Petty Officer Richard Symonds of the Royal Navy wears a Santa Claus outfit as he delivers mail and presents to troops around Helmand province.
Image by Sgt. Rupert Frere © Crown Copyright 2015

Another means of defining sacred time is to identify the functions that sacred time provides for believers. Like sacred space, sacred actors, or sacred objects (such as relics), sacred times allow believers to gain insight into religious meaning, to communicate with the divine, and to receive divine favors. This variety of functions and the diversity of holy days in any religious movement suggest that some sacred times are more significant than other times.

Yet estimating the relative importance of a holy day is no easy task. As a rule, holy days ascend in value the greater their ability to provide the three previously mentioned functions to believers. The more significant the historical or religious event commemorated on a sacred day, the greater the importance of the event. Salient dates tend to occur less frequently in the religious calendar, are often characterized by rules and practices that deviate more significantly from day-to-day behavior, and are accompanied by stricter penalties for transgression. Because of these penalties, as well as the potential favors to be gained on particularly potent sacred days, significant sacred days can often be recognized by the crowds they draw to rituals and sacred sites.

Whereas many religious movements provide a formal ranking of their sacred days, in practice believers may attribute value to a particular holy day based on a variety of idiosyncratic considerations. Thus, some Christians favor celebrating Christmas and Halloween over Easter, irrespective of the official position of their church, just as many Jews who fail to strictly observe Yom Kippur or the Sabbath nonetheless celebrate Hanukkah and Passover. A community's local-patriotic, emotional, or political attachment to a particular date, such as a local saint's day or the founding date of a local shrine, can elevate the value of even the most insignificant holy day.[4] Believers may care less about the formal ranking of a sacred date and, instead, esteem holy days that are particularly jubilant, associated with favored informal traditions, or linked to prominent political agendas. Thus any formal means of prioritizing sacred days can provide only a rough heuristic. Comparisons of ranking across religious groups—or even subgroups—are of limited utility. Indeed, a conflict can also affect the meaning and significance of the holy day it coincides with, thus complicating the calculation significantly.

Exploiting Sacred Time

The rituals and symbols associated with sacred time can advantage or disadvantage the party that has chosen to conduct combat on a sacred day by acting as force multiplier or force divider. In the absence of other constraints on the timing of conflict, leaders may face the temptation of exploiting sacred dates in the calendar to their advantage. Decision makers will time their attacks to coincide with sacred dates if the force-multiplying effects of sacred time, motivation and exploitation, outweigh the force-dividing effects of sacred time, inhibition and provocation.

Sacred time affects combatants in two primary ways. Certain sacred times create a constraining religious environment. Holy days that require soldiers to congregate, isolate themselves, fast, abstain from work, forgo sleep, or consume intoxicants, for example, will affect the ability of soldiers to engage in combat. This can have an inhibition effect on one's own soldiers, but it can also affect the opponent, creating opportunities for exploitation, particularly when sacred time and sacred space overlap. Other sacred times create an enabling religious environment. Holy days designed to venerate martial deities, mourn martyrs, or celebrate religious triumphs can have a positive influence on the fervor with which combatants pick up arms and fight. I call this encouraging effect *motivation*. When an attack on a sacred day provokes indignation from third parties, I refer to the effect as provocation (see table 2.1).

A holy day may exert several of these effects simultaneously. The challenge faced by decision makers is to untangle these outcomes and weigh

Table 2.1   Sacred time as a force multiplier

		RELIGIOUS ENVIRONMENT	
		CONSTRAINING	**ENABLING**
Target	Self	A. Inhibition (e.g., Christmas, 1914)	B. Motivation (e.g., Operation Badr, 1973)
	Other	C. Exploitation (e.g., Tet Offensive, 1968)	D. Provocation (e.g., Blue Star, 1984)

them against one another. Leaders will time their attacks to coincide with sacred dates if the force multipliers, motivation and exploitation, outweigh the force dividers, inhibition and provocation. This is likely to occur under the following three conditions.

First, the utility of coordinating combat operations with sacred time grows with the significance of the relevant holy day. As previously discussed, this significance is context specific. Leaders should care less about the formal ranking of sacred time and more about prevailing customs and practices in the relevant target audience. This, in turn, will require a familiarity with the religious profiles of combatants on both sides of a conflict. An overlap between sacred time and other aspects of religion, such as sacred time coinciding with sacred space or the presence of a religious leader at a sacred ceremony, will further enhance the effects of sacred time.

A holy day will have a more immediate effect on soldiers' willingness to engage in combat if its military implications are unambiguous. The less tentative the link between a holy day and military practices, the smaller the risk that soldiers will interpret religious symbols in unexpected ways or will ignore them altogether. Martial symbols associated with holy days that commemorate mythical-historical conquests or defeats, such as Purim for Jews, Vidovdan for the Serbian Orthodox, or Ashura for Shi'a, will be more salient to participants than holy days that merely allude to spiritual conquests or defeats, such as Ramadan for Muslims or Easter for Christians.

Second, decision makers will prefer to align offenses with holy days when they expect the relevant rituals to have a positive impact on military effectiveness. Military effectiveness denotes the ability of armed forces to translate resources into battlefield power and success.[5] Following Risa Brooks and Elizabeth Stanley, the properties essential for military effectiveness can be grouped under several headings, two of which in particular—responsiveness and skill—are amenable to the influence of sacred time.[6] Responsiveness defines the ability of a military to adapt its tactics and activities to new information, adjusting and compensating for constraints where appropriate. A responsive military is effective in tailoring its doctrine to exploit enemy weaknesses while modifying its own force structure as new challenges and threats arise. Skill, in turn, measures the proficiency of a military at executing doctrine to achieve a particular task. A skillful military is effective in motivating its soldiers to excel in combat by instilling a sense of commitment and initiative.[7] Rituals that require soldiers to abstain from nourishment, work, or sleep, for example, are more likely to affect military effectiveness than rituals that proscribe clothing, ceremonies, or liturgy.

Military discipline can mitigate the negative effects of sacred time on battlefield effectiveness. The more disciplined a military force, the more likely it is to have learned from its vulnerability to the effects of sacred time and to have established means of protecting against those weaknesses. Indeed, highly disciplined organizations can exploit expectations of susceptibility by initiating conflicts on sacred dates on which they are expected to be vulnerable. For example, the Israeli Air Force has occasionally initiated attacks on the Jewish Sabbath in hopes of catching opponents off guard because "Israel isn't supposed to start wars on the Sabbath."[8]

Third, decision makers will take advantage of sacred time in conflicts that cross religious lines. To ensure that only their own troops are subject to the motivation effects of a sacred day, or to ensure that only their opponents are susceptible to the exploitation effects of a sacred day, decision makers are likely to time attacks on significant dates in the calendar that are not shared across conflict lines. Doing so also ensures that third parties, whose support is deemed crucial to the success of a campaign, do not respond with outrage to this strategy. When third parties do share a religious identity with one's opponents, as might be expected when insurgents seek to recruit support from outside the combat zone or when counterinsurgents seek to implement a heart-and-minds campaign, the use of sacred time in strategic planning is likely to be minimal.

For example, as I show in chapter 6, Islamic insurgents in Iraq have not exploited the Ramadan season to escalate their attacks on coalition troops and Shi'a opponents, despite the motivating effects of the sacred month, due to the outrage that such timing would provoke among potential Muslim supporters outside Iraq. These insurgents have deliberately targeted Christians' religious centers on Sundays, however, because the vulnerability of their victims to such attacks easily offsets any concern over outrage among Christian audiences outside Iraq.

In conclusion, decision makers will choose to coordinate conflict initiation with sacred dates in conflicts that occur across religious divides, when the sacred day is unambiguous in significance and meaning, and when rituals connected to that day are likely to undermine the opponents' military effectiveness.

The Effects of Sacred Times on Conflict Initiation

The effects of sacred time on conflict initiation deserve closer scrutiny. Here I explore the four effects of sacred time—inhibition, motivation, exploitation, and provocation—to show their impact at work, even in conventional war between modern professional military forces.

Inhibition

Combatants may refuse to fight when they perceive a dissonance between the significance of a sacred day and their participation in combat. This tension may be grounded in the religious beliefs of the participants themselves, as illustrated in examples from the U.S. Civil War and World War I, or they may stem from efforts to respect an opponent's or audience's sacred time, as demonstrated later in my discussion of the recent Iraq War.

SABBATH OBSERVANCE DURING THE U.S. CIVIL WAR

Civil War generals and decision makers routinely issued orders calling for soldiers to respect the Sabbath and to limit military operations as much as possible on that day. Abraham Lincoln's General Order of November 15, 1862, proclaimed, "The importance for men and beast of the prescribed weekly rest, the sacred rights of Christian soldiers and sailors, a becoming deference to the best sentiment of a Christian people, and a due regard for the Divine will, demand that Sunday labor in the army and navy be reduced to the measure of strict necessity. The discipline and character of the national force should not suffer, nor the cause they defend be imperiled, by the profanation of the day or name of the Most High."[9] Robert E. Lee's General Order No. 15 called for "a proper observance of the Sabbath . . . not only as a moral and religious duty, but as contributing to the personal health and well being of the troops." Duties were to be limited to what was "essential to the safety, health and comfort of the army."[10] Generals Braxton Bragg and Nathan Bedford Forrest issued similar orders.[11]

These restrictions were often ignored, but that was not always the case.[12] General William Rosecrans, who led the Army of the Cumberland, objected to any but the most indispensable moves on Sundays, even though it was "apparently detrimental to his success."[13] At the Battle of Stones River in January 1863, he refused to pursue his beaten foe on a Sunday to give his army a Sabbath rest.[14] In a telegraph to Secretary of War Henry Halleck, he explained, "Tomorrow being Sunday we shall probably not fight unless attacked."[15]

Such restrictions were motivated in part by a belief, explicit in Lincoln's order, that fighting on the Sabbath sullied the cause for which the army was fighting. Upon assuming command of the Army of the Potomac, General George B. McClellan ordered that the "holy cause" in which the North was engaged required Sabbath observance and divine services in the camps. No less important a factor was the significance of Sabbath observance to troop morale. Keeping the Sabbath holy was the most frequently mentioned religious concern in soldiers' diaries and letters. Soldiers would complain when they were asked to march, do fatigue work, or even fight on Sundays.[16] Upon hearing of Lincoln's proclamation, "the news was hailed with no small delight by the troops."[17]

Finally, it is impossible to ignore the prevailing belief among soldiers and officers alike that combat on the Sabbath offended God and could bring divine retribution. General Oliver O. Howard argued that one of the causes of defeat at the First Bull Run had been the federal decision to attack on a Sunday morning. McClellan's Sabbath order, he argued, would ensure God's blessing to the Union because violations of the Sabbath weakened the spirit of Christian soldiers.[18] Others believed that the Confederates had lost at Pittsburg Landing (Shiloh) on April 6, 1862, because they had attacked on the Sabbath. One Union soldier wrote in May 1862, "I hope our Army will not attack the enemy tomorrow as it is Sunday and our men seem to have a dread of going to battle on that day unless in defence. The terrible Sunday at Pittsburg is pointed to and the reason given that the enemy was defeated because they commenced the fight on that day."[19] Soldiers that had to participate in battles on Sundays did so in the hope that God would understand and "forgive what sin there has been committed by us."[20]

The overall decline in U.S. and British Sabbath observance in the late nineteenth century came to influence military practices as well. Clerics protested military maneuvers and exercises on the Sabbath in the lead up to World War I, and chaplains expressed dismay at the lack of respect for the Sabbath during the war, but to no avail. By the time World War II had begun, U.S. regulations merely required commanders to minimize military duties on Sundays so as to enable personnel to attend religious services. The widespread revulsion against fighting on the Sabbath among U.S. and British troops was gone.[21]

CHRISTMAS IN NO-MAN'S LAND

The prominence of Christmas saw no such decline; literary and popular culture in both the United States and England supported the successful commercialization of Christmas. The reorientation of religious celebrations from church to home allowed the middle class to incorporate Sunday into its family-oriented weekend and to focus Christmas around children and gift giving.[22] This growing association of Christmas with domestic joy contributed to the most famous example of warfare constrained by the religious calendar: the Christmas truce of 1914.

Pope Benedict XV had pleaded, in vain, for a temporary armistice during Christmas.[23] Concerned that the armistice would further prolong the war, commanders began prohibiting ad hoc cooperative arrangements that had developed across the trench lines, such as the cessation of firing during meal times or the mutual collection and burial of bodies.[24] Nonetheless, through an improvised signaling process, sporadic acts of fraternization across the trenches developed into impromptu temporary truces during Christmas along the Western front. German soldiers placed small Christmas trees and placards bearing Christmas greetings on the parapets of their trenches and began singing Christmas carols.[25] Rifleman Graham Williams reported, "First the Germans would sing one of their carols and then we would sing one of ours, until when we started up 'O Come All Ye Faithful' the Germans immediately joined in singing the same hymn to the Latin words Adeste Fidelis. And I thought, well, this was really a most extraordinary thing—two nations both singing the same carol in the middle of a war."[26]

These signals, combined with the near absence of firing, culminated in direct meetings between commanding officers in no-man's-land, exchanges of gifts, and even improvised games of soccer. On the next day, however, firing resumed, accompanied by threats of disciplinary action against units involved in fraternization.[27] Thereafter, strict orders prevented the recurrence of truces—with occasional and minor exceptions.[28]

The dynamics of trench warfare and the shared religious proclivities of the participants that made the Christmas truce possible were not replicated in subsequent wars. Yet, in at least three contemporary instances, Christmas has demonstrated its continued ability to introduce reluctance into the conduct of war.[29] Having determined that "Christmas time is the most sensitive and emotional period for guerrillas," the Colombia Ministry of Defense joined forces with an advertising agency in Bogota to launch Operación Navidad, an effort to demobilize Colombian guerrillas by invoking the holiday spirit. In December 2010, the guerrillas were dumbfounded to discover ten 80-foot

Christmas trees, decorated with Christmas lights, along strategic paths in the heart of the jungle. Movement sensors lit up the trees as well as banners announcing, "If Christmas can come to the jungle, you can come home. Demobilize. Everything is possible at Christmas." Three hundred thirty-one guerrillas attributed their decision to demobilize to this encounter in this jungle.[30] The campaign continued the following year with Rivers of Light, in which 6,823 Christmas messages from families, inviting insurgents to come home for the holidays, were floated down rivers in illuminated capsules. This prompted 180 insurgents to leave the jungle. In 2012, Operation Bethlehem sought to help insurgents find their way home by means of powerful light beacons in town centers and strings of light dropped into the canopy along key routes out of the jungle. Colombian radio stations played rewritten Christmas carols that ended with the words: "This Christmas, follow the light. Demobilize." About two hundred guerillas did so.[31]

Motivation

Conversely, timing an attack to coincide with a sacred day can foster support among participants if they interpret the religious symbolism of the date as reinforcing the rationale behind the conflict. Combatants can be expected to fight with greater eagerness, ferocity, or enthusiasm on a holy day that reso- nates with their *casus belli*. War initiators can also expect civilians, observers, and third parties who share their interpretation of the religious symbolism of the date to support their cause and mobilize in its defense.

For example, the assassination of Archduke Franz Ferdinand of Austria in 1914 coincided with the feast of Saint Vitus, known in Serbia as Vidov- dan. This solemn Serbian Orthodox holiday commemorates the defeat of the Serbs by the Ottomans in the Battle of Kosovo and the heroic assassina- tion of Ottoman Sultan Murad by the Serb hero, Milos Obilic—events that have come to assume tremendous symbolic significance in Serbian nationalist mythology. The archduke's decision to select that sacred day for his visit to Sarajevo was perceived by many Serbs as a calculated insult.[32] The Bosnian conspirators who plotted the attack were able to frame the assassination on Vidovdan in 1914 as a symbolic reenactment of the assassination on Vidovdan in 1389.[33] Slobodan Milosevic later mobilized Serbian nationals against Koso- var Albanians by delivering his 1989 "Gazimestan speech" on the battlefield of Kosovo on Vidovdan, six hundred years to the day after the fateful battle.[34]

Irish Republicans rebelling against British rule during the Easter Rising of 1916 sought to exploit traditional Easter parades as a cover for anti-British mobilization. Moreover, the symbolic meaning of the holiday, the "blood sacrifice" of Christ on the cross and his subsequent "rising" from the tomb, served as a powerful metaphor for the resurrection of Irish independence.[35]

ASHURA AND THE BATTLE OF BADR

The Shi'a commemoration of Ashura, on the tenth day of the Muslim month of Muharram, provides an interesting parallel to the symbols and practices associated with Easter. Ashura commemorates the martyrdom of Hussein, grandson of the Prophet Muhammad and third Shi'a imam, who was ruthlessly killed by Sunni adversaries during the Battle of Karbala in 680 C.E. For Shi'as, Ashura is not merely a day of fasting and mourning, often involving public lamentation and self-flagellation, but also a day associated with passionate and heroic resistance against oppression.[36] Consequently, disenfranchised Shi'a communities in the Muslim world have exploited processions and pilgrimages during Ashura to organize mass uprisings against oppressive regimes that, in turn, have tried to ban observance of this sacred day. Ashura processions have provided launching points for anti-shah rebellions in pre-revolutionary Iran; mass protests against the Saudi government in 1979; sectarian clashes during the Lebanese civil war; anti-Israeli protests in southern Lebanon; uprisings in Bahrain in the 1990s; the anti-Ba'athist rebellion in 1972, in 1974, and after the First Gulf War; and sectarian violence in Iraq in the aftermath of the Second Gulf War.[37]

Throughout Shi'a history, the repeated experience of violence during Ashura has produced an interesting feedback effect, mirrored in other religious movements: not only can a religiously significant date influence how conflict is perceived, but the occurrence of conflict can also shape the symbolic meaning of the religious date. Just as Vidovdan evokes memories of the Battle of Kosovo, the assassination of the Austrian archduke, and the onset of the Kosovo War, Easter has become fused in Irish political consciousness with the events of 1916 and repeated sectarian clashes in Northern Ireland during the Marching Season.[38] Many Israelis have come to associate the Jewish holy day of Yom Kippur with the 1973 Arab-Israeli War that began on that day; they cannot think of one without recalling the other. The timing and name of the war conjure up connotations of judgment, doom, and the settling of accounts but also of guilt and remorse.[39] For Shi'as, Ashura evokes not only the seventh-century religious-historical battle but also subsequent instances of heroism and sacrifice that occurred on the same day. Conflict thus translates religious time into civil-religious time.[40]

Whereas Ashura carries particular meaning for Shi'a Muslims, Ramadan and the Battle of Badr resonate with all Muslims, regardless of sect. Both the Egyptian invasion of the Sinai Peninsula at the outset of the 1973 Arab-Israeli War and the Pakistani infiltration of Kashmir in the 1999 Kargil War were named Operation Badr to evoke the battle fought by the Prophet Muhammad against the Meccan tribe of Quraish on the seventeenth day of the month of Ramadan in 624 C.E. These references were symbolically loaded because the Qur'an presents the Battle of Badr as a decisive military victory against all odds guided by divine intervention.[41] Because the Battle of Badr also formed the first stage in Muhammad's reacquisition of territories from which he had been expelled by non-Muslims, Badr offered an apt metaphor for Egyptians and Pakistanis who wished to present their actions as defensive in nature, designed to regain lost sovereignty and, by implication, lost honor.[42]

The Saudi jihadists who launched the attack in Riyadh in May 2003 also named their operation Badr al-Riyadh, a symbolism that permeated multiple aspects of the attack.[43] Iranian leaders may have named their invasion of Iraq in July 1982 Operation Ramadan to invoke similar sentiments, rally unprecedented human wave attacks totaling 100,000 participants, and spark a Shi'a uprising in Iraq that would topple the Baath regime. Operation Ramadan was the first battle in the Iran-Iraq War fought on Iraqi soil and amounted to one of the largest land battles since World War II.[44]

In Judaism, it is Purim that is associated with political turmoil more than any other holy day. Purim commemorates a failed plot to exterminate the Jews of Persia in the sixth century B.C.E. and the ensuing Jewish retribution against the perpetrators. Jews have traditionally accompanied this feast with boisterous festivities, rowdiness, and the burning of anti-Jewish figures in effigy.[45] Elliott Horowitz has documented how Purim revelry by Israeli settlers in Hebron repeatedly led to anti-Palestinian violence, culminating in the massacre of Palestinian worshippers by a settler in a disputed sacred site in the heart of Hebron in February 1994.[46] Stretching the meaning of the Jewish holiday to its extremes, the perpetrator, Baruch Goldstein, timed his killing spree at the Cave of the Patriarchs to coincide with both Purim and the month of Ramadan, when he knew the site would be crowded with Muslim worshippers. "He couldn't have picked a better day," a friend of Goldstein later commented, "Purim, when Jews fight back."[47]

Exploitation

Initiators of conflict will hope to benefit from timing their attack on an opponent's sacred day if they expect religious practices associated with that day to hamper the target's mobilization or combat performance. Exploitation is the flip side of inhibition; it is the effort by an initiator to take advantage of an opponent's inhibition to conduct combat on a sacred day.

The Jewish constraint against combat on the Sabbath offers one classical example. Egyptian King Ptolemy I is said to have encountered no resistance when he conquered Jerusalem in 320 B.C.E. because he attacked on the Sabbath, a day on which the Jewish residents of the city refused to fight. Agatharchides of Cnidus, an early Egyptian historian, found the military implications of this Jewish practice derisible: "These men, in observing this mad custom of theirs, instead of guarding the city, suffered their country to submit itself to a bitter lord; and their law was openly proved to have commanded a foolish practice."[48] A century and a half later, the Maccabees, the Jewish rebels who attempted to overthrow Seleucid rule over Judea, were similarly hampered by their refusal to defend themselves on the Sabbath until their leaders decreed that "whosoever shall come to make battle with us on the Sabbath day, we will fight against him; neither will we die all, as our brethren that were murdered."[49]

A more recent example of an attack timed to exploit an opponent's religious observance occurred during the Flagstaff War, the Maori uprising against British rule in New Zealand in 1845. British troops attacked both Ohaeawai Pa (on June 23) and Ruapekapeka Pa (on December 27) on Sundays, knowing all too well that their Maori targets were devout Christians and would be at church during the assault.[50] These and similar cases demonstrate that reliance on sacred time as a force multiplier need not occur across religious lines.

PEARL HARBOR, 1941

The Japanese decision to attack Pearl Harbor on December 7, 1941, provides another example of an attack executed on a Sunday with the expectation of enemy vulnerability. Although Thomas Schelling has argued that "our stupendous unreadiness at Pearl Harbor was neither a Sunday-morning, nor a Hawaiian, phenomenon,"[51] Japanese deliberations prior to the attack suggest otherwise. As Hajime Sugiyama and Osami Nagano, Japanese chiefs of staff, explained to Emperor Hirohito in an imperial audience on December 2:

> The primary reasons for scheduling December 8 as the date to initiate military action have to do with the phase of the moon and the day of the week. In order for the army and navy to implement the first air strike with ease and make it effective, a moonlit night between midnight and sunrise with the moon about 20 days old would be appropriate. A Sunday would be best for the naval task force's attack on Hawaii: relatively high numbers of warships will be berthed at Pearl

Harbor, Sunday being a day of rest and recreation. Therefore we have selected December 8, a Sunday in Hawaii, with the moon 19 days old. Of course, the 8th will be a Monday in the Far East, but we have put the emphasis on a surprise attack by the task force.[52]

The phases of the moon provided the primary constraint on timing the attack, but this still left Japanese decision makers with a two- to three-day window of opportunity, within which the American Sunday observance provided a secondary consideration. Chief of Staff Ryūnosuke Kusaka elaborated the logic behind Sugiyama and Nagano's reasoning, "It seems unlikely that battleships would leave on Saturday or Sunday," so a Sunday attack allowed military planners to assume that intelligence gathered the previous day was still accurate.[53]

Japanese decision makers may also have expected the battleships to be undermanned on a Sunday.[54] Captain Mitsuo Fuchida, who commanded the airborne attack, later said that he had "never, even in the deepest peace" seen such unprotected targets.[55] Servicemen had been given their customary Saturday evening liberty.[56] According to Rear Admiral Edwin T. Layton, at the time the combat intelligence officer in charge of the Pacific Ocean area, "the battle force was just awakening to the relaxed routine of another Sunday. Only three quarters of the crews were aboard and many ships had scuttles and watertight hatches unclipped."[57] This despite the awareness among U.S. intelligence agencies as early as April 1941 that "the Axis Powers often . . . [attack on] Saturday or Sunday or on national holidays," and recommendations that commanders put "proper watches and precautions . . . in effect."[58]

THE TET OFFENSIVE, 1968

In 1968, U.S. forces were caught off guard once again during a surprise attack timed with a religiously significant date. General Vo Nguyen Giap launched the Tet Offensive against U.S. and Army of the Republic of Vietnam (ARVN) forces during Tet Nguyen Dan, the most important holiday in the Vietnamese civil-religious calendar, as well as a period of truce between northern and southern forces.[59] The surprise was effective: "No one really expected the enemy to launch an attack," admitted General Earle Wheeler, chairman of the Joint Chiefs of Staff during the offensive, "because . . . this is a very sacred time to all the Vietnamese, North and South."[60] "I frankly did not think they would assume the psychological disadvantage of hitting at Tet itself," admitted General William Westmoreland. His staff had discounted the likelihood of an attack on Tet Nguyen Dan, in part because they expected such a sacrilegious act to constitute a public relations blunder for the North Vietnamese.[61]

Holiday leave had reduced ARVN troop presence to about half its regular strength, at best.[62] Soldiers could not be recalled on short notice; with newspapers closed for the holidays, radio was the only means of mass communication with soldiers on leave, many of whom ignored orders to return to their units and continued celebrating the feast.[63] The holiday bustle afforded the Viet Cong the opportunity of introducing combatants in civilian clothing into population centers, as well as smuggling arms and explosives, some hidden in trucks ostensibly carrying fruit and flowers for the celebration.[64] To confuse matters further, the Vietnamese tradition of setting off firecrackers during Tet seems to have encumbered attempts by South Vietnamese security forces to pinpoint combat zones in urban areas.[65]

Mutual initiation of conflict in conjuncture with both Muslim and Christian holy days characterized the Yugoslav civil war as well. Serbian paramilitaries commenced their ethnic cleansing campaign in Bosnia in 1992 on Eid al-Fitr, the Muslim holiday of sacrifice, a day on which their Muslim victims were preoccupied with celebrations and Bosnian police were off duty.[66] Bosnian Muslim forces based in Srebrenica, in turn, launched a massive attack against the Serbian village of Kravica on Orthodox Christmas Day in 1993 as villagers were preparing for the festive Christmas meal.[67]

Provocation

Attacks designed to exploit an opponent's holy day can backfire if they cause targets or third parties to be outraged. The provocation effect of conflict initiation in sacred time can thus be conceived as the cost that decision makers pay for abusing the exploitation effect of conflict initiation in sacred time. Given the real costs of alienating a local civilian population or an international audience, we should expect leaders to hesitate to time their attacks on holy days, particularly during wars of occupation or insurgencies that include a hearts-and-minds component.

Americans reacted with indignation to the attack on Pearl Harbor, not only because it was not preceded by a formal declaration of war but also due to its "dastardly" nature.[68] In emphasizing the "infamy" of an attack that "suddenly sliced through a peaceful Sunday morning and brought war to America," Roosevelt was invoking a "religiously tinged language of retribution."[69] The symbol of the "massacre on a Sunday morning"[70] remained potent throughout the War in the Pacific.[71]

Vietnamese observers were similarly alienated by the timing of the Tet Offensive. "The Tet offensive was the best opportunity to see the Viet Cong insurgents and their North Vietnamese accomplices in their true light," wrote one Vietnamese analyst. "The Communists show absolute contempt for the people's welfare in starting an unprecedented offensive at the height of the nation's most sacred holiday."[72]

Jews worldwide were outraged at the Arab assault on Yom Kippur. According to Abba Eban, "The choice of Yom Kippur for the Arab attack seemed at first to be diabolic; it added the crime of sacrilege to the sin of aggression."[73] Many U.S. Jews first heard of the attack during Yom Kippur services in their synagogues and quickly rallied to organize donations for the Israeli war effort.[74]

Yet other attacks are timed to coincide with an opponent's sacred day precisely because the initiator wishes to provoke outrage. On March 27, 2002, in an attempt to derail a peace initiative by the Arab League and thwart U.S. mediation efforts, a Hamas suicide bomber attacked the dining room of an Israeli hotel in the middle of the Passover Seder (ceremonial meal). The explosion, which killed thirty worshippers, became known as the Passover Massacre and incensed Israelis across the political spectrum.[75] "It's not a coincidence that the idea was to hit during Passover Seder, one of the most important moments in Jewish life," commented a spokesperson for the Israeli government. "It sends a double message to Israel and the Jews of hate, and to the Arabs, a message of extremism."[76] Within two days of the attack, Israeli Prime Minister Ariel Sharon issued the largest call-up of reservists in twenty years and launched Operation Defensive Shield, the largest Israeli military operation in the West Bank since 1967.[77]

Even attacks at minor religious events can unleash this response. In November 2014, a Palestinian terror attack on a Jerusalem synagogue caused outrage not only because of the sacred site and the innocence of the victims but also because the targets were at prayer when they were assaulted. Media images of bloodied prayer shawls sprawled across the synagogue floor encapsulated the triple sacrilege to space, community, and time.[78]

Even when the religious calendar plays no role in the planning of an attack, carelessness in the timing of a military offensive can provoke indignation, as Indian authorities learned during their disastrous confrontation of a Sikh insurgency in the Golden Temple complex in Amritsar. In 1984, Indian Special Forces began planning a complex operation focused on eliminating insurgents who had sought refuge inside this most sacred Sikh temple. The operation, code-named Operation Blue Star, was a disaster on all fronts.[79] Sikhs were outraged not only by the extensive damage to their most sacred shrine but also by the insensitivity of the Indian government, as demonstrated by the date chosen for the operation. When the attack occurred, Amritsar was crowded with visitors who were there to commemorate the day on which the Sikh guru and founder of the temple, Guru Arjun, was martyred. The attack also coincided with the fifth day of a lunar month, a particularly auspicious day for bathing in the temple pool. One thousand pilgrims lost their lives during the attack.[80] Although the religious date of the attack did not determine its timing, it did influence the casualty rates and, consequently, the public uproar in response to the operation. Six months after Operation Blue Star, Indian Prime Minister Indira Gandhi was assassinated by her Sikh bodyguards, unleashing months of sectarian riots across India.

Demonstrating Causation

Attributing significance to conflicts based on their coinciding with religiously salient dates poses two problems. The first problem is selection bias. Because, in hindsight, any given date in the calendar can be seen as holding religious significance for the followers of some religious movement or other, how can we demonstrate persuasively that the concurrence of combat and sacred time is not coincidental?[81] Accidental concurrences are particularly difficult to rule out when either a large number of violent attacks or a wide range of religiously significant dates is present. Spurious correlations pose a second problem; even if particular incidents of violence correlate consistently with sacred dates, such a correlation may not amount to causation.

The challenge is to demonstrate persuasively that the sacred nature of a particular date influenced choices made by decision makers ex ante. Consider the timing of the largest amphibious assault in the Pacific Theater during the World War II, the Battle of Okinawa, on April 1, 1945. The assault coincided not just with April Fool's Day but also with Easter Sunday, the Christian commemoration of the Resurrection. Although soldiers' descriptions of "the war's greatest Gethsemane" are tinged with allusions to the events of the Passion, we can be as confident that U.S. commanders did not choose the date with Easter in mind as we can be that they did not choose it with April Fool's Day in mind. The timing of the Battle of Okinawa with Easter, like the coinciding of the final Japanese attack on Bataan with Good Friday in 1942, was unintentional.[82]

There are two means of addressing selection bias and spurious correlation: statistically analyzing comprehensive empirical data on conflict across time and examining statements made by decision makers during the planning of an attack. I demonstrate the former in chapter 6, where I analyze patterns of Iraqi insurgent attacks during Ramadan. Exploring statements made by conflict initiators allows us to corroborate whether these decision makers consciously elected to time their attacks with dates of religious significance in mind; however, such testimonial evidence is not always readily available. For example, given the direct and significant impact of Tet on ARVN military effectiveness, it stands to reason that General Vo Nguyen Giap was aware of the religious implications of his decision to time the Tet Offensive with the Vietnamese New Year.[83] But due to the dearth in North Vietnamese archival material pertaining to the Tet Offensive as well as reluctance to be interviewed by Cecil Currey, his foremost biographer, we have no smoking gun to establish whether Giap chose January 31, 1968, as the date for the Tet Offensive because it was the date of the Vietnamese New Year.[84]

The Yom Kippur War

In other cases, the causal link between sacred time and combat is amply documented. Statements by the four most important members of the Egyptian high command, for example, suggest that the religious implications of Jewish Yom Kippur observance were a factor, although by no means the most important factor, in the Egyptian decision to select October 6 as the launch date for the surprise attack on Israel in 1973.

Egyptian President Anwar el-Sadat confirmed that, once other tactical, operational, and strategic constraints had been taken into account, the religious significance of October 6 provided a tiebreaker between viable attack dates: "General el-Gamasy, Director of Operations of the armed forces, submitted to us a notebook in which he had entered the dates most appropriate, from the military point of view, for starting a war in 1973. . . . The first a set of days in May 1973; the second in August and September 1973; and the third in October 1973. The most suitable of these for several reasons was the last. An attack could coincide with Yom Kippur—the Day of Atonement—on October 6 when all public services in Israel would be suspended."[85] Egyptian Commander in Chief of the Armed Forces Mohammed Abdel Ghani El-Gamasy elucidated the expected effects of the Jewish holiday on Israeli military effectiveness:

What was important to us was to know the effect each holiday had on general mobilization in Israel since their forces depended very largely on reservists for war. . . . We discovered that Yom Kippur fell on a Saturday and, what was more important, that it was the only day throughout the year in which radio and television stopped broadcasting as part of the religious observance and traditions of that feast. In other words, a speedy recall of the reserve forces using public means could not be made. Consequently, they would have to use other and slower means to mobilize the reserves.[86]

Egyptian Chief of Staff Saad al Shazly validated the vulnerability logic outlined by El-Gamasy but also emphasized the motivational effects of the date on Arab soldiers:

This was one of the deciding factors in choosing October 6 for an attack: on that day both religious and secular Jews fast, abstain from the use of fire or electricity (which meant transportation would be at a standstill), and much of the Israeli army would be demobilised. The sixth of October would also coincide with the tenth of Ramadan, which meant that Muslim soldiers would also be fasting. It was in Ramadan that the Muslims won their first victory at the Battle of Badr in the year 634. Opting for something more inspirational than High Minarets as a name, Operation Badr was chosen by Egyptian commanders as the codename for the assault.[87]

These statements by the Egyptian high command confirm that three of the four effects of sacred time were at play in the decision to initiate the 1973 War on October 6: an expectation regarding Israeli vulnerability due to the Jewish holy day, an anticipation of Egyptian motivation due to the Muslim holy day, and the speculation that Israeli decision makers would expect the Egyptian military to be constrained by the symbolic significance of the Muslim date.

In actuality, few of these expectations were realized. The timing of the attack did not seem to affect the speed of troop movements to the front, but it was one of several factors that led to Israeli hesitation in calling up reserves in the first place. The primary reasons for this reluctance had nothing to do with the holiday; they stemmed from concern over the costs of a redundant mobilization along with inadvertently provoking war and, thus, bearing responsibility for that war. The presence of Yom Kippur complicated this calculation further by hampering the broadcasting of a public alert and increasing the likelihood that the public would overreact to such an alert.[88] These considerations are evident in an exchange between Israeli Minister of Defense Moshe Dayan and the chief of staff of the Israel Defense Forces

(IDF), David Elazar, in a meeting the day before the war, as recalled by then chief of military intelligence, Eli Zeira:

> ELAZAR: [T]he problem is that during this holy day the entire country is dead.
>
> DAYAN: That won't stand in our way.
>
> ELAZAR: It will, if something happens and we want to openly mobilize or issue alerts.
>
> DAYAN: There will be no mobilizing unless it really starts. The roads are empty today.
>
> ELAZAR: But we have no radio. We've been thinking, perhaps we should instruct the military's radio station to read psalms every two hours?
>
> DAYAN: Then we would have to tell everyone to listen to the military's radio station. That would cause a great panic. If we don't, who would tune in to listen to psalms? Nobody would turn on the radio.[89]

There is some anecdotal evidence of Israeli soldiers praying or fasting when the attack began but no indication that this affected their ability to fight. Orders to break the fast, accompanied by rabbinical sanction, were issued rapidly and obeyed immediately.[90] Some Israeli soldiers, perhaps as many as a quarter of those stationed at certain units along the front, had been given holiday leave.[91] Yet air raid sirens immediately after the attack alerted Israelis to turn on their televisions and radios, which started broadcasting the call to arms half an hour after the initial Egyptian assault.[92] This alert was backed up by phone calls and couriers, who were able to locate reservists readily at their homes or nearby synagogues.[93] As Dayan had recognized, vacant roads due to the norm against driving on Yom Kippur facilitated both the movement of couriers and the rapid deployment of troops to the front.[94] As a result, the majority of units reached the front within forty-eight hours, the standard time allotted by the Israeli military for mobilization, and many did so within twenty-four hours.[95]

In sum, Egyptian analysts were correct in attributing great significance to Yom Kippur as a date of religious centrality in the Jewish calendar. They were also correct in their assessment of the salience of the day for Israelis, regardless of piety. The widespread observance of Yom Kippur rites prevails in Israeli society across social, ethnic, and economic divides. Egyptian planners erred, however, in expecting that these practices would have a significant effect on IDF capabilities. Israeli commanders were quick to override any such impact by implementing alternative means of mobilization, aided by the taboo on driving, of which their Egyptian counterparts seemed unaware.

Israeli intelligence fared much worse, given its inability to predict the timing, means, or scale of the combined Egyptian-Syrian assault. Ironically, the Israeli failure to give credence to advanced warnings about an impending Arab attack may have stemmed, in small part, from a misreading of Muslim sacred time. The surprise attack on Israel coincided not only with Yom Kippur but also with the holy Muslim month of Ramadan. According to El-Gamasy, the expectation that Israeli leaders would dismiss the likelihood of an assault during this holy Muslim month also figured into Egyptian calculations: "The enemy would not have expected us to carry out an attack during the month of fasting."[96] El-Gamasy seems to have overestimated the extent to which Israeli analysts were aware of Muslim fasting practices or were willing to incorporate those into their estimates. To the contrary, a report prepared by the Research Department of the IDF military intelligence branch a day before the war noted recent Egyptian orders that prohibited soldiers from observing the Ramadan fast yet failed to realize the significance of this key indicator.[97]

Israeli analysts also failed to recognize the salience and the impact of the symbolism of the holiday for Egyptian soldiers. October 6 was not just Yom Kippur but also the anniversary of the Battle of Badr, as previously discussed a symbol of decisive military victory against all odds guided by divine intervention.[98] Launching an attack on the anniversary of the Battle of Badr was "a good omen," in the words of Egyptian Minister of War Ahmad Ismail, and "to the moral and psychological advantage of our own forces," according to El-Gamasy.[99] Rather than handicapping Egyptian forces, the symbolism of Badr propelled them into battle.[100] Israeli decision makers, on the other hand, remained wedded to the conception that Ramadan posed a vulnerability for their adversaries. The aforementioned intelligence report explained unusual Egyptian troop movements in terms of "Egyptian apprehensions of an Israeli intention to exploit . . . the Ramadan feast for an offensive."[101] In other words, the Israeli assumption was that, if sacred time mattered at all, it did so to the detriment of Egypt, not Israel.

Why did the Egyptians and Israelis fail to correctly assess the impact of sacred time on their opponents? Any answer must rest on speculation. One possible hypothesis is that both errors stemmed from a mirror imaging of religious practices. According to this premise, Egyptians overestimated the effects of Yom Kippur because they analyzed it through the lens of Ramadan. The Ramadan fast extends for a month and has a higher effect on fatigue than the day-long Yom Kippur fast. Muslims work during Ramadan and gather in mosques in the evenings, whereas Jews spend all of Yom Kippur at home or in synagogues. Ramadan increases traffic, whereas Yom Kippur brings traffic to a standstill. Israelis, on the other hand, may have misread the implications of Ramadan on war initiation because they analyzed the Muslim holy day through the lens of the Jewish holy day. Unlike Ramadan, the symbolic association of Yom Kippur is not with victory and solemn festivity but with repentance and trepidation.

Sacred time may not have produced the results that Egyptian military planners hoped for. Nevertheless, the false expectation that sacred time would hamper the IDF shaped Arab and Israeli behavior both before and during the war. The 1973 Arab-Israeli War is thus remarkable because it demonstrates the relevance of religious practices in a secular contemporary war between secular professionalized armed forces.

Lessons from Sacred Time

Sacred time has encouraged and discouraged participation in conflict, facilitated and hampered mobilization, and stimulated and dampened the enthusiasm with which combatants have fought. Yet the study of conflict and the religious calendar poses significant challenges. Even if analysts can accumulate the archival evidence required to document a causal link between the two, they face the challenge of determining the salience of sacred time in conflict. Assessing the impact of a particular timing on the outcome of a given conflict requires delicate counterfactual analysis because sacred time rarely determines success or failure in battle. How critical were Vietnamese New Year celebrations to the surprise of the Tet Offensive? What degree of surprise would the Japanese have achieved had they attacked Pearl Harbor on a weekday? Might Arab militaries have fared better against Israel in 1973 had they chosen not to attack on Yom Kippur?

To some extent, these questions obscure the true contribution of the study of sacred time to the analysis of international conflict. The coinciding of Yom Kippur with the Arab assault on Israel should be of interest to political scientists not because it influenced the outcome of the 1973 War but because it highlights the role of religion in contemporary, secular, interstate war. The Jewish Day of Atonement may only have affected mobilization, combat readiness, and battlefield performance at the margins; however, it did so in a war between two secular states, defended by professional and conventional armed forces, neither of which fought for religious reasons or sought to achieve religious goals. Religion can be more than just a cause for war. Religious identity matters in conflict, not only across the civilizational battle lines proposed by Samuel Huntington but also when rivals share a common religious identity. As the Christmas truces of World War I suggest, even shared religious sensibilities can shape war, for better or worse.

CHAPTER 3

Where?

Sacred Space and War

For religious practitioners, geography is not uniform. Salvation can more easily be obtained at some sites, where the sacred breaks through into the human realm and becomes accessible. Sacred shrines perform this function and, as a result, become religious centers. They are places with a divine presence at which worshippers can expect blessings, healing, forgiveness, and spiritual merit. At the same time, religious practitioners seek to protect that sacred presence by circumscribing access to holy places and behavior within them. A transgression of these rules, or any damage to the structure itself, is tantamount to desecration.

Like sacred time, sacred space can influence decision making by military forces—even when those military forces are not pursuing religious objectives. The most important sacred shrines are large, ornate, and architecturally vulnerable monuments, located in city centers that teem with worshippers. Because they have physical properties, sacred shrines are susceptible to harm. This sets sacred space apart from sacred time. Religious practices performed in sacred time are vulnerable to desecration, but the sacred time itself is not. Each sacred space, on the other hand, has a global religious appeal precisely because each space is unique. One cannot desecrate Christmas; one can desecrate only a particular Christmas ritual in a specific location. But to desecrate Rome is to provoke Western Christianity as a whole.

The force-multiplying effects of sacred space are weak; in conventional interstate conflict, shrines provide a minor motivation for combat. Any advantages that might be gained from exploiting an opponent's reliance on sacred space are outweighed by the costs of provoking both local and global outrage. Thus, unlike sacred time, which can have a motivating or constraining influence on combat, depending on context, sacred space tends to exert a uniform effect on professional militaries: their soldiers will seek to minimize the damage to sacred sites and to the worshippers in their vicinity. Because sacred space forces armies to constrain their resorting to force, it is a force divider. As I show in this chapter, twentieth-century militaries have neither targeted nor tried to exploit their opponents' sacred space to their advantage, and as a consequence, they have not provoked religious outrage for intentionally damaging such sites. This respect for religious sites is reflected in, and bolstered by, Article 27 of the 1907 Hague Convention, which requires armies "to spare, as far as possible, buildings dedicated to religion, art, science, or charitable purposes, historic monuments, hospitals, and places where the sick and wounded are collected, provided they are not being used at the time for military purposes."[1]

If these legal instruments treat sacred places as one category, among many, of structures that deserve protection, why would we expect decision makers (or scholars, for that matter) to afford them unique treatment? In other words, what is religious about protecting sacred space? Did the destruction of St. Martin's Cathedral in Ypres during World War I have implications that set it apart from the destruction of the famous Ypres Cloth Hall in that war?

The answer is yes, for two reasons. Damage to sacred sites provokes a broader audience, and it does so to a greater extent than damage to other types of monuments and public buildings. With the exception of particularly ancient or artistically valuable structures, most public buildings and monuments are valued only by local communities. Religious sites broaden and deepen that audience. Not only are they revered by global communities of faith, but the rules governing the desecration of religious sites are crisp and unambiguous.

Moreover, their vulnerability compounds many of the specific reasons that make secular structures susceptible to risk. Public structures, such as hospitals and schools, are sensitive because civilians tend to congregate in them. Cultural assets are sensitive due to their artistic and historical value. Government buildings and historical monuments have nationalist appeal. Religious centers exhibit all these characteristics together; they have historical, artistic, and nationalist appeal, but they also attract noncombatants in large numbers, particularly when sacred space overlaps with sacred time. On holy days, sacred places teem with worshippers and make tempting targets for those seeking to maximize harm. Indeed, sacred sites in many religious traditions have the official status of sanctuaries, places protected from even the most legitimate sources of violence.[2] If museums, universities, and theaters are deserving of discrimination at times of war, churches are deserving a fortiori. One of the implications of this logic during World War II was that the Allied committees that sought to protect cultural treasures focused the lion's share of their attention on churches.

In this chapter, I explore this logic by tracing the particular ways in which sacred space influenced British and U.S. combat during World War II. In contrast to previous chapters, in which I illustrated the logic of religion as a force multiplier by means of a range of examples across the nineteenth and twentieth centuries, here I offer a single, crucial, and detailed historical case study, drawing on archival evidence to showcase Allied decision making regarding sacred sites in Europe. This in-depth approach is sensible because, unlike sacred time, sacred space has exerted only one primary effect on modern combat. The analysis of U.S. and British policy during the Second World War permits me to probe the constraining effects of sacred space in an unexpected setting. This level of scrutiny also allows me to rely on primary sources to uncover precise motivations, mechanisms, and implications. I rely in particular on materials that document the deliberations among high-ranking U.S. and British leaders, as well as documents amassed by the American Commission for the Protection and Salvage of Artistic and Historic Monuments in War Areas (also known as the Roberts Commission).

In the first section, I briefly survey the three minor effects of sacred space on modern combat. I argue that holy sites have rarely acted to motivate interstate conflict in modern times, although occasionally highly visible sacred places have provided some degree of hope and comfort for civilians and combatants. More surprisingly, given the central role that sacred places play in the religious practices of so many societies, twentieth-century armies have not sought to exploit their opponents' sacred sites. Even when British Bomber Command began pursuing a policy of "morale bombing," sacred places played no part in their calculations. As a consequence, despite some public outrage, the incidental destruction of sacred places did not lead to retaliation in kind.

In the second section, I show how sacred space constrained the use of force by analyzing Allied deliberations about the bombing of Rome and, further, by tracing the consequences of those deliberations. In the third section, I document the broader Allied effort at identifying, protecting, and restoring cultural monuments and religious structures more specifically. I explore the origins and procedures of the Roberts Commission and evaluate the effect that it had on the conduct of war.

Motivation, Exploitation, and Provocation in Modern Interstate War

Motivation

I have examined instances of conflict provoked by sacred space elsewhere.[3] These have tended to involve nonstate actors driven by religious ideology and are thus excluded from the cases analyzed in this volume. In contemporary conflicts between professional armies, sacred space has rarely acted as an important motivator.

The three battles over Jerusalem in the twentieth century are a rare exception. Due to the extraordinary religious symbolism of the city, even seasoned commanders and soldiers expressed a mixture of religious and nationalist enthusiasm at the thought of possessing the city and dismay at the prospect of losing it. In 1917, David Lloyd George encouraged General Edmund Allenby to seize Jerusalem "as a Christmas present for the British nation," leading some British soldiers to think of themselves as modern-day crusaders.[4] Ordered to retreat from Jerusalem, Field Marshall Erich von Falkenhayn cried, "I lost Verdun and now you ask me to evacuate the city which is the cynosure of the world's attention. Impossible!"[5] In 1967, Israeli leaders and commanders spoke in messianic terms of their liberation of Jerusalem on behalf of the Jewish people, a "moment of redemption" that atoned for the sins of the war of 1948, when they had lost the city to the Jordanians. Meanwhile, in Jordan, King Hussein wept for having to bear the responsibility of defeat.[6] But even in these cases, strategic calculations trumped religious nationalism: Falkenhayn's officers persuaded the general to evacuate the city, which had no strategic value, and the Israeli cabinet approved the conquest of Jerusalem after much deliberation and only after victory in the war as a whole had been secured.

Such motivation as holy places did impart on participants in modern wars was subtle, often as a symbol of hope. Shrines did not encourage conflict but, instead, motivated soldiers and civilians to endure its challenges. Soldiers erected protective shrines near outposts and even in the walls of their trenches.[7] Because sacred structures were particularly vulnerable to the ravages of war, their survival represented the comforting stability of religion and perhaps even a modicum of divine presence amid the chaos of the battlefield. Soldiers attributed miraculous powers to churches, crucifixes, and calvaries that survived the shelling and bombing. They sought shelter in churches, not only because these were often the sturdiest buildings around but also because soldiers believed that providence might render them immune from enemy attack.[8]

Such was the case with the famous "Leaning Virgin" of Albert, a colossal gilded statue of the Virgin and child atop the Basilica of Notre Dame de Brebieres, which became a symbol of hope during World War I. The church—along the route that hundreds of thousands of soldiers took on their way to the Somme—had sustained a direct hit from a German shell and had begun to crumble. The statue hung precariously off its dome, bent below the horizon, but did not topple. Passing soldiers attributed agency to the statue, imagined that she was offering her child as a peace offering, that she was saving the child from falling as she would save the soldiers too, or that she was intent on destroying herself in despair. British, French, and German troops shared in the belief that whichever side might cause the statue to finally fall would lose the war, thus finally putting an end to the fighting.[9]

The miraculous survival of churches played a more influential role yet during World War II, which left so many city centers in ruin. No religious structure played a greater symbolic function than the Cathedral of Saint Paul in London, its white dome famously peering through the smoke during the Blitz: "an island of God, safe and untouched."[10] St. Paul's became the embodiment of British spirit during the Battle of Britain, "a national icon of faith, hope, endurance and unity" and an emblem of Christian triumph over German "neo-paganism."[11]

It is precisely because St. Paul's emerged unscathed from German attacks that it came to symbolize British fortitude. "You know, mate, I ain't a religious bloke," a London printer confessed, "but I should hate to see dear old St. Paul's hurt or damaged. Somehow—you know what I mean, mate—somehow—well blast it all, it's *London,* ain't it?"[12] Dorothy Barton, an office worker, saw the cathedral towering over the smoking ruins London: "I felt a lump in my throat because, like so many people, I felt that while St Paul's survived, so would we."[13] This is how a homemaker from Bethnal Green described her experience of the Blitz: "I could see St. Paul's standing there, and the fire all around, and I just said: 'Please God, don't let it go!' I couldn't help it, I felt that if St. Paul's had gone, something would have gone from us. But it stood in defiance, it did. And when the boys were coming back, the firemen said: 'It's bad, but, oh, the old church stood it.' Lovely, that was."[14]

This survival was not entirely miraculous. British authorities grasped the charismatic hold that the building exerted on their citizens, exploited it for propaganda purposes, and did everything in their power to protect the structure. Special units of the Air Raid Precautions guarded the cathedral around the clock and extinguished its frequent fires—this despite its irrelevance to the civil defense of the city. A propaganda film from the period, "Guardians of St. Paul's," reassured viewers of the "sacred trust" with which these men protected "the mother church of the empire."[15] The British National Firefighters Memorial, erected near the cathedral in 1991, commemorates their success in protecting this particular building rather than any other structure in Britain. It represents two firefighters aiming a water hose at the cathedral while a third gestures toward it in alarm.

Elsewhere in the United Kingdom, churches carried a similar message of reassurance, even when they succumbed to destruction. In a Belfast church, the survival of a single stained-glass window showing Christ and the Apostles was taken to mean that "God after all was still on the side of the city." An undamaged Jesus statue in a demolished Plymouth church and candles still burning on the altar of the bombed-out Royal Military Chapel in London offered encouragement, not despair.[16] After the war, several important churches were left in a semi-ruined state. Coventry Cathedral, the Frauenkirche in Dresden, the Nicholas Church in Hamburg, and the Kaiser Wilhelm Church in Berlin, all reminded survivors of the ordeals they had endured, reminded perpetrators of the price they had exacted, and reminded everyone else of the threat of war to European values.[17]

Exploitation

The positive influence on public morale that sacred places exerted—regardless of whether they were intact or destroyed—combined with the legal prohibition on targeting churches expressed in international conventions helps to explain why professional armies so rarely exploited their opponents' reverence toward sacred sites. Commanders tended to respect these rules and often added restrictions of their own to prevent soldiers from offending local religious sensibilities. Even in early modern wars, soldiers were warned not to mock religious sites, ceremonies, or officials, particularly when the religious identity of the occupier differed from that of the local population.[18] Commanders in both world wars also prohibited their chaplains from conducting ceremonies in enemy churches without the express permission of local clergy, a rule that even Wehrmacht officers enforced in occupied Russia.[19] Prior to the Allied invasion of Italy and again prior to the liberation of France, Eisenhower issued orders (see chapter 1) to protect churches and other monuments, as well as orders prohibiting the use of thousands of ecclesiastical structures for any military purpose.[20] Such orders coincided nicely with the prevailing superstition among soldiers—held even in World War II—that the misuse of churches would bring bad luck.[21]

When units did choose to exploit religious structures, it was the physical features—not the religious value of these buildings—that they targeted. Churches tended to be the sturdiest buildings in smaller towns. They were also uninhabited, which made them ideal structures for housing the sick and wounded, bolstered by the hope that the enemy would not target such structures intentionally. But the respect that most combatants showed toward religious buildings created concerns that opponents would exploit that reluctance to their advantage.[22] This was particularly true of church steeples, which made for good observation posts for sentries, snipers, and observers calling in target coordinates to artillery batteries or mortar operators. Once an enemy was spotted in a bell tower, commanders required tremendous restraint not to target the structure. In Pisa, tragically, German soldiers chose to direct artillery fire from the Leaning Tower, and Allied commanders did not refrain from firing on their position.[23] On occasion, retreating units destroyed churches to prevent their opponents from exploiting their steeples or to create roadblocks.[24] Some soldiers looted or vandalized churches, stored ammunition in churches, or booby-trapped them—particularly during shameful retreats—but these incidents were exceptions to the norm.[25]

The targeting of churches in bombing campaigns was even more incidental to their religious function. Air crews aimed their payloads at churches not to maximize deaths among worshippers or to undermine morale but because churches were the most visible human-made landmarks available; they were tall structures, located in city centers, and liable to survive several rounds of bombing. In actuality, British pilots could not have targeted churches intentionally had they chosen to; bombing at night, from high altitude and with unsophisticated bombsights, permitted no such precision.[26] But the practice of using churches at the center of cities as targets ensured the eventual destruction of these structures regardless of accuracy. British bombers sent to destroy Cologne (May 1942), Hamburg (July 1943), and Kassel (October 1943), for example, were instructed to use the spires of churches in the city centers as visual guides and to drop their payloads within a 3-mile radius of those churches.[27]

Remarkably, in all their discussions of "morale bombing," the members of Bomber Command or the Air Ministry made no reference to the desirability of targeting churches. This omission is noteworthy given the stated goal, as Sir Charles Portal put it to Winston Churchill, of a "general dislocation of industrial and social life arising from . . . all that goes to make up the general activity of a community."[28] The controversial Lindemann Memorandum on dehousing and morale, which had a significant influence on Churchill's support for area bombing, makes no mention of churches.[29] We might attribute this silence to the lessons the British had learned about the motivational impact of churches from their own experience during the Blitz: some sacred sites offered encouragement regardless of their integrity. The city bombing campaign was also under scrutiny by several leaders of the English clergy, for example, the bishops of Chichester and Birmingham and the former archbishop of Canterbury, who would have protested an official policy of targeting churches.[30]

Finally, British decision makers may have had sincere scruples about targeting Christian shrines, even if they were on German soil. The sole reference to churches in Air Ministry documents of this period suggests as much. At least, it suggests that decision makers expected air crews to express misgivings about the intentional targeting of churches. When Arthur Harris made his most provocative statement about "morale bombing," suggesting that its aim was "the disruption of civilized life throughout Germany," the ministry recoiled: "What is in dispute is whether, in order to maintain the morale of Bomber Command air crews and avoid unfair comparison with the methods adopted by the U.S.A.A.F. in their daylight attacks, it is necessary to include in the definition of avowed targets for direct attack civilian workers and the whole of a city including dwelling places and cultural and religious monuments. The Council cannot agree that it is."[31]

Provocation

Because professional armies have done little to purposefully exploit sacred places in the course of military operations, they rarely provoked a widespread outcry of substantial impact. The sole exception in the twentieth century was the uproar incited by German atrocities in Belgium in 1914. Much of that outrage was directed at German brutality against civilians, but the wanton desecration of multiple Belgian churches—most famously the burning of the Catholic University library and church in Leuven—contributed to the "Rape of Belgium" narrative that mobilized British and U.S. public opinion. A 1915 "Report of the Committee on Alleged German Outrages" by the Bryce Committee in the United Kingdom, which played an important role in persuading the United States to join the war, documented in lurid detail the German use of Belgian churches as prisons, stables, and outhouses, as well as the brutal killing of priests.[32] Accounts of the German occupation of Belgium published during the war described the destruction and desecration of churches in Heure le Romain, Gelrode, Aerschot, Campenhout, Rotselaer,

Lebbeke, Dinant, Malines, Visa, and Termonde, accompanied by photos.[33] A famous contemporary poem by Rev. Hardwicke D. Rawnsley, an official of the Church of England Peace League, captured the British mood at the time: "Religion, books, carved stone and storied pane, pleaded as vainly as the men you shot, wherefore our indignation burns red-hot, above the fiery ashes of Louvain."[34]

The shelling of Rheims Cathedral in France, where all French kings had been crowned since the Middle Ages, caused additional outrage. Images of the "Martyred Cathedral" in ruins were a recurring motif in propaganda posters of the period, intent on depicting the Germans as anti-Christian barbarians. L'Ange ou Sourir, the statue of a smiling angel recovered from the rubble of the cathedral, became a symbol of French endurance and German savagery. German authorities, in turn, claimed that they had responded to observation posts and machine gun fire from the cathedral tower.[35]

The general absence of any intentional targeting of sacred sites did not, however, prevent observers from assigning such intentionality to their adversaries. During the Second World War, the very same Londoners who attributed the survival of the Cologne Cathedral to the accuracy of Royal Air Force (RAF) bombers and the piety of the Bomber Command also attributed the targeting of St. Paul's to German savagery (and its survival to divine providence).[36] As mentioned earlier, however, given the altitude from which the RAF and the Luftwaffe were bombing, given their decision to attack at night, and given the crude state of their bombsights in the early years of the war, pilots would have been unable to target (or spare) particular churches had they chosen to do so.

Nevertheless, the perception that churches and other monuments were being targeted on purpose was bolstered by official propaganda, which sought to stir up hatred against an enemy intent on destroying one's culture, religion, and history. The German Propaganda Ministry downplayed the civilian casualties of British air raids but offered detailed descriptions of the churches destroyed by "the brutal gangsters" who were attacking "the irreplaceable values of European culture."[37] The Italian government published commemorative stamps and propaganda booklets—such as "What the English Have Done in Cyrenaica" or "The War against Art"—that displayed photos of ruined museums, churches, and palaces. Government officials painted the cynical message "handiwork of the liberators" on the wreckage of cultural monuments as a warning against collaboration with the Allies.[38] On the other side, in U.S. newspaper cartoons Germany was depicted as a giant looming over St. Peter's in Rome, with the landmarks of other cities burning in the background.[39]

These propaganda efforts had an impact on civilians. In December 1943, 64 percent of British people favored the policy of firebombing German cities, and 47 percent of British people polled listed "satisfaction" as their primary emotional reaction to city bombing in Germany because it gave the Germans a taste of "their own medicine."[40] Calls for retribution were at their loudest after the "wicked" destruction of the fourteenth-century Coventry Cathedral in November 1940 and the annihilation of most of the Restoration-era churches in London.[41] "My church is down," fumed one vicar, "but my blood is up."[42] A Londoner wrote to her U.S. pen-pal, "I think I'd give up half my salary if someone would drop a bomb on Cologne Cathedral, or some of Germany's precious monuments for what they did to our beautiful Coventry. . . . [People] can't go on like this for ever, unless they know that the Germans are taking the same medicine."[43] A visitor to the shell of Coventry Cathedral whispered to an RAF pilot standing nearby, "Please God you will avenge what was done to us that night."[44] And Arthur Harris, head of Bomber Command, who watched the fires going up around St. Paul's Cathedral from the roof of the Air Ministry, warned ominously, "Now they are going to reap the whirlwind."[45]

It is hard to tell how much such personal sentiments affected Allied decision making. Andy Rooney, who was a pilot during the war, certainly overstates the case when he describes the massive attacks on Cologne and Dresden as a "British 'take that' response to the raid on Coventry . . . revenge . . . chosen by the British as a way of breaking the German's hearts."[46] Churchill and Harris both denied that retribution was a significant factor in city bombing, but they also realized the positive effect on home-front morale that such retaliation exerted: "On every side there is the cry, 'We can take it,'"[47] Churchill spoke at the House of Commons, "but with it is also the cry, 'Give it them back.'"[48]

The attack on Coventry did have a tremendous psychological effect on the British government. Despite months of German attacks on London, the government "Official Narrative" of the strategic air offensive focused on the Coventry bombing as "an occasion of singular importance in the history of air warfare" because it marked the first use of massive airpower to obliterate a small city.[49] Anthony Grayling, in his study of civilian bombing in World War II, identifies it as the single event that may have provoked British city bombing as a strategy. The first British effort at area bombing, the attack on Manheim in December 1940, occurred less than a month after the German attack on Coventry.[50] Henceforth, the British media measured the damage to German cities in "Coventries," each "Coventry" amounting to approximately 20,000 dead, so that Hamburg, for example, was said to have had "the equivalent of at least 60 Coventries."[51]

Even if damage to churches did not provoke a desire for retribution, it weakened scruples regarding collateral damage to cultural monuments among some decision makers. This was apparent in the deliberations regarding the bombing of Rome, discussed below. When the pope requested that the Allies abstain from bombing Rome in 1943, the U.S. representative at the Vatican commented wryly to the Vatican secretary of state that it was regrettable that the pope "did not raise his voice clearly in some such manner as this when civilians and cultural institutions were being bombed by Germans in the early stages of the war."[52] U.S. Army Chief of Staff George Marshall argued that the Allies should have "no qualms about Rome" given the bombing of St. Paul's, Westminster Abbey, and the churches on Malta. And British Secretary of State for Foreign Affairs Anthony Eden declared in the House of Commons that "we have as much right to bomb Rome as the Italians had to bomb London."[53] These statements betray less of a desire for retaliation than a growing indifference to the fate of an opponent's sacred structures.

Mixed messages about retribution were voiced in Germany as well. There, it was the RAF attack on the Lübeck, a medieval city of little strategic value, that unleashed demands for revenge in March 1942. Baron Gustav Braun von Stumm, a propagandist working for the German State Department, responded to the attack by promising, "We shall go out and bomb every building in Britain marked with three stars in the Bädeker Guide," alluding to the popular tourist handbook of the period.[54] He was reprimanded for his statement, but the expression "Bädeker Blitz" soon became common parlance for the alleged German policy of targeting British cathedral cities of historical and cultural value, such as Exeter, Bath, Norwich, and York, all attacked in April. A second round of Bädeker bombings occurred in May, when Germany responded to the attack on Cologne with an assault on Canterbury.

Available records provide insufficient information about the mind-sets of German or British leaders for us to determine whether such attacks were indeed retaliatory and, if so, whether this desire stemmed from personal outrage or from a broader desire to placate public opinion and bolster morale. In either case, shock over the tremendous civilian casualties of these attacks would have overwhelmed any particular outrage about the destruction of ancient churches.

In recent conflicts in the Middle East, leaders have tried to provoke outrage by "framing" their opponents for the destruction of sacred sites. For example, during the First Gulf War, Iraqi forces removed the dome of a mosque in Al-Basrah to make it appear as if the building had been damaged by coalition bombing. The Iraqi military also constructed makeshift mosques in the heart of ammunition depots in an effort to protect these sites from attack.[55] As I show toward the end of this book, insurgents are drawn to set up bases in sacred sites not only because of the tactical advantages that such places offer but also because their destruction in the course of battle would be blamed disproportionately on their opponents. Finally, it stands to reason that the location of the Iranian uranium enrichment facility in Fordow was chosen with a *provocation* logic in mind. Iran is a sizable country, yet the facility was placed a mere 30 miles northeast of Qom, the primary center for Shi'a scholarship in the world.[56] Regardless of the accuracy with which an attack on that facility might proceed, Iranian officials would certainly present it to Shi'a audiences as an assault on the heart of Islam.

These exceptions notwithstanding, sacred sites have not tended to function as a force multiplier in twentieth-century interstate conflicts. Armies were not motivated to fight by the mere presence of sacred places, nor did they seek to benefit from targeting these places intentionally. The reasons for this pattern of behavior were multiple and mutually reinforcing: the laws of war, religious scruples, public opinion at home, international pressure (particularly from the Vatican), and the desire to avoid provoking soon-to-be liberated populations. In contrast, the strategic benefits to be gained from reckless bombing were few, and the likelihood of undermining enemy morale through the purpose-ful targeting of churches was slim. The same rationale led sacred places to exert a significant constraining effect on the conduct of war, prompting lead-ers to deliberate, hesitate, and even refrain from attacks and leading armies to take remarkable precautions to minimize harm to religious sites.

Nowhere were these effects clearer than in the lead up to the bomb-ing and liberation of Europe. In the case of Rome, decision makers at the highest ranks debated the risks of accidental damage to shrines and placed severe constraints on pilots executing bombing missions over the city. More generally, the American Commission for the Protection and Salvage of Artistic and Historic Monuments in War Areas made mapping, protecting, and rebuilding the churches of Europe its objective and sought to constrain warfare in and around those sites with some success.

The Bombing of Rome

Deliberations

The Allies started debating the idea of bombing Rome in fall 1940, after the placement of bombers in Malta made targeting the city a realistic pros-pect. The Allies were divided over the issue, with Churchill favoring an attack and Franklin Roosevelt in opposition. Electoral politics played a role in these deliberations. Churchill's electorate consisted of few Catholics or Italians, whereas Roosevelt was preparing for reelection with a significant Democratic base consisting of both demographics.[57] In addition, the Allies disagreed on the costs and benefits of such an operation. The British wished to "hold themselves free to bomb Rome at any time they saw fit," while the Americans pushed for restraint, concerned over public opinion as well as the legal status of the Vatican, officially a neutral party to the war.[58]

Such disagreements were reflected in the respective war cabinets as well. In the United Kingdom, the Air Ministry and the RAF under Air Marshall Charles Portal were eager to launch bombers toward Rome, as were their U.S. counterparts, the U.S. Army Air Forces under Henry H. Arnold. The British War Cabinet and the Foreign Office worried that an attack would provoke worldwide Catholic condemnation. In October 1941, Portal conceded to the Foreign Office, "[T]he selection of the right moment to bomb Rome is clearly a matter of some delicacy." He also confessed to the secretary of state for air, Archibald Sinclair, that there was some reluctance among Bomber Command crews about bombing Rome. Sinclair had no patience for such scruples and scribbled on the margins of a memorandum about the bombing of Rome, "We must not hedge our airmen round with meticulous restrictions." He was even curter in a message to the archbishop of Canterbury, William Temple, who had inquired about the status of Rome. The Allies, Sinclair explained, would not refrain from bombing a military objective just because it was near old or beautiful buildings.[59]

Across the Atlantic, Secretary of War Henry L. Stimson joined Roosevelt in pushing for Rome to be recognized as an "open city" rather than a target to be bombed, whereas General Arnold felt that Eisenhower should make the decision about bombing Rome without regard for politics or religion. Army Chief of Staff George C. Marshall sided with Arnold and was determined that no "outside considerations" be allowed to interfere with "the firm prosecution of the war," telling the combined chiefs of staff that, although it would be a tragedy if Saint Peter's were destroyed, it would be a "calamity if we failed to knock out the marshalling yards."[60]

The Vatican tried to exert relentless pressure on this decision-making process. The pope repeatedly threatened the U.S. envoy to the Vatican with public protest should the Allies bomb Rome, emphasizing the damaging effect that the destruction would have on Catholics throughout the world, particularly in Latin America.[61] With the Allied invasion of Italy looming, the Vatican representatives continued to press for the recognition of Rome as an open city, emphasizing the deep-seated antagonism that the destruc-

tion of Rome would create worldwide. Public opinion polls lent some credence to concerns about how such attacks would be received even within
the United States and the United Kingdom. A majority of Americans polled
in April 1943 assumed that it was religion that had prevented the Allies from
bombing the city, and a majority of U.S. and British citizens supported that
policy.[62] The Vatican even went as far as to suggest that air strikes would
lead to spontaneous Roman rioting against the diplomats inside the Vatican
and could play into the hands of communist sympathizers lurking inside the
city.[63] In May 1943, Pope Pius sent a personal message to Roosevelt pleading
that Italian shrines of religion and art be spared ruin.[64]

These arguments proved less persuasive in the weeks leading up to the
invasion of Sicily due to concerns that the Germans would be relying on the
rail yards in Rome to move troops to southern Italy.[65] Churchill and Roosevelt had agreed at the May 1943 Trident Conference not to bomb Rome
without prior consultation. In early June, Churchill began trying in earnest
to persuade Roosevelt that the marshalling yards in Rome had to be targeted.
To assuage Roosevelt's fears, he emphasized that the Vatican was far from the
targets and on the opposite side of the Tiber, so if the bombing were carried
out in daylight, "there would be a small chance of damage to Rome itself,
and none of damage to the Vatican."[66] Roosevelt relented on June 14 but
emphasized, "Prior to launching these attacks, all pilots concerned must be
thoroughly instructed in the geography of the area, the location of the Vatican, and directed that they must not permit any bombs to fall in the Vatican
City." Roosevelt also conveyed to Churchill his intention of notifying the
pope of the attack and of the precautions that would be taken.[67]

Roosevelt's message to the pope the next day affirmed that "Americans
are among those who value most the religious shrines and the historical
monuments of Italy" yet insisted that military necessity might compel an
attack on Rome, in which case special precaution would be taken not to hit
Vatican City. He added a note of concern regarding Axis efforts to unleash
(what I have termed) a *provocation* effect: "I cannot feel assured that the planes
of the Axis would not manufacture an opportunity to strike Vatican City
with the purpose of charging Allied planes with the brutalities which they
had committed themselves."[68]

As the date of the bombing neared, questions about the precise nature
of the sacred sites that had to be taken into account during the raid came
to occupy a significant part of the correspondence between Roosevelt and
Churchill. Neither leader knew much about the religious landscape of the
city, and the committees that would later provide the Allies with crucial
information on the location and significance of sacred places had not yet

been formed. "His letter to me was not a request not to bomb Rome," Roosevelt wrote to Churchill about the pope, "but he spoke of the historic places and also spoke of the Holy See, which, I suppose, includes the Churches outside the Vatican."[69] Churchill offered his best guess in response: "I think we ought to instruct our pilots to observe all possible care in order to avoid hitting any of the Papal buildings in the city of Rome listed in Article 13 of Lateran Treaty, especially St. John Lateran."[70] The Lateran Treaty of 1929 affirmed that three basilicas—St. John Lateran, Sta. Maria Maggiore, and St. Paul—were Vatican property, in addition to the Basilica of St. Peter in the Vatican. These were the four Major Basilicas in Rome.

The treaty was drafted to stipulate the legal status of various Vatican properties, but it was a poor source of information on Catholic religious practices. It made no mention of the three Minor Basilicas that, together with the four others, formed the Seven Great Pilgrim Churches of Rome—the seven oldest churches that every pilgrim was expected to visit. These seven churches were also the sites at which pilgrims could receive plenary indulgences during the Jubilee Year. Missing from the Allies' list were the churches of Santa Croce, San Sebastiano, and San Lorenzo. Unbeknown to decision makers, that last basilica stood just northwest of the rail yard that had taken its name, the San Lorenzo rail yard, the target of the July raid.

The Vatican, meanwhile, sought to expand as much as possible the religious protection requested by the pope. In a letter of June 25, the Vatican delegate to the United States, Amleto Cicognani, explained, "it is not a question merely of Vatican City but of the entire city of Rome, the Episcopal See of the Holy Father."[71] Roosevelt acknowledged this point in his reply: "We fully realize all that the pope has said about Rome as a whole and that we have no desire to destroy any church property or historic monuments."[72] He also requested Churchill's permission to convey his personal reassurances to the pope "because of the large percentage of Catholics here, and because the pope and I have a rather personal relationship." In his message to the pope, Roosevelt promised that "churches and religious institutions will, to the extent that it is within our power, be spared the devastation of war during the struggle ahead."[73]

The Raid

Jimmy Doolittle, who had commanded the daring raids over Japan in retaliation for Pearl Harbor, was given the task of leading the bombing of Rome. He is said to have winced when he received the order, realizing the propaganda costs of a single misdirected bomb, and to have sought advice from his Catholic chaplains. When these chaplains approved the raid, Doolittle excused Roman Catholic pilots from participating in the attack. No pilots accepted his offer.[74]

The measures taken to protect the four major basilicas of Rome were remarkable. One commander later wrote, "I never briefed crews quite as carefully and flew a bombing run through flak as meticulously as on this raid."[75] The most experienced pilots were selected for the task, and a cloudless day was chosen for its execution. Maps distributed to air crews pinpointed the four churches.[76] The words "MUST ON NO ACCOUNT BE DAMAGED" appeared four times on the map, once next to each church (see figure 3.1). Pilots were given strict orders not to fly within three-quarters of a mile of the churches marked on the map.[77] They were also instructed not to dodge anti-aircraft fire: "No evasive action was the order, to ensure that the placing of the bombs should be accurate."[78]

The permissible axes of attack, far east of the Vatican, ran north and northwest over the San Lorenzo rail yards. Because the rail tracks ran east, northeast, and west, this meant that bombers were flying over the tracks crosswise, which reduced the likelihood of direct hits on the tracks.[79] A bomb run along the tracks would have offered a greater concentration of fire on the target, but it would have forced the bombers to fly over two of the basilicas that commanders were aware of. Doolittle's biographer concludes, "Never was a raid more carefully planned. . . . This was by far the greatest example of precision bombing the world had ever seen."[80]

It was also deeply flawed. The axes chosen for the attack led the bombers directly over the Basilica of San Lorenzo. Herbert L. Matthew, a *New York Times* correspondent who had attended the briefing and participated in the raid, later wrote, "Our only mistake on the Rome raid (on which I flew) was to make our bombing run in such a way that we were bound to hit the Basilica of San Lorenzo, and that got us some grievous publicity."[81] The briefing maps failed to highlight San Lorenzo.[82] Matthew confirmed, "There was no mention whatsoever of San Lorenzo. . . . San Lorenzo could have been saved along with other buildings indicated had anyone on the staff been aware of its importance."[83]

Virtually the entire Northwest African Strategic Air Force of the U.S. Army appeared in the skies above Rome that day. Five hundred bombers dropped 2 million pounds of explosives on the Littorio and Ciampino airdromes and on the railway marshaling yards at Littorio, all at the outskirts of the city, and on the marshalling yard of San Lorenzo, in the heart of the city (see figure 3.2). The raid destroyed the marshalling yards, but bombs that missed their target killed over 2,000 people. The raid also placed a single 1,000-pound, high-explosive bomb in the nave of the Basilica of San

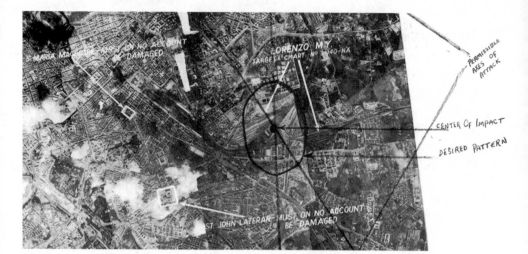

FIGURE 3.1   Excerpt from a map, distributed to U.S. air crews prior to the bombing of Rome. Black lines mark "permissible axes of attack" and the center of the San Lorenzo marshalling yard is circled. The basilicas of St. John Lateran and Santa Maria Maggiore are outlined and annotated "MUST ON NO ACCOUNT BE DAMAGED." The vaulted roof of the Basilica of San Lorenzo is visible under the first letter "T" in the words "Target Chart."
NARA

Lorenzo. The explosion caved in the roof and the front façade of the church, destroying thirteenth-century frescos and fourteenth-century mosaics, in addition to severely damaging other parts of the Basilica.[84]

The pope, who watched the bombing from the windows of his study, rushed to the San Lorenzo neighborhood, his first foray from the safety of the Vatican in three years. Propaganda images, such as the one published by the Italian weekly *La Tribuna Illustrata*, showed the pope in front of the burning church, surrounded by a throng of local survivors, his arms raised in a desperate gesture of benediction. He returned to the papal apartment that evening with a bloodstained cassock.[85] The next day, the pope wrote to Roosevelt, "We have visited and with sorrow contemplated the gaping ruins of that ancient and priceless Papal basilica of St. Laurence, one of the most treasured and loved sanctuaries of Romans, especially close to the heart of all Supreme Pontiffs. . . . We feel it our duty to voice a particular prayer and hope that all may recognize that a city, whose every district, in some districts every street, has its irreplaceable monuments of faith or art and Christian culture, cannot be attacked without inflicting an incomparable loss on the patrimony of Religion and Civilization."[86] A similar remonstration followed from the cardinal secretary of state, Luigi Maglione, to the U.S. representative in the Vatican, stressing that Rome was "as though covered with" sacred structures that required protection.[87] Harold H. Tittmann protested feebly

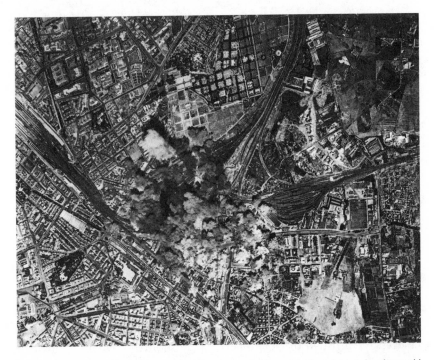

FIGURE 3.2 Bombs explode on the San Lorenzo marshalling yard. One of these bombs would eventually demolish the Basilica of San Lorenzo.
NARA

that the Basilica of San Lorenzo was not mentioned in the Lateran Treaty but soon learned that it was indeed Vatican property, enjoying extraterritoriality, and that it was the fifth most important basilica in the city to boot.[88] The orders to Eisenhower about the protection of religious structures in preparation for the liberation of Rome rectified this mistake. They emphasized that protection extended not just to the Vatican but also to "a number of other churches and buildings in Rome, which are situated outside the boundaries of the Vatican City but are the property of the Holy See."[89]

The Liberation of Rome

The bombing of Rome unleashed a propaganda battle between the Axis, castigating the "barbarous Yankees," and the Allies, disseminating images of the salvaged churches of Rome and stressing the military importance of the marshalling yards.[90] These efforts were aimed at international audiences as well as at troops in the field. *Impact Magazine*, a classified internal publication of the Army Air Force, offered airmen detailed descriptions of the San Lorenzo raid, billed as "a test of what our bombers could miss as well as what they could hit." The description was accompanied by photographs highlighting that the raid had left "San[ta] Maria Maggiore [and] St. John Lateran undamaged." Since these publications were classified as "secret," their purpose was not external propaganda but internal reassurance. These in-house documents seem designed to signal to soldiers that the military was conducting operations based on clear moral and Christian principles.[91]

Debates regarding the inviolability of Rome took on even greater urgency after the landings on the Italian mainland in September 1943 and the bombing of Cassino in February 1944 (discussed in chapter 1). Roosevelt reassured the pope that, if he managed to persuade the Germans to retreat from Rome without a struggle, the city would be spared.[92] Churchill, on the other hand, worried that declaring Rome an open city would hamper Allied efforts to pursue the Germans northward.[93] The pope, who had little sway over Adolf Hitler, insisted that the Germans had treated the Vatican and its property with far more respect than the Allies had.[94]

Some of the most vociferous debates about the status of Rome occurred in the House of Lords, pitting "Lords Spiritual" against "Lords Temporal." The bishop of Chichester warned that the destruction of Rome's churches would unleash "such hatred that the misery would survive when all the military and political advantages that may have accrued may have long worn off. . . . The destruction would rankle in the memory of every good European as Rome's destructions by the Goths or the sack of Rome rankled."[95] Viscount Trenchard (Hugh Trenchard), one of the founders of the Royal Air Force, wondered what cost the government was willing to pay to protect Rome from destruction. Reginald Fletcher, Baron of Winster, found the very idea of protecting religious and cultural assets to be puzzling: "Are we to understand that the Commander-in-Chief charged with achieving that objective ought to be guided by care for ancient monuments?" The Lord Chancellor John Simon shared the sentiment: "A man cannot be expected in the midst of a crisis, a noise, darkness and danger, to obey little instructions about not hitting that or avoiding if you can hitting something else." Lord Latham (Charles Latham), head of the London County Council and largely responsible for the civil defense of London, expressed this view more forcefully yet: "I am not a Philistine or a Vandal, but I wish to enter a strong protest against any policy being adopted by his Majesty's Government . . . in which proper military decisions and necessities are affected by considerations of culture or of aesthetics. . . . I want to say frankly that I would not be willing to sacrifice my son for any building there is in the world." Lord Lang (William Lang), the former archbishop of Canterbury, tried to balance military expediency with respect for cultural treasures, a "two-fold obligation—not by our care for these objects of interest and value and beauty, great as that care must be, to play into the hands of an unscrupulous enemy, and (I emphasize the word 'and') to see that, subject only to quite over-riding military necessity, these objects, these things of beauty, will be preserved from the ravages of war." The Bishop of Birmingham (Ernest Barnes) was exasperated: "I cannot think that the Christian position has been quite adequately understood by some noble Lords who have spoken. . . . These magnificent buildings, some of the finest achievements of European civilization, are Christian, and we cannot forget it."[96]

German attitudes vacillated similarly between respect for the city and disdain for both the Italian government and the pope. Hitler fumed at what he believed to be the role of the Vatican in overthrowing Benito Mussolini: "Do you think the Vatican bothers me? They will quickly be packed up, especially the entire diplomatic corps. . . . I could care less. . . . We'll remove every one of these bunch of swines. . . . Then we'll apologize afterwards." Despite urgings of restraint from his generals, Hitler demanded that General Karl Wolff, head of the SS in Italy, occupy the Vatican and escort the pope to Germany: "There will be quite an uproar worldwide but it will calm down. This will be quite a harvest." Wolff persuaded Hitler to abandon this bold plan, reasoning that an attack on the Vatican "would have so many negative repercussions for us as well as among the German Catholics at home and at the front."[97]

Meanwhile in Rome, the pope appeared before crowds in St. Peter's Square, appealing to both sides to spare the city "so that their names may remain a benediction, and not as a curse through the centuries on the face of the earth."[98] Formal appeals from the Portuguese, Irish, and Spanish governments called on the Allies to spare Rome, as did messages from Latin American and Australian church leaders, to the frustration of the Foreign Office, which was in no mood to "enter into polemical telegraphic and other correspondence with the Roman Catholic hierarchy in Ecuador and Peru."[99] Roosevelt, in a statement to the press, framed the looming battle over Rome as a battle over religious values and promised restraint: "Hitler and his followers have waged a ruthless war against the churches of all faiths. Now the German Army has used the Holy City of Rome as a military center. . . . We on our side . . . have tried scrupulously—often at considerable sacrifice—to spare religious and cultural monuments, and we shall continue to do so."[100] The public mood in the United States had shifted against such restraint; a month before the liberation of Rome, 74 percent of Americans polled approved of the bombing of religious shrines if deemed necessary by military leaders.[101]

We will never know how much restraint the Germans and the Allies would have demonstrated in fighting over Rome. On June 3, Hitler instructed

Albert Kesselring, "There must not be a battle for Rome."[102] Hitler may have acted on some mix of propaganda concerns, pressure from the Vatican, and the hope of conserving his forces to regroup along the Arno Line. Kesselring obeyed the order and chose to not defend the city during his retreat. On June 4, the Fifth Army entered Rome, encountering no resistance. To avoid accidental damage to monuments, fine arts experts, the "monuments men," entered the city ahead of combat troops. General Mark Clark ordered that Vatican officials be immediately informed of ongoing efforts to protect Church property. He also instructed that the Vatican receive copies of the handbooks used by the Army to identify and protect cultural treasures.[103] These were the handiwork of the Roberts Commission.

The Roberts Commission

Art scholars, historians, and museum curators had expressed grave concerns about the safety of the cultural heritage of Europe in the early years of the war and had formed various ad hoc committees to catalog these treasures and attempt to assess their condition. It was only in response to the extensive cultural damage caused by military operations in North Africa and in preparation for the invasion of Italy in June 1943 that the U.S. government formed an official committee to safeguard these treasures, the American Commission for the Protection and Salvage of Artistic and Historic Monuments in War Areas, known as the Roberts Commission after its chair, Associate Supreme Court Justice Owen J. Roberts.[104] Its operatives on the ground in European war zones, the Monuments, Fine Arts, and Archives (MFAA) Section of the Civil Affairs and Military Government Sections of the Allied Armies, were colloquially known as the "monuments men." The joint chiefs of staff gave the creation of the Roberts Commission a lukewarm reception. They did not expect it to provide any military advantage, but they agreed to cooperate with the MFAA as long as doing so did not interfere with military operations.[105]

Mission and Procedures

The Roberts Commission and its monuments men faced three difficult tasks: to identify cultural treasures and monuments so that these could be kept out of harm's way during Allied operations, to document and mitigate any damage that did occur, and to unearth and repatriate looted treasures after the war. The items to be protected ranged from museums and palaces to paintings, statues, and archives. But the largest category of protected treasures was religious: cathedrals, churches, and sacred objects. Although the commission couched its task in cultural language and justified its mission in utilitarian terms, its de facto role was to protect Europe's religious heritage.

To do so, the Roberts Commission in Washington, DC, had to first identify and locate the monuments, structures, and treasures that needed salvaging. The commission correspondence and minutes of meetings, now housed at the National Archives, allow us to piece together its procedures. Commission members established a master index of monuments by sending thousands of questionnaires to art scholars and educational institutions, and by scouring popular guidebooks and libraries. These data were compiled into authoritative lists by the Harvard Defense Group, a group of scholars led by Dr. Paul Sachs, in Cambridge, Massachusetts. The group completed its first list for Sicily and sent the list to the War Department on June 12—three weeks before the island was invaded. Other lists soon followed, usually just ahead of military progress: Albania, Austria, Belgium, Luxembourg, Bulgaria, Czechoslovakia, Denmark, France, Germany, Greece, Holland, Hungary, Italy, Yugoslavia, Norway, Rumania, Tunisia, Indochina, and the Netherlands East Indies. The group also prepared shorter lists for China, Japan, Korea, and Thailand. Experts ranked the priority of monuments by conferring one, two, or three stars to the most significant structures. Three stars, for example, marked sites of "the highest/greatest importance."

Lists for the eight most important countries were accompanied by handbooks that provided commanders and soldiers with historical background and instructions on respecting and preserving monuments.[106] These lists and handbooks were then forwarded to a second working group, the American Council of Learned Society, headquartered in the Frick Library and the Metropolitan Museum in New York. This group had the task of locating the Harvard Group monuments on 786 maps, supplied by the Army Map Service. The New York group outlined the monuments on the maps, annotated the maps with highlights from the monument lists, and bound them into atlases. By April 1944, its agents managed to produce 160 detailed city maps for Italy alone. Because the greatest danger to monuments was from the air, the commission also asked the Army Air Force to fly special reconnaissance missions over major Italian and French cities so that it could identify and outline key monuments on reconnaissance photos. These photo maps were used in planning strategic bombing campaigns and proved particularly useful in briefing crews because they enabled pilots and bombardiers to see the targets as they appeared from the air with the protected areas clearly defined and easily recognized.[107]

The Roberts Commission sent all these materials to the Civil Affairs and Military Government Sections of the Allied Armies, which forwarded them to the Supreme Headquarters of the Allied Expeditionary Force (SHAEF), from where they were distributed to the War Department in Washington, the Army Map Service, the Army Air Force, the Military Intelligence Division, and the Office of Strategic Services.[108] On occasion, the RAF requested copies of these lists and maps as well, as it did in preparing for D–Day, for example.[109] When General Eisenhower issued his order of January 1944 regarding the protection of Italian monuments, the order was distributed to troops along with copies of the commission handbooks.[110] The handbooks were also used by the monuments men—the representatives of the Roberts Commission who moved with the advancing Allied armies through Europe. They advised SHAEF in real time on all matters relating to monuments, repaired damaged monuments where possible, and returned thousands of stolen artifacts to collectors and museums in liberated areas. Over the course of the war, the monuments men gathered 15,000 photographs documenting damaged monuments in Europe and Asia.[111]

Priorities and Rationale

A survey of the monuments listed in these handbooks and atlases sheds light on the priorities of the Roberts Commission. Churches appeared as the first category in the commission definition of cultural treasures (followed by palaces, monuments, and cultural institutions) and as the first category listed in each handbook and atlas.[112] Of the 5,466 sites that the commission identified as particularly valuable, more than 40 percent (2,269 in all) were churches, monasteries, or abbeys—the single largest category by far. In comparison, the handbooks listed only 583 museums worthy of protection, amounting to only 10 percent of all sites (see table 3.1).[113]

Table 3.1 Sites identified as particularly valuable in the Roberts Commission handbooks

COUNTRY	ALL SITES	RELIGIOUS SITES	PERCENTAGE RELIGIOUS
Belgium	503	249	49
Denmark	160	66	41
France	2,558	1,052	41
Germany	946	417	44
Holland	170	34	20
Italy	950	378	40
Japan	60	25	42
Norway	119	48	40
Total	**5,466**	**2,269**	
Average			**42**

The predominance of French, Italian, and German sites on these lists suggests that, although the commission suffered from various cultural biases, it guarded itself against political bias. Indeed, the committee located more three-star monuments and more three-star churches in Italy and Germany than it did in any other country. But the narratives that accompanied the lists, handbooks, and atlases, and that sought to explain why locals valued these monuments, suggest a far deeper prejudice: whereas the authors presented Europeans as treasuring their sacred sites for national and economic reasons, they presented non-Europeans as being driven by religious fanaticism in protecting their shrines.

This bias cut both ways. First, it minimized European religion as a motive for cherishing sacred sites. The committee summaries presented the Czechs, Norwegians, and Danes, for example, as prizing churches for aesthetic, cultural, and historical reasons.[114] The French valued their cathedrals as a source of "national artistic supremacy," and were driven by "the materialistic considerations of an economically-minded people" to protect pilgrimage centers.[115] The Italians resented "damage to the things that tourists spend money to see."[116] Most often, the authors of the handbooks represented religious considerations as taken for granted. In France, "it goes without saying that all churches should be given whatever protection is possible," and in Italy, "it may be assumed that all churches, whether listed or not, are important."[117]

The opposite attitude is apparent in discussions of non-European monuments. The introduction to the Japan handbook begins: "Although only a relatively few important cultural monuments exist in Japan as compared with a small European country, the Japanese hold almost fanatical reverence for even the most humble shrine. It colors their entire way of life and it is this attitude which is one of the most difficult characteristics for a foreigner to understand."[118] This cultural bias explains why the commission identified fewer monuments and fewer religious sites worthy of protection in Japan than in any other country and why, at the same time, it ranked nearly half of the shrines on those brief lists as "extremely valuable." Outside of Europe, the concern of the committee was not with the destruction of cultural heritage but, rather, with desecration. The handbook continues:

To profane by our mere presence their holy buildings or the spots held in affectionate regard by these simple people might (in many cases certainly should) lead to immediate violence which would nullify the strategy of the High Command and set back for years our plans for peace, delaying the repatriation of our troops and obstructing negotiations. . . . A surly population, desperate at seeing their holy soil invaded for the first time in history, will be in a mood for suicidal defense of such places as the Imperial Palace Grounds (Gosho) or even of the humblest wayside shrine, when they see a fancied insult.[119]

The commission betrayed a similar prejudice in its analysis of monuments in Tunisia, Indo-China, and Siam. Of Tunisia, commissioners wrote, "The religious fanaticism of the Mohammedans is well known; since the great majority of the population consists of Mohammedans, immeasurable damage to American reputation in Mohammedan countries would result from any carelessness or disregard of the many large and small religious shrines and places of worship mentioned in the lists. At the same time, efforts at protection will defeat themselves if non-Moslems enter sacred Mohammedan buildings."[120] Monuments in Indo-China offered "little aesthetic value" but were nonetheless regarded "with religious veneration" by locals.[121] The Siamese, another introduction explained, attributed little significance to art objects or books, but held their temples in great reverence, thus obviating any concern over local vandalism.[122] No such concerns over religious fanaticism, outrage over desecration, or deeply rooted religious sentiments appear in discussions of Western monuments, despite the predominance of religious sites on the commission lists and despite the explicit intention of the commission to rank sites objectively, based on "the importance of these items in the eyes of the local population."[123]

How did the commission explain its own motivations, and how did it strive to persuade military decision makers to act on these motivations? Here, two arguments dominated the discussions and publications of the commission: a short-term utilitarian logic and a long-term concern with the Allied legacy after the end of the war. Both views were first expressed in one of the founding documents of the commission, a pamphlet written in summer 1942 by George Stout, an art conservation specialist, entitled *Protection of Monuments: A Proposal for Consideration.* Stout, who would later salvage thousands of artifacts stolen by the Nazis in his capacity as monuments man (and who was portrayed by George Clooney in the movie *The Monuments Men*), used decidedly religious language in his vision of the committee and its purpose:

> To safeguard these things will not affect the course of battles, but it will affect the relations of invading armies with those peoples and [their] governments. . . . To safeguard these things will show respect for the beliefs and customs of all men and will bear witness that these things belong not only to a particular people but also to the heritage of mankind. To safeguard these things is part of the responsibility that lies on

the governments of the United Nations. These monuments are not merely pretty things, not merely signs of man's creative power. They are expressions of faith, and they stand for man's struggle to relate himself to his past and to his God.[124]

Military and political decision makers echoed similar sentiments, albeit without Stout's religious references. At a meeting between commission members and representatives of the War Department in October 1943, Robert L. Sherwood, the director of overseas operations in the Office of War Information (in effect, head of the propaganda arm of the military), urged that the efforts of the commission be made public to counter Axis propaganda and to "reassure the world" that Americans were not "vandals and ignorant of European culture."[125] In their appeals for funding from Congress, commission members emphasized their role in protecting the Army from the blame for careless destruction.[126] But they also emphasized the long-term contribution of their efforts to the U.S. legacy: "It is a record of which we shall all be proud as Americans and that record should be available for future historians."[127]

The countering of Axis propaganda, a consistent theme in commission reports, gained significance over the course of the war as both the Axis and Allied sides learned to exploit the damage to cultural sites caused by their opponents' bombing campaigns. The existence of the commission "proved the falsity of German charges that the Allies lacked an appreciation of Europe's culture and assisted in combating German propaganda that vandalism and looting would follow the military success of our armies."[128] As if to confirm this point, Axis propaganda lashed out at the commission, which it described as "an organization consisting of thieves and Jews" that sought out artistic treasures only to loot them.[129]

The language that the commission used in its handbooks to persuade the Army to respect monuments was more pragmatic yet. It emphasized the positive influence that respect for monuments would have on the ability of the Army to effectively control occupied territories. The lists for Greece and Hungary and the handbooks for France and the Netherlands, for example, make an explicit connection among the preservation efforts, their positive effects on "the morale of the population," and the efforts of the Army in "enlisting their cooperation."[130] The commissioners thus conceived of their task as part and parcel of what we would today call a hearts-and-mind campaign. After the war, the final commission report cited its activities in France as an example: "The most important general aspect of MFA&A work in France is the most intangible, the exhibition of good will on the part of the military authority towards an aspect of French national life and sentiment of which the French themselves are especially conscious. The French have been given a feeling that their national possessions and sentiments are not a matter of indifference to us."[131]

Impact

The spectacular success of the Roberts Commission in tracking and recovering looted art in the final years of the Second World War is the stuff of legends. Books, documentaries, and star-studded Hollywood movies have documented how the monuments men salvaged art that the Germans had looted from European museums and had hidden in castles, salt mines, and Nazi lairs.[132] But these actions, occurring after the liberation of Europe, required little effort by the Allied armies. Was the Roberts Commission able to influence the conduct of war itself?

The commission did affect military planning and execution in several ways. At the most fundamental level, the lists and maps drafted by the commission provided pilots with the information necessary for avoiding historical, cultural, and religious structures if they so chose. Allied pilots were not always interested in or capable of taking advantage of such information, but in the absence of the commission, they would have caused extensive damage even in those cases—such as Rome—in which they did wish to preserve monuments from destruction.

The case of Rome is instructive. The maps used to brief pilots prior to the bombing of San Lorenzo showed only four churches of significance. The list drafted by the Roberts Commission, in contrast, identified 210 monuments of significance in Rome, 23 of which were categorized as "highly significant." Most of these were churches, and they included, of course, the Basilica of San Lorenzo. But the commission list arrived too late. It was completed on July 29, ten days *after* the city had been bombed.[133] It is safe to assume that some of the information from the commission list would have made it onto the maps used to brief the pilots prior to the bombing of Rome; it is equally reasonable to assume that it would have affected their bomb runs in some way. The destruction of the Basilica of San Lorenzo was the result of genuine ignorance regarding the religious landscape of Rome. The Roberts Commission was designed to prevent such hapless failures from recurring.

The bombing of marshalling yards in Florence in March 1944 offers a clear contrast to the Rome debacle. Prior to the attack, members of the commission pinpointed 58 of the most important monuments of Florence—half of which were churches—on an aerial reconnaissance photo (see figure 3.3).[134] The map used to plan the attack showed outlines of both the targets and these

FIGURE 3.3 Excerpt from an aerial reconnaissance photo of Florence on which members of the Roberts Commission identified the most important monuments of the city. One of the targets, the Santa Maria Novella marshalling yard, is outlined on the bottom of the photo. It is right across from the eponymous church (numbered "8"). The Duomo is numbered "17."
NARA

monuments. The map was accompanied by a list on which the monuments were ranked by priority.

To convince Churchill to authorize the attack, British Air Marshal John Slessor reassured the Air Ministry that only the most experienced U.S. air crews would be used and that the Duomo, the famous Florentine cathedral, would not be hit.[135] The detailed briefing of the air crews was documented by a film crew from the U.S. Army Signal Corps to show that all necessary precautions had been taken. Bomb runs were designed to skirt the Duomo altogether; the pilots were told to identify the cathedral by the gleaming white roof of its baptistery.

The thirteenth-century Church of Santa Maria Novella, ranked as a three-star site by the commission, posed a serious concern. It was embellished with the only renaissance façade in Florence and contained art by some of the most famous painters of the period. It was also 426 feet away from the eponymous railroad station, one of the primary targets of the bombing. Upon surveying the monuments on the map, one bombardier exclaimed, "Sure got a lot of things we can't hit."[136]

Bombsight technology had come a long way over the course of the war, and U.S. pilots, flying daytime raids at lower altitudes, had a vastly better accuracy record than their British counterparts.[137] Although the accuracy demanded for this mission bordered on the unreasonable, bombardiers could not have been asked to avoid structures that they were unaware of. Through some combination of luck and skill, Santa Maria Novella was spared, as was the Duomo. The attack "may well have been the most precise bombing mission of the war."[138] Seventy-eight aircrafts dropped 145 tons of high explosives on Florence, damaging all the targets without hitting any churches of significance. In contrast, an attack on the same day on the marshalling yards in Padua proceeded with little restraint and obliterated, among other things, the famous Church of the Eremitani.

The difference between Padua and Florence illustrates yet another way in which the Roberts Commission influenced war planning. Among the very first services that the commission performed for the Army was to assist in ranking Italian cities by cultural sensitivity. General Lauris Norstad, Mediterranean Allied air force commander, relied on this information to divide Italian towns into three categories that reflected a mix of cultural and military considerations. Rome, Florence, and Venice were classed as Group A cities and were consequently off-limits to any bombing without special authorization. Absent directives from high-ranking decision makers, their cultural value trumped their military value. Cities in Group B required particular caution; this group included Ravenna, Assisi, Como, and San Gimignano, places of some cultural significance that were considered to have little military importance. If possible, pilots were expected to avoid bombing these towns; however, if they considered it essential for operational reasons to strike any of them, they were permitted to do. So cities in Group C, for example, Siena, Verona, Bologna, and Luca, were located near important military targets.

Padua was included in that group. Any damage to these cities was deemed acceptable. Pilots were discouraged from bombing cities in Groups B and C if clouds completely obscured their objectives, but if operations occurred at night or under partially cloudy conditions, they were free to use their own judgment. Any German use of those cities for ground operation nullified these restrictions.[139]

Pisa was also in Group C; its strategic value trumped its artistic and religious value. Pisa was the most important railway and highway junction in western Tuscany, it controlled the Arno River, and it was stubbornly defended by the Germans.[140] Because of its Group C categorization, air crews were instructed to avoid its monuments, but they were also told that any collateral damage was acceptable. The destruction caused by the bombing of Pisa, in addition to artillery exchanges during the German retreat, harmed thirty-eight churches in the city, including the devastating damage to the Campo Santo cemetery and its invaluable frescoes. General Mark Clark, deeply concerned over the adverse publicity caused by the destruction, responded quickly to requests from local monuments men, rushing engineers, military personnel, and fresco specialists from Florence and Rome to salvage what they could in Pisa. This was the most significant contribution of the monuments men to salvaging European cultural heritage: documenting damage, preventing further deterioration (e.g., by preventing soldiers from billeting in protected structures), and initiating emergency repairs where needed. The Army did its part by providing the Roberts Commission with reconnaissance photos, taken after bombings, so that its experts could assess the scope of destruction in preparation for the arrival of the monuments men.[141]

Throughout the war, the commission also played an important advocacy role, striving to counter arguments about military necessity with claims about the pragmatic value of protecting monuments. One such exchange was captured in the minutes of a meeting between representatives of the War Department and members of the commission, chaired by Justice Roberts himself, on October 8, 1943.[142] Major General John H. Hilldring, chief of the Civil Affairs Division, struck the main theme of the meeting, the moral hazard of declaring certain sites off limits due to their cultural value: "We have a most important project and that is to beat the German Army. We don't want to permit this thing to interfere with that project. . . . if we said we wouldn't bomb art objects, we would be giving the enemy an advantage. . . . every time you tell a fellow you aren't going to bomb something, they are apt to put an ammunition dump there." Harvey H. Bundy, representing the secretary of war, made an even stronger case for unrestrained combat: "The best protection for the cultural monuments is to lick the Germans before they can destroy them." Moreover, Bundy reasoned, Allied constraint would be in vain because the Axis could always cause destruction and blame it on the Allies. Archibald McLeish, Roberts Commission member and a Pulitzer Prize–winning poet and librarian of Congress, presented the counterargument: "To win this war under terms and conditions which make our victory harmful to ourselves would hardly be to win it. . . . We might win the war in a way that would make our name a stench in history. I don't think that it is a starry eyed [sic] but realistic and of military importance."

Commission members used the meeting to push for a series of verbal assurances: that the care with which Rome had been treated would be extended to other valuable cities, such as Florence; that area bombing as practiced in Germany would not be extended to Italy; that Allied generals were being thoroughly briefed about the location of monuments; and that the commission maps were being forwarded to both U.S. and British bomber commands, despite the fact that the British were conducting night bombings and area bombings. Hilldring reassured the commissioners that their materials were being flown by special courier to Eisenhower, but he could offer no assurances regarding the British. He conceded, however, that it would be important to influence the British to share these concerns because "it really doesn't make a difference whether an historical monument is hit by a British or American bomb. It's blown up."

During the liberation of France, monuments men advancing with the Allied forces labored to convince unit commanders to protect the monuments listed in the commission handbooks. The guides for Normandy, for example, listed 210 protected buildings, a number deemed "too comprehensive and detrimental to battlefield maneuvers" by field officers. After much persuading, the list was ultimately approved.[143] A far more futile effort pertained to the indiscriminate bombing behind enemy lines that accompanied the advance of Allied forces across France. This prompted the Roberts Commission to issue a formal resolution, communicated to Secretary of War Henry L. Stimson and the Commanders of SHAEF, regarding collateral damage to French monuments. Carpet bombing far behind enemy lines, the commissioners argued, nullified all efforts to preserve monuments. If commanders could not restrict indiscriminate bombing to combat zones, then the signatories requested that they strive to "divert the tide of battle" from the areas surrounding the twenty-five greatest architectural treasures of France, "whose importance to the cultural life of the world as a whole is so outstanding as to admit no argument."[144]

This list of twenty-five monuments had originated with the French authorities in London, and it included ten of most important French cathedrals and churches. Of those religious structures, only one, the Cathedral of Rouen, was damaged during the course of the war. After the war, a French report on damage to national historic monuments praised the "prepared maps" produced by the commission for their "remarkable efficacy."[145] Commission members took credit for influencing military decision making in defense of cultural, artistic, and religious treasures. Francis H. Taylor, director of the New York Metropolitan Museum of Art, noted that "even in areas of heavy fighting, brilliant artillery direction and precision bombing from maps laid out by fine arts officers resulted in the saving of ancient buildings."[146]

It is hard to tell just how much of the preservation of the churches of Europe can be attributed to the efforts of the Roberts Commission and the monuments men, as opposed to military considerations and the vagaries of war. The final report of the commission, composed after the war, conceded this point: "It is difficult to estimate how far the comparative immunity of the greater cathedrals of France from damage was due to the efforts of the Allied Air Forces based on information supplied by SHAEF but certainly such information was sought by the air staff and supplied."[147] Where the fighting was fiercest, as in Rouen, the Army was able to make few concessions to sacred sites. In some instances, however, the information and advocacy provided by monuments men made a clear difference. At Caen, two churches were spared artillery fire even though nearby sections were devastated. Mont Saint Michel was spared, despite heavy fighting in the area. In Mantes, troops succeeded in destroying a bridge without harming the Church of Notre Dame, located 100 meters away.[148] In Magdeburg, Germany, monuments men helped guide artillery observers of the Ninth U.S. Army, who took "extreme care" to save the cathedral from shelling.[149] In these and many other cases, Allied units were able to follow the guidelines proposed by the monuments men without compromising military objectives.

The survival of Chartres Cathedral, one of the most beautiful and historically significant cathedrals in all of Europe, would be difficult to explain were it not for great efforts invested by Allied combatants at all levels to protect it from destruction. The thirteenth-century cathedral is a magnificent example of Gothic architecture in an excellent state of preservation, renowned for its stained-glass windows, statuaries, flying buttresses, facades, relics, and labyrinth in its nave. Built in a period of transition between two architectural styles, it is unique in boasting one Romanesque spire and one Gothic spire. All these merited separate entries in the commission handbook for France, each receiving a three-star rating. But the cathedral was also located less than a mile from an airfield that was used repeatedly by the Luftwaffe and that Allied bombers attacked multiple times in summer 1944. At the command level, decision makers responded to this challenge by carefully designing bomb runs and briefing air crews to identify and avoid the cathedral (see figure 3.4). It escaped these bombings with little to no damage.[150]

The cathedral was imperiled again when the U.S. XX Corps came under German artillery fire from the town and was ordered to target the spire to flush out German observers. Colonel Welborn Barton Griffith questioned the order and went behind enemy lines, accompanied by a single enlisted soldier, to inspect the cathedral. He climbed the bell tower and, finding it empty of enemy troops, rang the bells to alert his unit. For these actions, "with complete disregard of his own safety," he was awarded the Distinguished Service Cross.[151] When U.S. troops finally entered the town, the cathedral was salvaged again, this time by Stewart Leonard, demolitions expert and monuments man, who dismantled twenty-two explosive devices in the buildings and bridges around the cathedral. As his reward, he requested and received one hour alone in the cathedral.[152]

FIGURE 3.4   A U.S. air force bombing of the Chartres airport. Chartres Cathedral is at the bottom left of the image, across the river Eure.
NARA

Conclusion: Sacred Space and
Allied Operations in Europe

Given the scale of the destruction across Europe, more churches survived the Second World War than might have been expected. Military technology and the pace of combat were the primary determinants of the damage to sacred sites. Churches had little chance of surviving indiscriminate night-time bombing by the British or German air forces or fierce ground combat between entrenched adversaries. But when bomber doctrine permitted accurate targeting, as in the U.S. daylight campaigns over Italy and France, and when troops advanced more rapidly, the desire to protect churches influenced the use of force. In many cases, the decision to spare holy sites came at some military cost. Nowhere did the Allies target churches intentionally, despite the advantages that such attacks might have provided.

The damage to sacred places was heaviest in Britain and Germany, where most of the destruction was the result of massive night bombing from high altitudes by the Luftwaffe and the RAF. Thousands of churches in Britain and Germany burned to the ground, and many thousands of churches, monasteries, and convents in those countries were damaged over the course of the war.[153] The city of Würzburg, for example, lost thirty-five churches in a single RAF raid.[154] The devastation in Germany after the war was so extensive, and the needs of the survivors were so extreme, that the monuments men could do little to document, let alone repair, the churches.[155]

In contrast, in Italy, France, and the Low Countries, the scale of the damage depended primarily on the speed of the Allied advance and the amount of resistance put up by the Axis, which in turn depended on the terrain and on the proximity of cities to axes of attack.[156] In Sicily, for example, much of the damage to churches and monuments occurred in the bombardment prior to the Allied invasion (which destroyed more than sixty churches in Palermo) and in the east of the island, where the Germans dug in, but there was little damage to churches elsewhere.[157] On the Italian mainland, southern cities such as Naples suffered relentless bombardment and artillery barrages by both sides. But once the Allies broke through the Gustav Line at Cassino, few churches were damaged until well north of Florence, where the Germans entrenched behind the Arno Line and where cities straddled major roads. This explains why the beautiful cathedrals of Orvieto, Perugia, Siena, and Assisi survived the war while those in Lucca, Arezzo, and Pistoia were reduced to rubble.[158] In France, German resistance was the strongest in Normandy and Brittany, which is why both the Allies and the Germans caused damage to the cathedrals of Rouen and Orleans.[159] In southwest and central

France, however, rapid German withdrawals made it easier for both sides to refrain from targeting cultural and religious monuments. Finally, in southern Germany, those baroque churches not already decimated by Bomber Command were heavily damaged in the last fierce battles of the war.[160]

When units were able to exercise some caution, the care with which they treated sacred sites depended on the religious, cultural, and political significance of those sites. The more important the church, the more likely decision makers were to tolerate risks to spare the structure, and the more likely it was that experts would be able to guide combatants on how to protect the site. At times, as in Rome, Florence, or Chartres, great effort was expended in preserving sites due to a combination of religious and architectural value. But even when the ultimate decision was to destroy a shrine, as at Cassino, the sacred character of the target affected deliberations and the manner and timing of the attack.

CHAPTER 4

Who?

Sacred Leaders and War

Armies employ chaplains for a variety of reasons. Political leaders recognize that soldiers have the right to practice their faith, reasoning that the denial of such rights will have an adverse effect on recruitment and popular support for the war, particularly among religious minorities.[1] Church leaders hope that missionary activity among troops will bring soldiers into the fold and will influence church attendance after military service.[2] Most important and consistent among the justifications for maintaining a chaplain corps is the belief, voiced by military and political leaders alike, that the presence of chaplains will have a direct effect on the discipline, efficiency, courage, and morale of military units, not unlike the impact of political commissars. Indeed, when commissars assumed some of these roles, as in the Soviet and German forces during World War II, chaplains were restricted to liturgical roles or came into conflict with commissars due to overlapping responsibilities.[3] Throughout, the chaplain's role as motivator assumed a primary position, perhaps even the primary position, alongside his conventional ecclesiastical obligations. As one Second World War chaplain put it, "Chaplains are not in the Army because government is primarily interested in the saving of men's souls. The chaplain shares the mission of all other arms of the service to strengthen the will to victory. . . . Religion can and does make souls strong for battle."[4]

In this chapter, I propose four ways in which chaplains have affected combat in modern wars. Their primary impact was to enhance combat motivation by encouraging, guiding, and comforting soldiers. Chaplains performed this motivational function in a variety of ways, ranging from the provision of religious services to entertainment, counseling, teaching, and fiery battlefield sermons. I explore these skills in the first section of this chapter.

Surprisingly, chaplains have not coupled this motivating effect with an effort to moderate the conduct of war, even though their formal duties have often included advising commanders on matters of morality. As I discuss in the second section, there is no evidence of chaplains constraining, or even claiming to have constrained, war. Perhaps this is because the presence of chaplains on the battlefield is the result of military policy, not an exogenous environmental condition like the presence of sacred time or sacred space, or perhaps this is because particular chaplains voluntarily select into military service. As the deputy command chaplain of the U.S. Army Republic of Vietnam phrased it, "We do not debate the morality of the war in general or the morality of any particular war. Our job is to look after the spiritual welfare of the men."[5]

In the third section, I explore the effects of chaplains' vulnerability on combat. In the absence of intentional targeting of chaplains by the enemy, the chaplains themselves have prompted a variant of the *provocation* effect, encouraging the men in their units by voluntarily entering the battle zone unarmed. They have accompanied soldiers in attacks, tended to the wounded and dying under fire, and followed soldiers into prisoner-of-war (POW) camps. These acts of courage came at a great cost in life and limb but had a particularly strong effect on troop morale.

I conclude this chapter by offering three kinds of evidence demonstrating that chaplains have had a tangible impact on unit motivation. Soldiers have attested, time and again, to the crucial role that chaplains played in affecting their willingness to fight. Actions taken by POW-camp commanders to constrain chaplain functions bolster the claim that they, too, perceived chaplains as crucial sources of morale. Most significant are statements by military commanders, asserting that chaplains form the lynchpin of their morale-boosting efforts, with significant effects on battlefield performance.

As in prior chapters, my emphasis here is on religious practices, not merely religious beliefs. Given the paucity of comprehensive research on the motivating and constraining impact of chaplains, the evidence in this chapter has been culled from secondary sources and is often fragmentary in nature. My analysis focuses on the experience of Christian chaplains in the British and U.S. armed forces in the twentieth century because these are the cases least studied by scholars of religion and conflict yet they are the most relevant to our understanding of religion on the contemporary battlefield.

Motivation

The belief in the motivating power of chaplains is apparent in the earliest documents that sought to define their duties.[6] Indeed, it is explicit in the biblical origins of the practice, which called on priests to accompany the army, not to perform sacrifices, prayers or benedictions but to embolden soldiers prior to battle.[7] This recognition of the chaplains' motivating role appears more explicitly in twentieth-century documents. A World War I report by the British Committee on the state of the Anglican Chaplaincy recognized that "in addition to purely spiritual work which is their first and most important duty, Chaplains are of the greatest use on the social side and in helping forward the recreation of men when not actually in the trenches. As is well known the effect of this on the morale of the troops is of great value."[8] This morale-building role assumed greater significance after the First World War, when the use of the death penalty to deter cowardice and desertion was abolished. The War Office established a Morale Committee, which noted "the key role of chaplains in supporting and enhancing morale."[9] A U.S. army manual from the Second World War noted, "It is the chaplain's function to stimulate or inspire men through the medium of religion to an idealism which finds its fruition in loyalty, courage and contentment, the very essence of good morale. . . . He should neglect no opportunity to help both officers and men to maintain a cheerful and courageous spirit, with unshaken faith in the high cause which they serve. . . ."[10] The parallel British document from the same period advised chaplains to instill discipline, the will to win, and a "fighting spirit."[11] Cold War field manuals emphasized the chaplains' "moral advocacy" role, instructing them to consult with commanders regarding religion, morals, and morale and to "assist the commander . . . by providing periodic evaluation to the commander on the moral and spiritual health of the command."[12]

Morality, Discipline, and Morale

The pattern that emerges from these documents is a growing emphasis on chaplain activities that are either unrelated or indirectly related to their pastoral role and that are aimed at enhancing military effectiveness, very broadly defined. This conception varied, from vaguely defined "moral character" in the early days of the chaplaincy, to martial qualities such as discipline, efficiency, and courage in the nineteenth century, and to the equally vague "morale boosting" of the twentieth century. Commanders came to judge their chaplains based on the number and quality of nonchaplain duties they performed, reprimanding and eventually replacing those chaplains who insisted on restricting their activities to purely priestly tasks.[13] A recent British chaplain handbook, "The Unit Guide to Administration of Personnel in War," dedicates only five pages out of one hundred to the religious aspects of chaplaincy work.[14]

Initially, these tasks were defined as "reforming morality in the camp."[15] George Gleig, the principal chaplain of the British Army in the mid-nineteenth century, explained that chaplains protected not just the morals of individuals but the discipline and efficiency of the army as a whole.[16] U.S. Secretary of War Redfield Proctor made a similar point in 1890: "The higher the moral character of the army, the more effective it must be. . . ."[17] Examples of moral character included respect for civilians; honest dealing; abstention from gambling, swearing, and drinking; and the ability to better endure indignities and hardships.[18] Late-nineteenth-century U.S. chaplains were morale officers, given the task of maintaining "the social happiness and moral improvement of the troops" and reporting regularly on the "moral and religious condition" of their regiments."[19]

Other sources emphasized the chaplains' effect on military discipline. In a circular from November 1811, the Duke of York expressed the expectation that chaplains would provide "the most essential Benefits . . . as well to the discipline of the Army at large, as to the Conduct of Individuals of whom it is composed."[20] Similar language appears in a 1950 report by the President's Committee on Religion and Welfare in the Armed Forces: "Chaplains . . . are able to advise commanders on morale problems. Through inspirational talks, they inspire men to greater performance of duty. Through sympathetic counseling, they help solve personal problems and help servicemen perform their duties more effectively. Through leadership in character guidance programs, they help combat delinquencies and promote greater efficiency."[21]

At times, commander expected their chaplains to have a direct impact on combat motivation. Douglas Haig, the commander in chief of the British Expeditionary Force (BEF), believed that morale played a primary role in determining victory and ensured that his chaplains play a "direct and sustained role" in motivating front-line units to fight.[22] Field Marshal Bernard Law Montgomery called this "moral purpose" and considered it to be the single most powerful factor in war.[23] The 1964 U.S. chaplain field manual refers to this asset as "fighting capability" and noted that chaplains instilled "native bravery and thorough training" and "a spiritual sense of obligation to duty [that] will produce the very best type of soldier."[24] A recent U.S. Navy handbook expects chaplain to provide personnel with a moral foundation and sense of purpose as well as a "morally valid framework for judging and refuting the enemy's propaganda claims."[25]

The Many Tasks of Military Chaplains

How are chaplains expected to exert this impact on morale? At the most fundamental level, chaplains were given the task of supporting soldiers by performing religious ceremonies and rituals. They led prayers, performed Mass, offered communion, conducted funerals, heard confessions, pardoned sins, pronounced blessings, and offered general absolution to military units on the battlefield.[26] The purpose of these rituals was as military as it was religious. Commanders considered soldiers who had taken part in religious ceremonies to be more disciplined, more courageous, more accepting of hardships, and more likely to stand firm in battle (figure 4.1).[27]

Between battles, chaplains resorted to a colorful variety of nonreligious means to raise morale, divert soldiers from illicit activities, and attract them

FIGURE 4.1   At an outpost in Afghanistan, a chaplain leads six Marines in a prayer for themselves, their families, and their comrades.
U.S. Navy Photo by Lt. Marlin L. Williams, CHC

to religious services. U.S. Civil War chaplains wrote and mailed letters on behalf of soldiers; delivered news, gifts, and clothing from their families; maintained libraries, gardens, and bakeries; and offered literacy classes.[28] First World War chaplains ran canteens; distributed food, cigarettes, and gifts; and functioned as postmasters, librarians, athletic officers, and education officers, offering classes in citizenship, religion, history, geography, language, and ethics.[29] To channel the excess energy of his men in more positive directions, James Naismith, a chaplain, taught them a game he had invented in 1891, which he called "basketball."[30]

After the First World War, a growing recognition of the importance of morale led to the establishment of new military institutions dedicated to promoting troop welfare that took on many of the tasks previously fulfilled by chaplains.[31] World War Two chaplains were able to focus more of their time on their ministry, yet they continued to view the encouragement and education of soldiers as part and parcel of their duty. They ran errands on soldiers' behalves, led orchestras, organized boxing matches, screened movies, and wrote newsletters. They organized reading and debate clubs; lectured on citizenship, patriotic themes, or current events; and taught classes in reading, math, geography, history, and government. In moral leadership classes, they instructed officers in ethics, counseling, and human relations.[32] During the Vietnam War, chaplains also acted as drug counselors.[33]

Most crucial was their physical presence at the soldiers' side at times of need. Chaplains accompanied troops during training, marches, and deployment; provided company to tired sentries; and spoke words of encouragement to men in dugouts, trenches, and bunkers.[34] They visited the sick and wounded in the hospital to provide prayers and blessings, wrote and read letters on their behalf, and gave comfort in the operating room to those about to undergo surgery.[35]

The one task that chaplains performed in all wars in which they served, without exception, was the function that brought them into closest physical proximity to soldiers and to the horrors of war. This task was the burial of the dead. Like chaplains' efforts to reform morality, this function combined spiritual and medical considerations. Chaplains retrieved the dead from the battlefield, often at great personal risk, honored them with appropriate funerary rites, carefully marked and recorded the locations of their graves, and returned their personal effects to family members back home. They did all this without discriminating among the soldiers based on their religious affiliation. In so doing, the chaplains were able to reassure onlookers that they would be treated with similar respect if they fell in battle. Moreover, their efforts to clear the dead from the battlefield and inter them in demarcated cemeteries provided crucial hygienic benefits.[36]

Chaplains as Counselors

Chaplains supported soldiers in more intimate settings as well, anticipating the functions of military psychiatrists.[37] Soldiers recognized chaplains as intermediaries between the ranks, enjoying influence over officers and an informal relationship with enlisted men. As a consequence, soldiers were comfortable speaking confidently to chaplains about leaves, promotions, clashes with officers, or distressing thoughts about killing and dying.[38] Chaplains also interceded on behalf of individual soldiers, a task of particular importance in POW camps, where they were often punished for doing so.[39] "Tell it to the chaplain" became synonymous with "share your complaints with someone who cares," with multiple benefits to the military unit. Soldiers gained the peace of mind necessary for focusing on combat and training. Commanders recognized that soldiers distracted by personal problems would be less likely to perform well on the battlefield, and they found their chaplains to be the best source of information about the state of morale in their units.[40]

The uneasy mix of pastoral and morale-boosting duties is evident in an exchange between Frederick George Scott, the senior chaplain to the 1st Canadian Division in the First World War, and a soldier who had asked for a transfer to the rear. The chaplain recalls:

> I told him that he had the chance of his life to make himself a man. In the past he had been more or less a weakling, he could now, by the help of God, rise up in the strength of his manhood and become a hero. . . . His mother and sister no doubt had loved him and taken care of him in the past, but they would love him far more if he did his duty now, "For," I said, "All women love a brave man." I told him to take as his text "I can do all things through Christ which strengthen me," and made him repeat it after me several times. I saw that the young fellow was pulling himself together, and he shook hands with me and told me he would go up to the line and take his chance with the rest—and he did.[41]

Chaplain Irving Davidson told an Australian soldier, who was hesitant about running his enemies through with the bayonet, that "when the moment for decision comes you will know exactly what your duty is and you'll do it."[42] When Cold War RAF cadets expressed reservations about flying bombers loaded with nuclear bombs, their chaplain launched into an explanation about the "morality of deterrence" and organized a program of special training for other chaplains who might encounter similar reservations.[43]

In twenty-first-century conflicts, medical staff have called on chaplains to recognize, refer, and support mental health cases, including trauma, grief, and depression, in the hopes that doing so will help lower the incidents of desertion and suicide, and reduce the number of personnel taken out of action as a result of psychological illness.[44] During the First Gulf War, British chaplains provided counseling to soldiers burdened by military and marital hardships, and their U.S. counterparts made up for the shortage in mental health workers by screening and comforting soldiers suffering from battle stress.[45] U.S. chaplains are now trained to engage in trauma risk management (TRiM), offering soldiers a kind of "psychological first aid" in the immediate aftermath of traumatic events. They also participate regularly in "decompression" sessions designed to help soldiers adjust to civilian life after operational duties.[46]

Chaplains as Instructors

In addition to focusing on the souls and spirits of soldiers, chaplains also strove to directly impact their physical well-being by means of lectures focused on sex education and the curbing of misconduct. In these talks, the interests of morality and military efficiency went hand in hand. Generals John Pershing and Douglas Haig employed chaplains to promote abstinence and thus reduce venereal diseases in the ranks, a serious concern in the Expeditionary Forces, which had lost 60,000 soldiers to venereal disease in 1918. Chaplains battled against excessive drinking, gambling, cursing, and delinquency by means of lectures, sermons that emphasized purity and self-restraint, and alternative recreational activities.[47] Other chaplains took matters directly into their own hands. One eccentric chaplain conducted stakeouts from the piano in a French brothel to prevent soldiers from visiting the rooms upstairs. Another, in Italy, distributed pornography to soldiers to keep them out of local brothels.[48] The more conventional approach took the form of sex hygiene talks. Second World War recruits had to attend nearly three hours of "sex morality lectures" during basic training.[49]

As Anne Loveland has documented, these lectures grew into chaplain-led character guidance programs during the Cold War, in which U.S. chaplains sought to inculcate the religious, moral, and citizenship foundations of the "American way of life" and teach "godly patriotism."[50] In parallel, the British army introduced Padre's Hour, a dedicated period of time each week during which chaplains addressed troop concerns, the vast majority of which pertained to social issues, not to religion. Inspired by the U.S. model, these chaplain-led sessions were later recast as "character training."[51] Instructions to chaplains promised that teaching faith, self-reliance, courage, obedience, fair play, and persistence would "develop the kind of soldier who has sufficient moral understanding and courage to do the right thing in whatever situation he may find himself."[52] U.S. recruits were required to attend several lectures during basic training as well as an additional lecture per month for the rest of their tour of duty. Only with the increased skepticism regarding the efficiency of character guidance that accompanied the Vietnam War was the program abandoned in favor of the view that courage, motivation, and morale could be achieved surreptitiously by means of simple religious teaching.[53]

Chaplains as Preachers

Of all the services provided by chaplains, sermons provide the clearest insight into the means that chaplains used to motivate soldiers. Unlike the prayers, pep talks, and acts of kindness that chaplains offered on a daily basis, their sermons, held on Sundays, during religious services or in the minutes before an assault, were often recorded in chaplains' diaries and are thus relatively well documented. As with other chaplain functions, military interests assumed a primary importance in sermons that often equaled or even trumped religious content.

The most consistent and traditional theme in sermons, evident in early medieval orations, was the promise of divine protection. Chaplains sought to embolden soldiers by reassuring them that God's presence at their side would shield them from physical harm.[54] World War One chaplains spoke to troops about courage and obedience but also reminded them of God's providence and protection, in the hope that this would offer consolation, hope, and courage.[55] For example, Adrian Beausoleil, a Canadian chaplain, promised his men before battle, "He will not forsake you, not one hair will fall from your head without His permission. He has a splendid reward for those who might fall . . ." These words, he claimed, "steadied the high strung nerves of those boys by putting them face to face with the reality and by showing them where help and eventually an immediate reward could be gotten."[56]

Five decades later, the chief rabbi of the Israel Defense Forces used similar tropes to embolden soldiers fighting in the Six Day War: "Let not your heart be faint. Do not be afraid, do not tremble before them. For the Lord your God goes with you to fight on your behalf against your enemies and to save you. Today He will give us courage! Today He will make us great! Today our enemies shall be crushed beneath us!"[57] General Norman Schwarzkopf prayed for victory on announcing the launching of Operation Desert Storm in 1990. The general read to troops from a prayer that his chaplain had written: "As we now begin Operation Desert Storm, we humbly, but boldly ask for your blessing on our mission and our service members as we carry out the process of freeing Kuwait and its citizens. . . ."[58] The chaplain of the VII Corps during that operation went a step further; he assured General Frederick M. Franks that he had been anointed by God to lead the corps into battle as an instrument of God's righteousness and foresaw "victory without great casualties."[59]

A second theme common to modern battlefield sermons was the religious justification of military objectives, even when troops were facing opponents of similar religious persuasion. The presence of uniformed clergy on the battlefield implied to devout soldiers that their war was just. Chaplains made this point explicit in their sermons, linking religious duty with patriotism and presenting the military cause as synonymous with service to God.[60] One Catholic chaplain in the BEF exhorted his troops, "Inasmuch as you are doing your duty to your country, you are doing a good work for God. . . . Say to yourself: . . . By being here, I am doing my duty, I am serving God, I am earning heaven for myself."[61] One example, among many, of the appearance of this theme in World War II sermons appears in an address to soldiers by a British chaplain, A. R. Grant: "I believe that the present conflict is a just and righteous war, engaged as we are in a fight against the evil which is in the world through lust and false ambition."[62]

Yet other chaplains took patriotic preaching to an extreme. Their homilies blurred the distinction between religious and political symbolism, presented the conflict as a holy war and portrayed the opponent as heretics. British chaplains during the colonial wars, U.S. Civil War chaplains, and Prussian chaplains during the Franco–Prussian War emphasized the blasphemous behavior of the enemy, the purity of their own army, the sanctity of the national mission, and the heroic martyrdom of the battle dead.[63] After the Passchendaele offensive, Thomas Colwell, a Canadian chaplain, compared the battle to the crucifixion, the soldiers' packsack to the cross, their march across no-man's-land to the *Via Dolorosa*, and the death of their comrades to the triumph of the Resurrection.[64] The wars of ancient Israel and pivotal events in early Christian history featured as frequent metaphors for the suffering of soldiers. The enemy, in turn, assumed the form of Pharaoh, Herod, or Nero and stood accused of religious, moral, and sexual excesses.[65] General Montgomery encouraged his chaplains to read a 1943 army publication, calling on chaplains to highlight "the conflict of Good and Evil, the opposing standards of Right and Wrong, the just foundations of our Cause, the Presence of Christ, the value of prayer, the glory of sacrifice, the gift of eternal life, and such things as deepen their sincerity and confidence as soldiers gathered to battle by God."[66] The comparison between fallen soldiers and the crucified Christ was a particularly common theme in sermons, accompanied by rumors, prevalent in both world wars, that the enemy was crucifying captive soldiers.[67]

Most chaplains simply tried to preach on whatever they deemed necessary to rally their troops. Bishop Llewellyn H. Gwynne, speaking to soldiers during the Passchendaele offensive, praised the division for its accomplishments, sympathized with their desire to go home, but warned that if they did not "stick it," as their fallen comrades had done, then "all we have suffered is lost [and] our children will have to fight for what we could not finish."[68] Canon Frederick George Scott, preparing Canadian troops for a bayonet charge against a German position, reminded them that "they had a chance to do a bigger thing for Canada that night than had ever been done before. It was a great day for Canada boys. . . ."[69] In the midst of the Japanese attack on Pearl Harbor, Chaplain William Maquire tried to rally his men, shouting, "Keep our spirits high and carry on with all our heart and soul in the fight for victory."[70] And troops boarding planes bound for Panama in December 1989 heard their chaplains quoting from Joshua: "Be strong and courageous. Do not be afraid; do not be discouraged, for the Lord your God will be with you wheresoever you go."[71]

Constraint

Throughout the twentieth century, Christian leaders have often acted to constrain war. Pope Benedict XV tried, and failed, to broker peace in the early weeks of the First World War.[72] The archbishop of Canterbury, Randall Davidson, and several leading English bishops condemned reprisals against civilians during the First World War, as did many of their counterparts in the Second World War, leading to acrimonious debates within the Churches.[73] British church leaders condemned war as contrary to Christian teachings in 1924 and 1930, as did the Vatican in *Pacem in Terris* (1963) and *Gaudium et Spes* (1965). The pastoral letter *The Challenge of Peace: God's Promise and Our Response*, published by U.S. bishops in 1983, rejected offensive war and warned of the dangers of nuclear weapons. Individual religious leaders have intervened in conflicts, acting as peace-brokers, observers, intermediaries, and arbiters.[74] Even soldiers and officers have constrained violence, by reporting breaches of the Geneva Conventions, for example. But there is no evidence that any chaplain has ever done so or that any chaplain has even claimed to have done so.[75] This has led harsh critics to dismiss chaplains as indoctrination agents serving to legitimate the military enterprise.[76]

Clerical anti-war activism outside the ranks could have provoked a conflict of interest among clergy in the military, torn between Christ's teachings and war-making, conflicted between their duty to the Church and their loyalty to the state, insecure in their noncombatant status among soldiers, ambivalent about their rank as officers and its trappings, or constrained by their inability to proselytize.[77] But it did not. We might also have expected official guidelines, such as those published by the U.S. military starting in 1977, to support chaplains in their role as moral compass. These guidelines made explicit the expectation that chaplains would act as a moral check on commanders by criticizing decision making, policies, and leadership when necessary. The 1984 and 1989 manuals required chaplains to report immoral practices during combat, such as the dehumanizing treatment of prisoners or civilians and disrespect for human life.[78] If chaplains have ever acted in that capacity, their actions have left no trace in the official record.

In actuality, ethical tensions, insofar as they were felt by chaplains at all, do not seem to have affected their actions. British and U.S. chaplains raised no objections to the bombing of German or Japanese cities, the internment of Japanese-Americans, or even the destruction of Monte Cassino Abbey. Of the two hundred chaplains surveyed about their attitudes toward the atomic bomb at the time of its dropping on Hiroshima and Nagasaki, only 15.5 percent condemned the event and 65 percent endorsed it outright.[79] The Military Chaplains' Association of the United States declared the war in Vietnam to be "just," and the Roman Catholic military bishop, Francis Cardinal Spellman, noted during his Christmas visit to troops there that "in this situation in Vietnam, our country is in my opinion right by every test I know."[80]

Few chaplains have felt that it was their responsibility to place moral constraints on combat. They interpreted their moral-guidance obligation as a reactive and interpersonal task, a response to individual soldiers seeking council. The goal of the chaplain was to make the soldiers' lives easier, not to initiate a moral dispute with the establishment.[81] Asked about their stance on the killing of civilians during World War Two or the Vietnam War, chaplains surveyed responded, "That's not our job." "A man of discernment has to give his government the benefit of the doubt," "You don't consider the justice of the war," or "A chaplain should never let himself come into a situation where he takes a position against military authority."[82]

In a 1952 survey of seventy-one U.S. chaplains, across denominations, the majority of chaplains surveyed saw no conflict between military regulations and their faith. They compartmentalized their tasks in a manner that allowed them to focus on moral contexts only when performing their religious services. The overwhelming majority saw no moral content to the killing of enemy soldiers and no conflict between Christ's injunction to "turn the other cheek" and war. Most stunning of all was the finding that many chaplains seemed not to have given these questions much thought at all.[83] The author of the survey concludes, "None of the respondents would of his own volition raise questions concerning the morality of killing, or of war in general, or of tuning the other cheek, or any question concerning the relationship between religion and war. . . . Many respondents had not attempted to answer such questions even in their own minds prior to the interview. . . ."[84]

These sentiments are attributable to self-selection and socialization among chaplains. Clergymen volunteering for service are likely to have favorable attitudes toward the military. Selection committees and review boards weed out individuals who are likely to criticize their superiors on moral grounds.[85] In addition, chaplains are socialized through training as well as personal involvement in their role to internalize military values such as discipline, loyalty, and pragmatism in the face of war.[86]

A 1969 survey of RAF chaplains bolstered these findings. Most chaplains surveyed perceived no moral conflict between their religious and military duties. Those who did resolved such tensions in favor of their military obligations. The chaplains questioned explained that their moral authority focused on personal, family, and sexual issues, such as swearing, drunkenness, and prostitution, and not on military matters. When it came to military decision making, they put their full trust in the judgment of military authorities.[87] For example, two-thirds of the RAF chaplains interviewed stated that they considered large-scale civilian bombings to be justifiable, outside their prerogative to judge, or deplorable but something one had to resign oneself to. Those few who did consider protesting against military policy felt that their protest would have no impact and would thus be a waste of time.[88] The principal Roman Catholic chaplain of the British Armed Forces echoed this skepticism about the ability of chaplains to act as whistle-blowers.[89]

Several near-exceptions illustrate how ineffectual the constraining effect of chaplains has been. In the First World War, John Groser, a chaplain, refused an order to lead a unit that had lost its officer. On the insistence of his commanding officer, he relented provided that he did not have to carry arms.[90] One British chaplain who found that he could not support the use of the army in Russia, in Ireland, and to repress industrial protests in England waited until the armistice in 1919 before resigning.[91] Prior to the Allied invasion of Normandy, the assistant chaplain-general of the Second Army, John W. Steele,

expressed alarm over the indiscriminate nature of the flame-throwing Croco-
dile tanks. The fruits of his labor was a religious ceremony at which officers
were invited to promise that they would use the tank only "for the purpose
which is intended."[92] In 1982, Chief of Chaplains Kermit Johnson prepared
a memorandum for the army chief of staff in which he criticized U.S. policy
regarding nuclear weapons and the conflict in El Salvador; the fruits of *his*
labor was the offer of early retirement, which he accepted.[93] These six self-
confessed instances are the only examples of chaplains expressing reservations
about combat that I could find in my survey of twentieth-century U.S. and
British war-making.

This is not to say that chaplains did not, at times, agonize over the moral
dilemmas they were faced with. They merely failed to take effective action to
change outcomes. Reverend Richard Collins was outraged by British carpet
bombing and described it, after the war, as an "evil policy." But during the
war, he served as the official chaplain for Bomber Command and did not
resign his post.[94] A Wehrmacht chaplain responded with anguish to reports
that wounded POWs were being executed: "We priests suffer from the para-
doxes that we are faced with. All the physical challenges posed by war would
be easier to bear were it not for that internal dilemma."[95] He did nothing
beyond expressing that anguish in his diary. U.S. chaplains in Vietnam heard
about the My Lai massacre from participants who sought their counsel, but
they failed to notify the relevant authorities about what they had learned.[96]
Even British chaplains who represented churches that officially opposed the
Iraq War joined the troops deployed there, arguing that their role was "to
support the troops, not to condone or support the war."[97]

Indeed, commanders took exception to chaplains who strayed from the
official line in their addresses to troops. Haig instructed his chief chaplain,
Gwynne, to ensure that chaplains were emphasizing military and political
objectives in their sermons and complained that the chaplains "were too
narrow in their views. They must be enthusiasts to do good."[98] In his diary,
Haig noted, "We must have large minded, sympathetic men as Parsons, who
realize the *Great Cause* for which we are fighting, and can imbue their hear-
ers with enthusiasm. Any clergyman who is not fit for this work must be
sent home."[99]

When chaplains struck the wrong tone in sermons, military leaders were
quick to voice their displeasure. General Sir William Thwaites, commander
of the 141st Infantry, instructed his chaplain to deliver a bloodthirsty sermon prior to engagements "and would not have any texts from the New
Testament."[100] Another World War I general urged his padres to preach on
"High ideals of Honour, Duty, and Discipline" and was outraged to hear

the padre talk about something that had happened in Jerusalem 2,000 years ago, "as if that had anything in the wide world to do with us in the 20th century!"[101] One colonel mocked his chaplain for telling the men that their actions should be inspired by love and not hate. The colonel wanted to confirm that the chaplain approved of "sticking Germans" as long as one loved them at the same time.[102] In another instance, a soldier recalled a sermon on the eve of the Battle of Arras: "The Padre preached to us on the text *Love your enemies, do well to them that do spitefully use you*. Afterwards the Colonel gave us a little heart-to-heart talk about the desirability of remembering that we had bayonets on our rifles and using them accordingly. . . . The Church cannot be allowed too much rope lest we lose the war!"[103] German chaplains serving in the Wehrmacht received similar warnings against "too much pious talk." One such chaplain was reminded by his superiors that "a commander should speak like an officer and not like a pastor."[104] Instructions by the German High command to its chaplains in 1942 put the matter bluntly: "The primary function of the chaplaincy is to strengthen the fighting ability of the unit. . . . It cannot represent the interests of the Church but should help the German soldier to find the inner strength required to complete his difficult task. Like all Germans, the chaplain must direct his entire efforts to achieving the great goal of winning this war."[105]

Vulnerability and Provocation

Despite the chaplains' seminal role on the battlefield and their inability to defend themselves, there is little evidence of purposeful efforts to target chaplains in modern war. Rather than increasing their vulnerability, the unique religious status of chaplains made them invulnerable to intentional targeting, a trait that commanders soon learned to use.

The invulnerability of chaplains rests on three foundations: the normative, the strategic, and the institutional. Normatively, chaplains' religious calling, their faith-based motivation, and their perceived charisma have led soldiers to respect men of cloth on the battlefield. Combatants have shared the intuition that "holy men" serve a higher cause, even when they are uniformed and part of a military hierarchy. This recognition was particularly powerful when soldiers on both sides shared an allegiance to a transnational religious movement, personified in the figure of chaplains of the same denomination on both sides of the conflict. But it has also held true in conflicts that coincided with religious divisions, given the widespread acceptance of the norm of chaplain immunity. This deference was, in part, strategic. As I argue later in the chapter, chaplain deaths produced an intense outrage effect that matched the motivation contribution of living chaplains. Soldiers soon realized that, unlike the intentional targeting of officers, efforts to single out chaplains were likely to have significant blowback effects that could end up boosting, rather than harming, the target's morale. These two intuitions, the normative and the strategic, were bolstered by the gradual legalization of chaplain immunity in international treaties. Respect for clergy was enshrined in the first Geneva Convention (1864), which afforded chaplains and medical personnel a neutral status, and culminated in the Additional Protocols (1977), which emphasized the noncombatant rights and obligations of chaplains.

Consequently, most of the fatalities among chaplains in modern wars have been the result of either indirect fire aimed at military units with chaplains in their midst or the willing participation of chaplains in assaults under conditions that made it impossible for opponents to discriminate between chaplains and other officers. After all, chaplains wear the same uniforms and ranks, and are often distinguishable only by a small insignia. Rare exceptions occurred prior to the widespread acceptance of the norm against targeting chaplains or in cases in which combatants openly defied international treaties. Occasionally, chaplains came under attack when the enemy chose to target religious services, such as funerals or open-air ceremonies, because these concentrated large numbers of combatants in one space, a practice that led to a ban against religious services in the front-line trenches during the First World War. Several U.S. and British chaplains carried weapons during the War in the Pacific due to the impression that Japanese soldiers would not respect chaplain immunity, a suspicion strengthened by the exceptionally rough treatment that chaplains received in Japanese POW camps, as did German chaplains facing Russian partisans. Yet even under those circumstances, there is no evidence of intentional targeting of chaplains or indications that these chaplains fired their weapons.[106]

Because participants in modern wars abstained from intentionally targeting enemy chaplains, chaplains did not elicit a provocation effect. Instead, it was the chaplains' own decision to expose themselves to enemy fire, voluntarily and unarmed, that provoked this response. This added measure of risk, which chaplains imposed on themselves, had a tremendous effect on troop morale. Personal courage became yet another instrument in the chaplains' toolkit. An Australian chaplain who served in Gallipoli put it this way, "The influence of a chaplain over the men depends on one thing—his obvious physical bravery. Everyone can value courage, for all know the meaning of fear. All things can be forgiven to the chaplain who shows himself prepared to share their dangers; nothing can mitigate the failure of the man who is not."[107] The prohibitions in the Geneva Protocols on direct chaplain participation in combat proved no impediment to the chaplains' willingness to assume risks on behalf of their troops. In fact, by barring chaplains from carrying or using weapons, the prohibitions provided the necessary foundation for the provocation effect that these chaplains caused. As one World War II sergeant told his chaplains, "If you were armed, Sir, it would spoil everything."[108]

Religious and military leaders were quick to grasp that the physical presence of chaplains among the troops in the heat of battle provided an important source of encouragement for combatants, precisely because they were not under orders to be in the front lines. A citation for the Military Cross, awarded to a British chaplain for operations in Yemen in 1967, captures this well: "By virtue of his appointment he has not been able to retaliate or even to defend himself, nevertheless he has shown complete disregard for his own safety, and has displayed a coolness and air of confidence which has inspired every officer and soldier around him."[109]

Chaplains took great risks in the heat of battle. In disregard of danger, they performed sacred rites under fire, such as the general absolution that Father William Corby famously pronounced over his unit at Gettysburg under a hail of bullets.[110] Chaplains assisted medical units on the battlefield, comforted and prayed alongside the wounded and dying, and carried casualties out of the field on their backs.[111] At times, they joined the attack, unarmed, went "over the top" with their men, parachuted with them into enemy territory, and followed them into captivity.[112] More rarely, chaplains carried battle flags, took command of troops that had lost their officer, supplied ammunition, saved ships from sinking, took prisoners, and even fired weapons.[113] During the First Gulf War, one U.S. chaplain even managed to convince a troop of eighty armed Iraqis to surrender, but such active participation became increasingly rare in the twentieth century.[114]

These and other acts of courage brought 405 military honors to British chaplains in World War I, 85 decorations to U.S. chaplains in World War I, and 2,453 decorations to U.S. chaplains in World War II.[115] They also came at the price of ninety-seven British and eleven U.S. chaplains killed in action in the First World War and ninety-six British chaplains and sixty-three U.S. chaplains killed in action in the Second World War.[116] In terms of World War II casualties (as a percentage of personnel), the U.S. Army chaplaincy ranked third in the entire army, behind the Air Force and the infantry.[117]

Only rarely were chaplains ordered into the line of fire (a policy known among German chaplains as "Uriah's Law").[118] Why, then, did chaplains brave the heat of battle? The primary justification given was a desire to "share so far as we might in what the troops endured."[119] Like all soldiers, chaplains empathized with the plight of their comrades and worried about letting them down, appearing cowardly, or disappointing loved ones back home.[120] A U.S. chaplain who took part in the Allied invasion of Normandy explained the advantages of parachuting into Europe with his men: "He could truly say that he was one of them, and the men, for their part, liked to feel that the chaplain was undergoing the same trials as themselves, and their mutual feeling of discomfort, nervousness, and exhilaration, were equally shared."[121] In contrast, a chaplain who was barred from the front lines at Gallipoli glumly observed the support trenches from afar, noting, "I am quite sure this was just the place I should have been."[122]

The chaplains also recognized a unique opportunity to offer encouragement and inspiration. One chaplain, reprimanded for coming within 50 yards of the German lines in Flanders, replied, "I just wanted to keep the men cheery."[123] Across no-man's land, a German chaplain "sought out his comrades where the danger was at its greatest and steeled their hearts with his word and with his exemplary courage and determination."[124] Another was "constantly among the men, cheering them up." Yet another "went around cheering and encouraging the men."[125] A chaplain to a unit that had lost its officers absolved his men and said, "Now, out you go, there's only one order: take the trench and after that the roll call up above!" He then led his men over the top and was the first killed.[126] The troops, in turn, could be heard going "over the top" whispering excitedly "the padre is with us" or pointing him out to others: "That's our priest."[127]

These practices persisted during the Second World War and beyond. Joseph Lacy, a chaplain, accompanied soldiers onto Omaha Beach on D-Day: "Every time we caught it really bad it was the padre who was in there when the stuff was worst."[128] To strengthen the nerves of his men, a chaplain attached to the 1st Irish Guards at Anzio in December 1943 left his dugout during a heavy bombardment and paced the battalion lines reading his breviary.[129] At the Battle of Imjin River, April 25, 1951, Sam Davies, a chaplain, "walked about talking to men, trying to appear relaxed and hopeful, and feeling for encouraging words."[130]

Chaplains also found service on the battlefield to be in line with their religious duty, message, and ministry. If faith was to be a source of courage in the face of danger, as they had so often preached, then the chaplains' presence among fighting units was a means of practicing what they were preaching.[131] The risks of service under fire reminded chaplains that "the church was ready to go where the men had to go," and it reminded the soldiers that chaplains were the only ones "not under orders to be there, and as such could hardly fail to encourage the rest, who had no option in the matter."[132] A German chaplain serving with the Wehrmacht in the Caucasus concluded, "A priest who stays in the headquarters or the medical station will never enjoy the right contact with soldiers. Only by staying at their side will he earn their trust. . . ."[133]

One of the most famous of all British chaplains in World War One, Rev. G. A. Studdert Kennedy, insisted that a padre should seek out the most dangerous spots on the battlefield as an expression of the church's message to the troops.[134] In an oft-quoted statement to a fellow chaplain, the Rev. Theodore Bayley Hardy, he advised:

> Live with the men; go everywhere they go. Make up your mind you will share all their risks, and more if you can do any good. You can take it that the best place for a Padre . . . is where there is most danger of death. Our first job is to go beyond the men in self-sacrifice and reckless devotion. . . . The more padres die in battle doing Christ-like deeds, the better for the Church. . . . The line is the key to the whole business. Work in the front and they will listen to you when they come out to rest, but if you only preach and teach behind you are wasting your time. . . . The men will forgive you for anything but lack of courage and devotion.[135]

Hardy followed this counsel faithfully, in one case spending thirty-six hours in no-man's-land at the side of a wounded soldier who could not be extracted from the mud. He became one of the most decorated noncombatants of the war before he was killed in action in October 1918.[136]

As mentioned in chapter 1, for Catholic chaplains the opportunity of offering soldiers the essential sacraments—confession, communion, and extreme unction—added yet another incentive for being present in the thick of battle.[137] Novelists of the Great War, such as Robert Graves, Guy Chapman, and Siegfried Sassoon, often wrote disparagingly of chaplains and their ineffectiveness. Yet they praised the Roman Catholic clergy for its willingness to accompany the men into battle.[138] Sensing the visible impact of this presence on the morale of soldiers and on the status of the Churches in the ranks, other denominations soon emulated the example set by Catholic chaplains. Any differences between denominations regarding the willingness of their chaplains to accompany men into battle dissipated long before the First World War was over and were absent altogether in the Second World War.

Assessing Chaplain Effectiveness

In twentieth-century wars, British and U.S. chaplains played an important morale-boosting role. Similar functions are evident in the chaplaincies of contemporary militaries; modern Canadian, Russian, Australian, and Israeli chaplains provide moral and psychological counseling to soldiers, exhort soldiers by means of rituals and prayer, and link religious duty to military duty in their sermons.[139] These chaplains contribute to establishing and proclaiming the justness of the wars they participate in (the *ius ad bellum*) at the expense of constraining or even commenting on the ethics of military practice in the field (the *ius in bello*).[140]

What evidence is there to support the notion that the efforts that chaplains invested in boosting morale, their sermons, and the risks they assumed on the battlefield have had an impact on the performance of armies in battle? There is no hard evidence linking the activities of chaplain to unit morale (let alone data linking morale to success in war, a surprisingly understudied relationship). But there is much circumstantial evidence to suggest that this relationship holds. This evidence assumes three forms.

First, as already discussed, frequent statements by soldiers testify to the effects that chaplains had on their willingness to take risks, face death, and continue fighting. Here is yet another of these statements, as recalled by Rev. John McKie Hunter:

> Some years after the war a man stopped me in Princes Street, Edinburgh, and asked me if I had been on the march from St. Valery. Then he told me that, at one of the halts, when he was sitting with his head in his hands—at the lowest depths of physical misery and spiritual despair—I had come up to him and said "Cheer up, boy, God will do his stuff yet!" He had never answered me but, from then on, he had taken a grip of himself, and acquired a more hopeful outlook which carried him through the years of captivity which lay ahead. I had entirely forgotten the incident.[141]

A second, if unconventional, source of evidence regarding the efficacy of chaplains can be found in the treatment that chaplains received at the hands of their captors in POW camps. German, Turkish, and Japanese camp commanders, in both world wars, expressed little interest in individual religious practices but seemed to recognize, quite wisely, the dangers of communal services and the disruptive potential of chaplain–soldier relations. Their concern was both that group gatherings would provide opportunities to organize unrest and that "the men derived some moral power from the services which they didn't understand."[142] Indeed, so great was the German belief in the influence of chaplains during the First World War that they employed Muslim chaplains of their own in POW camps in an effort to persuade North African prisoners to defect based on religiously motivated loyalty to the Ottoman sultan.[143] In Turkish camps, British chaplains were prevented from ministering to their soldiers altogether. Japanese POW camp commanders regularly obstructed chaplains in their work, leading to a palpable decline in morale. German, Japanese, and Soviet POW camp commanders required chaplains to seek official permission before any religious services or addresses could be held. Chaplains had to submit their sermons in advance for censorship, and an interpreter from the commandant's office had to be present at every religious gathering. Prayers for victory or in support of the Allies or the royal family were prohibited. Fascinatingly, although German commanders permitted private conversations between chaplains and soldiers, they prohibited chaplains from hearing confession, suggesting that the Germans regarded the spiritual nature of the exchange, in particular, as dangerous.[144] As one chaplain, who spent years in German captivity, explained, "The main reason why the Germans were so reluctant to distribute the padres among the camps is fairly obvious. . . . They had no concern with the morale of prisoners—except that it should be kept as low as possible—in order that our men would more easily accept their political propaganda. They did the padres the honour of believing that we could do something to raise morale, and so they kept us away from the men as long as they possibly could."[145] Judging from chaplain activity during the Korean War, these perceptions were justified. In Korean POW camps, chaplains, sermons, and religious services took on political content and became the focus for resistance and defiance, prompting captors to punish chaplains for "using religion as a cloak for political activity."[146] Post-war analyses suggested that British susceptibility to communist indoctrination in Korean POW camps was far lower than those of their U.S. counterparts due to "strong religious faith," prompting the development of moral education classes in the U.S. military.[147]

The third, and most compelling, evidence comes from commanding officers. Low-ranking officers expressed their appreciation for their chaplains in citations, official reports (such as the British "despatches"), and recommendations that accompanied requests for honors. For example, one U.S. Civil War officer noted, "We count our chaplain as good as a hundred men in a fight, because the men fight so much better when he's with them."[148] A British officer on the Western front in the First World War praised a chaplain who "on all occasions afforded me the most valuable help in keeping up the moral[e] of fighting troops."[149] A Second World War citation for the military cross, awarded to Father Patrick Bluett, who ministered to casualties in the fighting north of Naples, stated that "his disregard for danger had a most invigorating effect on the company."[150] Written statements of this sort, linking chaplain action to commendable results, are too numerous to count.

More telling yet are statements by senior military leaders that laud the chaplains' contributions to military discipline and morale, starting with the claim by the Duke of Wellington (Arthur Wellesley) in 1811 that chaplains were necessary "not only from the desire which every man must have, that so many persons as there are in the Army should have the advantage of religious instruction, but from the knowledge that it is the greatest support and aid to discipline and order."[151] Sir Henry Horne, commander of the First Army of the BEF, recommended his senior chaplain for the Distinguished Service Order for demonstrating "how much chaplains can do to raise and maintain morale."[152]

Haig notified his deputy chaplain general, Llewellyn H. Gwynne, that his was one of the most important positions under Haig's command and that "a good chaplain is as valuable as a good general."[153] In a subsequent letter of August 1916, Haig thanked the chaplain, noting, "That the troops are in such splendid heart and morale is largely attributable to our chaplains who have successfully made our men realize what we are fighting for and for the justice of our cause."[154] General Herbert Plumer later credited Gwynne with having done more than anyone else to ensure the Allied victory in the First World War.[155] In a June 1916 letter to King George V, Haig explained:

> Everywhere I found the troops in great spirits and full of confidence in their ability to smash the enemy when the moment for action arrives. Several officers have said to me that they have never known troops in such enthusiastic spirits. We must, I think, in fairness give a good deal of credit for this to the parsons. I have insisted on them preaching about the cause for which we are all fighting and encouraging the men to play their part. Some parsons too that were no use have been sent home. But, taken as a whole, they have done well and have been a very great help to us commanders.[156]

Haig's U.S. counterpart, General Pershing, concurred: "Their usefulness in maintenance of morale, through religious counsel and example, has now become a matter of history and can be accepted as having demonstrated, if need be, the wisdom of the religious appeal to soldiers."[157]

Field Marshall Bernard Montgomery established close relationships with his chaplains, who became the lynchpins of his campaign to raise troop morale in the Eighth Army. After the war, Montgomery wrote, "Moral purpose is the most powerful single factor in war. . . . The moral brief must come from the Church. The Church must tell the soldier not what is, but what should be behind their going forth. . . ."[158] On the U.S. side, General Brehon Somervell, commanding general of the Army Service Forces in World War II, praised chaplains for providing "one of the greatest morale factors in the war" and as a source of soldiers' strength and courage.[159] Fleet Admiral Chester W. Nimitz, commander in chief of U.S. forces in the Pacific in World War II, emphasized the chaplains' services as counselors: "No one will ever know how many young men were diverted from acts of depression by a heart-to-heart talk with the 'padre.' . . . By his patient, sympathetic labors with the men, day in, day out, and through many a night, every chaplain I know contributed immeasurable to the moral courage of our fighting men."[160] Field Marshal Wilhelm List praised his chaplains for providing his troops with the strength and morale necessary to endure perilous situations.[161] A British War Office report on the role of morale in the Second World War concluded, "There is no doubt that religious faith will increase the powers of endurance and self-sacrifice of soldiers who possess it. . . . By fostering these sentiments, and in many other ways, a good chaplain may help to raise and maintain the morale of a unit, particularly in action, as many commanding officers have testified."[162]

Leaders may well have misattributed their battlefield success to chaplains or, in their gratitude for divine intervention, exaggerated the impact that religious leaders had on troops. They could not base their assessments on systematic data linking the efforts of their chaplains to unit morale and linking unit morale, in turn, to military effectiveness. Nor would such evidence have mattered. What did matter was that they, their officers, and their troops believed that chaplains had the ability to motivate troops. This sincere perception in and of itself sufficed to turn chaplains into a powerful force multiplier. Consequently, throughout the twentieth century, decision makers recruited, trained, and deployed chaplains and placed the responsibility for the religious and emotional health of soldiers in their hands. Without their chaplains, their soldiers felt lost, spiritually and morally. Accompanied by their chaplains, they went to battle emboldened and reassured. They continue to do so to this day.

CHAPTER 5

How?

Sacred Rituals and War

On June 15, 1098, the starved, exhausted and outnumbered crusaders besieged in Antioch made a miraculous discovery: In a pit under the cathedral, they found the Holy Lance, the tip of the spear that had pierced the side of the crucified Christ. Inspired by this divine relic, as well as visions of Christ, the Virgin Mary, an ominous meteor, and saints Andrew, George, Demetrius and Maurice, they charged out of the city gates, led by Raymond of Aguilers, who brandished the lance. Their enemies fled before them.[1]

I suspect that scholars of religion and war like to tell and retell such stories about the Crusades to remind ourselves of how much the religion of Western soldiers has changed since the Middle Ages and how different these modern professional soldiers are from the religiously motivated opponents they face. Yet miracles are a just as common in modern wars.

General George Patton is said to have produced one such miracle himself. In winter 1944, Patton's Third Army was mired in northern France, unable to advance against the German 7th Army due to low supplies and incessant rains. In his despair, the general summoned his chaplain, James H. O'Neill, and ordered him to write a prayer to stop the rains. The prayer, composed on December 14, read, "Almighty and most merciful Father, We humbly beseech Thee, of Thy great goodness, to restrain these immoderate rains with which we have to contend. Grant us fair weather for battle. . . ." By Patton's order, 250,000 copies of the prayer were printed and distributed to the soldiers of the Third Army with instructions to pray fervently: "Pray when fighting. Pray alone. Pray with others. Pray by night and pray by day. Pray for the cessation of immoderate rains, for good weather for battle. Pray for the defeat of our wicked enemy whose banner is injustice and whose good is oppression. Pray for victory. Pray for our Army, and Pray for Peace." On December 20, the rains ceased, and Patton awarded his chaplain a Bronze Star, commenting, "Well, Padre, your prayers worked. I knew they would."[2]

During the First World War, visions of angels and saints were frequent and had a positive impact on recruitment and morale.[3] British soldiers reported miraculous crucifixes, chapels, and statues of the Madonna that survived shelling, dripped blood, or spoke words of prophecy.[4] Russian soldiers saw the Virgin and Child prior to a successful counterattack against German forces in Augustów.[5] Some French soldiers beheld visions of flaming swords in the skies; others witnessed tricolor stars.[6] Here is how one French soldier described the appearance of Saint Therese of Lisieux on the battlefield:

> It was at a very hard moment, for the guns were roaring at each other full blast. . . . I said to Sister Therese: "My sister Therese, bring me back, I beg you, to my wife and my children, and I promise you I'll go to your tomb. . . ." Scarcely had I uttered this prayer that I saw a cloud open above me and the face of the saint stood out against the blue sky. I thought I was the victim of a hallucination. I rubbed my eyes over and over, but I could not doubt what I saw, for her face got clearer and more resplendent as I gazed. . . . Since that time I have no longer felt alone.[7]

Along similar lines, Israeli soldiers conducting house-to-house combat during the Operation Cast Lead reported that Rachel, the biblical matriarch, appeared to them in the heat of battle, in the form of a beautiful young woman, to warn them about of explosives, booby-trapped houses, and terrorist ambushes.[8] Other soldiers attributed a divine origin to a miraculous rainfall that prevented enemy explosives and mortar bombs from going off and that collapsed terrorist tunnels.[9] During the 2014 war in Gaza, a predawn patrol that risked being exposed by daybreak was shrouded by a miraculous fog: "Suddenly a cloud protected us," recounted an officer. "It really was a fulfillment of the verse 'For the Lord your God is the one who goes with you to give you victory.'"[10]

Enlisted soldiers are not alone in sensing a divine presence on the battlefield. General Alexander von Kluck, commander of the German First Army during the World War I, attributed the repulsion of his advance on the Marne to divine intervention because it coincided with the French celebration of the Nativity of the Virgin. His French opponents dubbed it "the Miracle of the Marne" and credited it to fervent prayers at Sacré-Cœur in Montmartre.[11] General Douglas Haig thought himself to have been divinely ordained to lead the BEF, believed that all his battles were directed from above, and sought divine guidance prior to battle.[12] Winston Churchill credited Almighty God for saving him during his escape from a Boer POW camp and for protecting England time and again, from preventing the Germans from following up on their success at Dunkirk to calming the sea to facilitate the invasion of North Africa.[13]

Scholars of religion on the battlefield have not developed the tools to make sense of these events. We do not even know what the appropriate questions are that we ought to ask, let alone what the answers to these questions might be. Does it make sense to ask whether Patton believed in the miraculous power of prayer? Or are Patton's efforts better understood as an effort to boost unit cohesion by means of a group ritual? How did the chaplains and soldiers in the Third Army understand the order to pray? How did the seeming efficacy of the prayer, in turn, affect the religiosity of soldiers in the Army? Because we are bewildered by prayers and miracles on the modern battlefield, we have developed neither the tools to analyze these behaviors nor an intuition about how much they matter, if at all.

My goal in this chapter is to begin addressing these lacunae in two ways. First, I highlight the continuity of religious practices in Western militaries across time. By focusing on the religiosity of extremist "others"—insurgents and terrorists—scholars imply a discontinuity of religious practices, as if the religious rituals that characterized premodern Western armies have been relegated to the past. I show that this is not so, that soldiers continue to bear relics into battle, venerate amulets, seek priestly benediction over units and weapons, and participate in auspicious group rituals.

Because the topic of religious rituals among contemporary military forces is vastly underexplored, my second purpose is to draw on such meager evidence as does exist to suggest hypotheses, raise further questions, and stimulate further research. In the second part of this chapter, I ask questions about prayer, a research topic of baffling paucity. When do soldiers pray? What do they pray for? I present anecdotal evidence from twentieth-century wars to showcase the range of conditions under which soldiers pray, the primary themes that recur in these prayers, and their self-professed effects on practitioners.

The practices and prayers I explore in the first part of this chapter raise two interrelated questions. First, how does the religion that soldiers practice affect their performance on the battlefield? Put more bluntly, why should scholars of war and peace care about the rituals and prayers of soldiers? In the third section, I take a first cut at this question by exploring the effects of religiosity on resilience. In doing so, I borrow from a handful of analyses that investigate the religiosity of trauma victims, inside and outside the military, to suggests preliminary findings on the positive relationship between religiosity and resistance to shock.

The second question turns the first on its head: How does combat, in turn, affect the religiosity of soldiers? Do religious practice and military practice enjoy a mutually reinforcing relationship or is one likely to undermine the other? We have no answers to any of these questions, but to illustrate the possibility and utility of taking on such puzzles, I offer some initial evidence for the inconsistent effects that war has had on the religiosity of participants. I conclude the chapter with a series of open-ended questions about religion and war that deserve scholarly attention. Primary among these is the under-explored relationship between religious practice and unit cohesion and its implications for military effectiveness.

This chapter is exploratory, and my findings are tentative and often speculative. My goal is not to deliver decisive answers to the "how" of religion in modern war because neither the data nor the methods necessary for producing such answers are available. Rather, my goal is to provoke scholars to embark on research programs that will shed light on the mutual interaction between sacred rituals and the conduct of war.

How Little Has Changed

Historians of medieval warfare, led by David Bachrach, have beautifully documented the many curious and fascinating ways in which medieval soldiers practiced their religion on the battlefield: they prayed, alone and in groups; participated in religious rituals (benedictions, fasts, and absolutions); marched into battle with clergy bearing relics; wore religious insignia; witnessed miracles on the battlefield; and employed religious war cries.[14] These descriptions paint a colorful picture of a period in history in which all aspects of warfare were infused with religion. But the description also runs the risk of making these practices seem exotic, tinging them with an aura of mystique and distinctiveness, as if to suggest that religion has long since ceased to play this eccentric role in Western armies. Readers can be forgiven for concluding that, even though religious rites on the battlefield may characterize contemporary insurgents, radicals and terrorists, modern armies no longer express their religiosity in this manner.

Nothing could be further from the truth. In all aspects, public and private, the religiosity of contemporary militaries mirrors that of their medieval predecessors. The rituals may have changed in form but not in purpose. Some of these rituals are formal religious practices, such as benedictions, liturgical prayers, and religious ceremonies. Others are personal practices, including private prayers that soldiers compose to suit their individual needs. Yet others mix piety with superstition in what Alphonse Dupront has called "everyday religion."[15] These are informal, but no less important, rites such as the wearing of protective charms or the performance of small auspicious routines prior to battle, akin to those that professional athletes perform prior to competitions.[16]

Protective Charms

Consider the propensity of soldiers to carry bibles, sacred amulets, or magical talismans in the hopes of protecting themselves from enemy fire. World War I soldiers wore rosaries, religious trinkets, and talismans and circulated stories of bibles stopping bullets. The search of soldiers' bodies prior to burial revealed that approximately one-third of British soldiers and more than half of French soldiers carried bibles, crosses, or amulets.[17] Paul Fussell, a cultural historian who has studied the symbols of the First World War at length, writes, "No front-line soldiers or officer was without his amulet, and every tunic pocket became a reliquary. Lucky coins, buttons, dried flowers, hair cuttings, New Testaments, pebbles from home, medals of St. Christopher and St. George, childhood dolls and teddy bears, poems or Scripture verses written out and worn in a small bag around the neck like a phylactery, Sassoon's fire-opal—so urgent was the need that no talisman was too absurd."[18] Catholic soldiers protected themselves by means of scapulars, pairs of holy images worn over the chest and back and tied together over the shoulders.[19] German wives and mothers pronounced ritual verses and spells over men leaving for the front and offered them *Schutzbriefe*, heaven-sent letters of protection, to carry on their persons.[20] One of the most popular amulets of the war, the "Touchwood Charm" sold 1.2 million copies in the first year of the war alone.[21] Successful amulets that were deemed to have saved a soldier's life were sent to local churches as missals to provide public evidence of miraculous intervention.[22]

The faith in the protective power of sacred items, and the fatalism that accompanied it, continued into the Second World War.[23] John Steinbeck observed this widespread reliance on amulets among U.S. troops, and Spike Milligan, a British comedian, joked that he would have weighed 280 pounds had he worn all the holy medallions he had received from friends and family members.[24] Soldiers carried crosses, good luck charms, bibles, rabbit feet, and medals, some blessed by the unit chaplain, others blessed by the pope.[25] In Britain, the archbishop of Westminster blessed 50,000 Bakelite crosses for distribution among Catholic troops.[26] In the United States, the military distributed 11 million copies of the bible with an endorsement from President Roosevelt commending the reading of the Bible to all soldiers as "a fountain of strength. . . ." Multiple photos from this period show soldiers triumphantly displaying the punctured bibles that had saved them from an otherwise deadly bullet.[27]

When Operation Desert Shield was launched in 1990, chaplains arrived in Saudi Arabia armed not only with crucifixes, rosaries, communion wafers, and sacramental wine (labeled "tea") but also with 300,000 bibles with camouflage covers, donated by the American Bible Society.[28] Many U.S. soldiers now wear a "Shield of Strength," a dog tag with the words "One Nation Under God" engraved on one side and a verse from the Book of Joshua engraved on the other: "I will be strong and courageous. I will not be terrified, or discouraged; for the Lord my God is with me wherever I go." The creator of the shield, Kenny Vaughn, claims to have produced over 3 million copies for British and U.S. soldiers.[29]

Sacred Relics

A similar continuity of practice is apparent in the bearing of sacred relics into battle. Medieval priests carried the bones of saints or holy talismans (fragments of the cross, relics of the Passion, or the personal effects of saints) into war in the belief that these would provide divine protection as well as encouragement to soldiers. The Russian military continues to do precisely that; except for a brief interlude during Joseph Stalin's reign, Orthodox priests routinely bear relics to the front, as they did during the First World War.[30] General Fyodor Ushakov, canonized as the patron saint of the Russian Navy in 2000 and the patron saint of Russian nuclear-armed strategic bombers in 2005, is physically present on all naval vessels in the form of a blessed icon.

In the Indian military, Sikh *granthis* accompany forces while carrying the Guru Granth Sahib, the holy scripture and physical embodiment of the gurus, on their heads.[31] When Argentine forces invaded the Falklands, they bore a statue of Our Lady of Lujan, the patron saint of Argentina. In good Roman tradition, the victorious British troops took the statue with them and installed it at the Royal Garrison Church in Aldershot, England.[32]

In Shintoism, the parallel protective function is performed by altars, *kamidana*, present on all airplanes and naval vessels of the Japanese Self-Defense Forces. These are designed to physically house the spirits of the vessel and to allow soldiers to make offerings, such as candles and food, to avert mishap. To purify these vehicles and populate their shrines with spirits, Shinto priests perform dedication ceremonies (*kigansai*) that have to be repeated prior to training exercises or after accidents. In smaller vessels, such as trucks or helicopters, soldiers substitute an *o-fuda*, an amulet inscribed with the name of a spirit or shrine that transfers part of the god into the object on which it is attached and provides protection. Many soldiers also carry a personal protection amulet (*o-mamori*) that contains the spirit of a god. A pilot, for example, may carry an amulet from the Hikō Shrine in Kyoto, whose god protects those who fly.[33]

Whereas Protestant traditions have rejected the veneration of saints, relics, and amulets altogether, Catholic soldiers in Western militaries do bear relics into battle, although in an attenuated form. Consecrating the eucharist to celebrate mass requires an altar, and this, in turn, requires altar stones or an altar cloth containing relics or fragments of relics.[34] Father William Corby, who famously blessed the troops during the Battle of Gettysburg, carried hosts and an altar stone on the field.[35] Chaplains who did not carry altar stones had to carry a limited supply of already consecrated hosts and wine, and soldiers took inordinate risks to protect these sacred objects in battle.[36] Father Charles F. Suver landed with his mass kit on the beaches of Iwo Jima and set up an altar on Mount Suribachi to celebrate mass minutes after the mountain was captured.[37] Chaplain John Maloney, who parachuted into France with a mass kit, was henceforth known by the nickname "the Bread from Heaven."[38]

Benedictions

Orthodox priests, from Romania to Yugoslavia, routinely bless rifles, tanks, attack helicopters, naval vessels, and soldiers by sprinkling them with holy water (figure 5.1). Russian Orthodox priests have even sprinkled holy water on nuclear bombers and nuclear missiles.[39] This is not without precedent in the U.S. armed forces; George Zabelka, the Catholic chaplain on Tinian Island, blessed the crew of the *Enola Gay* prior to its departure to Hiroshima, although he later insisted that it was the crew he blessed, not the plane or the bomb.[40]

On the whole, British and U.S. forces have displayed a more ambivalent attitude about priestly blessings of weapons, although the benediction of soldiers has continued unabated. In 1862, Father Thomas Mooney was recalled from duty after it was discovered that he had baptized the big guns at Fort Corcoran with holy water.[41] But Northern and Southern ministers were entirely

FIGURE 5.1   A Russian Orthodox priest blesses new Kalashnikov rifles in Stavropol, January 2008.
Danil Semyonov/AFP/Getty Images

comfortable blessing companies of soldiers setting off to the front and consecrating their regimental flags.[42] This practice has continued uninterrupted in the British army, where chaplains consecrate the "colours" by means of a prayer of protection. For example: "Let thy gracious favor rest on those who shall follow the Colours. . . . give them courage, and may their courage ever rest on their sure confidence in Thee. . . . Guide the counsels of those who shall lead them, and sustain them by Thy help in the time of need. . . ."[43] During the First World War, clergymen offered prayers for protection against air raids and submarines, uttered prayers at the "baptism" of tanks and field ambulances, prayed that German mines would be rendered inoperative, and prayed to stop winds from spreading poison gas into the British lines.[44]

In the British and U.S. armies, attendance at certain religious rituals was compulsory until quite recently: Chapel services were obligatory at West Point until 1908 and at other military academies until 1972, when a lawsuit prohibited the practice.[45] Church parades, considered beneficial to discipline, morale, and esprit de corps, were still enforced in the British armed forces during the Second World War.[46] To this day, every regiment and corps of the British Army, Navy and Air Force has its own regimental prayers, known as collects, invoked at public ceremonies.[47]

During battle, commanders found that rituals calmed fears and distracted their men from a preoccupation with danger, cleared their consciences, and offered them a sense of spiritual tranquility.[48] Prior to the Battle of Vimy, the senior chaplain to the 1st Canadian Division wrote that "the assurance of pardoned sins through the Blood of Christ, gives a cheerfulness, a hope and a Divine courage in the face of death which military training alone cannot secure."[49] General Bernard Montgomery's chaplain felt that Monty's prayer prior to the Battle of El Alamein consecrated the Army and boosted its confidence: "It was a formidable task, but we had confidence. We had the Cause, the Leadership, the Men, the Stuff and we had more: we had the consciousness that God was calling us."[50] As a consequence, unit-wide ceremonies such as mass, group prayers, or general absolution were practiced widely by U.S., French, German, and British troops during the First and Second World Wars. These ceremonies were held as close to the moment of battle as possible, when soldiers were at their most needy, reverent, and receptive.[51] A contemporary British chaplain put the matter bluntly, "In times of actual or anticipated combat, trade was brisk."[52]

In their memoires, soldiers reported that these were moving events that could transcend age, class, and even denominational differences.[53] Receiving absolution just prior to an assault, testified Rudyard Kipling, "is a powerful tonic."[54] Prior to D-Day, for example, all the principal British officers participating in the assault took part in a pre-invasion service held at Portsdown.[55] Allied soldiers also used religious services to celebrate their victories. Victorious soldiers flocked to local churches and cathedrals to participate in large thanksgiving masses after the liberations of Libya, Italy, and France as well as—by special order of General Douglas MacArthur—the liberation of Manila.[56] Today, even though prayers at mandatory gatherings in the U.S. military are deemed unconstitutional, they continue to feature widely at official events, including change-of-command ceremonies; prior to lights-out on all U.S. Navy vessels; at meals in the Naval Academy; and at the mandatory Fall Convocation of the Naval War College.[57]

Public Prayer

Religious ceremonies in the military were often backed by officially mandated public ceremonies on the home front. Congress ordered such a day of "fasting, humiliation and prayer" on May 15, 1776, to "incline the Lord, Giver of Victory, to prosper our arms," and it ordered a public day of thanksgiving after John Burgoyne's surrender at Saratoga.[58] Abraham Lincoln and Jefferson Davis both proclaimed national days of prayer, fasting, humiliation, and thanksgiving during the course of the Civil War. This followed the widespread belief among Civil War soldiers that the prayers of their families and neighbors could spare soldiers' lives, particularly if they coincided precisely with the timing of a battle.[59] The thanksgiving proclamation that Lincoln issued on October 3, 1863, to celebrate "the advancing armies and navies of the Union," decreed Thanksgiving a national holiday and determined the date on which it is still celebrated to this day.[60] During the Franco-Prussian War, German pastors on the home front arranged days of repentance (*Busstage*), days of prayer (*Bettage*), days of military celebration (*Kriegsfeiertage*), and, after victories, special thanksgiving services (*Dankgottesdienste*).[61]

British monarchs declared national days of prayers repeatedly during both world wars as a "means by which the State expresses its recognition of God and the need of Divine help and guidance."[62] On New Year's Day 1916, Jewish congregations in England joined all churches, established and Nonconformist alike, in a wartime prayer and intercession.[63] The royals also proclaimed and participated in national thanksgiving services at the conclusion of both wars.[64] In the United States, religious leaders across denominations wrote special prayers to be offered in all churches on "invasion day."[65] So positive was the influence of home-front prayers on the morale of U.S. soldiers in the field that Secretary of War Henry Stimson instituted a fifteen-minute noontime prayer in the Army, to allow soldiers at the front lines to coordinate their prayers with those of military staff and families praying for their welfare.[66] Patton argued that his army had avoided defeat, famine, and disease "because a lot of people back home are praying for us."[67] More recently, chaplains to troops departing for Saudi Arabia placed a roster with the names of 22,000 deployed soldiers on it in a bible so that their family members, left behind at their home base in Germany, could pray for the soldiers.[68] Religious communities in the United States regularly bless congregants prior to enlistment (e.g., in the form of "laying of hands") and pray for community members in uniform while they are stationed abroad.[69]

Prayer

These public prayers are mirrored and amplified by the prayers that soldiers utter in the trenches. When and where do soldiers pray? Rarely do they find the time to pray during battle, when their primary focus is physical action in response to physical threat. Periods of calm, waiting, and inaction provoke a helplessness that often motivates soldiers to pray. Soldiers pray between battles, as they enter the battlefield, and after battle to express thanks.[70] Others pray as part of a daily schedule in an effort to preserve the routines of civilian life or to wish for the healing of a wounded or dying comrade in arms.[71] The only systematic survey of prayer in the military found that 70–83

FIGURE 5.2   U.S. Marines at a forward operating base in Afghanistan pray before heading out on patrol, October 2010.
Scott Olson/Getty Images

percent of U.S. soldiers were "helped a lot" by prayer during World War II. Prayer was particularly helpful for surveyed soldiers who had experienced stressful and difficult conditions, such as the loss of a friend or massive artillery attacks, or for soldiers who had experienced fear or a loss of confidence in battle.[72]

Prayer also fulfills a social function, drawing together members of military units to enhance unit cohesion and provide a collective calm and focus. Here the practice of group prayer seems to matter no less than the particular content of the invocation. A British soldier from the Second World War recalled, "We did not worship together in France just because we were afraid. Worship had a meaning and a reality for us because we lived together. We shared the same hopes and the same fears."[73] Chaplains recorded Irish Guards kneeling as a group in prayer, just prior to an attack on a German position, with "a look of absolute joy on their faces"; prisoners of war, after a forced march of 20 miles, finding energy and hope in group prayer and hymn-singing session; and wounded soldiers in a field hospital joining in the singing of the hymn "Abide with Me."[74] Marines in the U.S. military today often fashion small-group rituals that allow members from different religious traditions to sing, quote from scripture, and pray together.[75]

What do soldiers pray for? One contemporary best-selling military accessory for U.S. soldiers serving in the Middle East suggests some answers to that question and highlights the range of aspirations that soldiers express in their prayers. It is the "Psalm 91 Camo Bandana," a gray-and-white speckled cloth imprinted with the full text of the psalm and designed to be affixed over or under the helmet for added protection. "It's not magic," explains one military-apparel website selling the cloth. "It just gives you a touch of comfort and security to know someone's watching out for you."[76]

The particular psalm chosen for the "Camo Bandana" encapsulates four primary motifs in battlefield prayer. The first and most obvious is protection from physical harm: "No evil shall befall you, nor shall any plague come near your dwelling, for He shall give His angels charge over you, to keep you in all your ways."[77] The second theme is victory on the battlefield: "A thousand may fall at your side, and ten thousand at your right hand." The third is courage: "You shall not be afraid of the terror by night, nor of the arrow that flies by day, nor of the pestilence that walks in darkness, nor of the destruction that lays waste at noonday." The fourth, least obvious yet very common among soldiers' prayers, is the simple comfort of God's presence: "Because he has set his love upon Me, therefore I will deliver him; I will set him on high, because he has known My name. He shall call upon Me, and I will answer him; I will be with him in trouble."

We know little of what soldiers pray about because so few have been able to record their thoughts on the battlefield. Even chaplains, who are otherwise careful to note down their sermons, rarely commit impromptu prayers to paper. An audio recording of an unknown chaplain, archived at the Imperial War Museum, offers a unique glimpse into these same four motifs during an informal prayer session by men of the Royal Welch Fusiliers prior to an attack near Roermond, Netherlands, in 1944:

> O God, our Father, we put ourselves into Thy care and in Thy keeping today. Grant, we beseech thee, as we go forward into this battle, that we may have a sense of Thy presence with us. Give us, we beseech Thee, such success that, when we overcome the enemy, help us to set forward that final victory, which will bring back peace and happiness, truth and justice, liberty and freedom, unto all mankind everywhere. We ask for Thy help and for Thy protection, not only for ourselves but for all our comrades. We know that we are in Thy keeping. Grant us, therefore, such courage that we may do our duty faithfully, we may not shrink from danger but feeling that Thou art beside us we may conquer weariness and overcome all perils. Have mercy, we beseech Thee, on those who shall be wounded. Bring Thy comfort unto all who, in this battle, will lay down their lives and hasten the time when war shall be no more through Jesus Christ our Lord Amen.[78]

Naturally, the fervent hope for safety, protection. and survival is a dominant theme in these prayers. In the trove of personal messages left by First World War soldiers at the sanctuary at Noulette, for example, the wish to survive the war and be reunited with one's family is a common motif, often expressed on behalf of an entire unit or even all parties to the conflict: "Preserve me against the disasters I risk every day, and I beg you, stop as fast as you can this terrible carnage that makes so many corpses. . . ."[79] Airmen in the Second World War and riflemen in Vietnam were united in the simple wish: "Please God, I don't want to die."[80] For some soldiers, such protective prayers took on the form of magical mantras, as in the French World War I prayer "against firearms," which promised to defend the reciter from all peril: "Ecce, Crucem, domini, fugite, partes, adverse, vicis, l'eode, Tribu, Juda, make the sign of the cross, radix, clavo."[81]

Commanding officers often express an additional sentiment in their supplications: the strength to bear the burden of command and the wisdom to make the right decisions. The actor Jimmy Stewart, who was a squadron commander during the Second World War, prayed because he feared for the lives of his crew: "We all prayed a lot. . . . I didn't pray for myself. I just prayed that I wouldn't make a mistake."[82] Similarly, Colonel David Shoup, the officer in charge of the Marine assault on the Tarawa Atoll, asked his chaplain to pray "that I don't make any mistakes out on that beach; no wrong decisions that will cost any of those boys an arm or a leg or a hand, much less a life."[83] During the Falklands War, Lieutenant Colonel Chris Keeble suddenly found himself in command of the 2nd Battalion of the Parachute Regiment after his commander was killed in action during the Battle for Goose Green. Keeble reports finding the strength to lead after kneeling in prayer and surrendering his will to God.[84]

The most common theme in soldiers' prayers is more nuanced: a wish to be reconciled with God and ascertain his companionship during battle and, if need be, after death. "In our prayers before entering combat, these boys and I had not asked to escape unscathed or to come out alive," explained Chaplain Joseph O'Callahan regarding prayers on the *USS Franklin* prior to battle. "We had reminded ourselves that, should death come, in whatever form, it would be a happy death if we died in the friendship of God."[85] In his study of faith in the U.S. military, Stephen Mansfield observes, "The focus during crisis becomes simply, 'Is God with me?'" Mansfield recounts the request of a U.S. soldier preparing for a convoy in Iraq: "I wanna' know that Jesus is in my Humvee."[86] An anonymous poem, hidden in a foxhole in North Africa during World War II conveys the same idea in a more poetic manner: "Stay with me, God, the night is dark, the night is cold.

My little spark of courage dies. The night is long. Be with me, God, and make me strong."[87]

Religion, Morale, and Mental Health

Why should we care whether soldiers pray, carry amulets, or believe in God? What are the effects of these ritual practices, and the ideas associated with them, on military units and their ability to operate effectively? I offer several speculative answers in the conclusion to this chapter; the impact of rituals on unit cohesion or military effectiveness has not yet received scholarly attention. The one aspect that leaders and scholars alike have commented on, although superficially, is the relationship between religion and mental health. Commanders have treated religion as conducive to discipline, moral fortitude, and morale. The health sciences have backed this claim up to some extent with initial research that links religiosity to the mental health of trauma survivors.

Nineteenth- and twentieth-century commanders were comfortable conflating religiosity, morality, morale, and discipline. George Washington, in his "Farewell Address," warned against the supposition "that morality can be maintained without religion."[88] British Standing Order RB 1801 proclaimed that "true religious fortitude generally makes the best men, and consequently the best soldiers. A man without religion is generally a disobedient, a drunken, a cowardly and of course a cruel man. . . ."[89] In justifying his request for chaplains at frontier posts, Lieutenant Colonel Josiah Voss wrote to the Department of War, "Nothing will add so much to the respectability and efficiency of our army as the appointment of chaplains and the regular public worship of God at our military posts on the Sabbath. . . . When the Sabbath is properly observed, and public worship is held, there are fewer desertions, less intoxication, and a more healthy and efficient command. . . ."[90]

"Morale Reports" issued by the Third Army in 1916 and 1917 used religious statements from the letters that soldiers sent home as an indicator of morale and listed religion, alongside dedication, discipline, and camaraderie, as the lynchpins of victory.[91] The U.S. chief of staff during World War II, General George C. Marshall, stated: "Morale can only come out of the religious nature of a soldier who knows God and who had the spirit of religious fervor in his soul."[92] A guidebook, detailing chaplain duties in World War II, noted the chaplain's dual concern with moral and spiritual welfare and went on to state, "Moral qualities include discipline, the fighting spirit, the will to win, self-control, self-respect, loyalty and a high sense of honour. . . . these are in the realm of character and character is in the realm of religion. . . . Morale has its basis in religion."[93] In 1989, the U.S. Army Character Training program emphasized that Christian faith and tradition provided the foundation for service, courage, and discipline, a position that is expressed in U.S. military manuals to this day.[94] For example, the Marine Corps guidelines for chaplains explain that "in times of stress or crisis, overlooking basic religious needs—such as required sacramental or ritual observances—and essential faith practices can have a negative impact on personal readiness and unit morale."[95]

Mental health research lends some support to the link between religiosity and resilience, particularly as regards the ability of soldiers to cope with and recover from trauma. Several studies of stress and post-traumatic stress disorder (PTSD) outside the armed forces have found that religiosity and religious involvement are significantly associated with a reduced likelihood of depression, anxiety, alcohol or drug abuse, stress, and trauma.[96] For PTSD sufferers in particular, religion provides a positive coping mechanism that can result in mitigated symptoms. Religion and spirituality can act as buffers against the impact of trauma and can encourage post-trauma growth. These studies suggest that patients recovering from shock who rely on religion enjoy better social relationships, fewer unpleasant thoughts, fewer temper outbursts, and a more positive outlook on life.[97]

The relationship between religion and coping with trauma also finds confirmation in a handful of studies involving veterans. In a poll of one hundred U.S. veterans of the Iraq War, the respondents revealed that religion was the most significant factor in helping them accept the physical and psychological challenges of being a veteran.[98] Israeli soldiers from religious backgrounds who fought in Lebanon in 1982 reported fearing death less than their nonreligious counterparts and experienced a lesser elevation in fear when exposed to risk.[99] A study of Iranian veterans of the Iran-Iraq War has found that religious coping provides a significant contribution to PTSD management, and a study of Bosnian veterans has found that religious beliefs are negatively correlated with PTSD severity.[100]

The contribution of religion to suicide prevention among soldiers is particularly remarkable. Among Croatian War veterans with PTSD, suicidality is inversely correlated with intrinsic religiosity and spiritual, existential, and religious well-being. Those veterans who expressed feeling close to God, loved by God, and satisfied with their relationship with God were the least likely to attempt suicide.[101] U.S. veterans with PTSD confirmed that, although thoughts of family and friends ranked first among the reflections that helped them through suicidal episodes, thoughts of faith, religion, or spirituality ranked second.[102]

How does religion effect these outcomes? Religion may exert its influence indirectly by enhancing social support. Religious rituals offer a group setting in which troubled individuals can speak about their concerns and anxieties in an open manner without fearing social reproach. In one survey of soldiers who discussed their suicidal thoughts with others, 40 percent attested to seeking out a friend, 35 percent sought out a spiritual advisor or clergy member, and only 30 percent spoke to a spouse or significant other.[103] As discussed in chapter 4, chaplains can help soldiers cope with stress, guilt, and trauma by hearing their confessions, forgiving their sins, or initiating constructive conversations about justice and culpability. These practices led post-war U.S. psychiatrists to recommend that armies enlist the aid of chaplains to supplement psychotherapy as a means of alleviating war guilt.[104]

At the same time, mental health research suggests that the role of religion extends beyond the provision of basic social outlets. Religious coping seems to contribute to the mental health of PTSD sufferers to a greater extent than mere social support does by itself.[105] One hypothesis in the mental health literature is that religious beliefs provide an external attribution for traumatic events. Insofar as feelings of guilt, helplessness, or incompetence contribute to PTSD, these can be mitigated by attributing difficult events to "the will of God" or "fate"[106] Among Sri Lankan veterans with combat trauma, for example, a belief in reincarnation acted as a buffer to prevent further traumatization. The victims believed that their physical and psychological symptoms were due to karmic actions in the past lives. This helped them to find meaning in their suffering and to come to terms with their trauma.[107]

These effects are not just a matter of belief but of practice as well. The repetitive and meditative nature of religious rituals can provide stress-relieving benefits. Two studies of U.S. veterans have found that repetition of a mantra improved the subjects' spiritual well-being and helped them manage PTSD symptoms.[108] Unlike rituals, religious beliefs can prove to be a double-edged sword when it comes to preventing or treating trauma because particular beliefs can have an adverse effect on healing.[109] Individuals who view their spirituality, faith community, or higher power as sources of support, validation, and acceptance are better equipped to recover from trauma. In contrast, those who view religion as a source of judgment, punishment, or rejection are handicapped in the recovery process.[110] The former is referred to as "positive religious coping" and includes mechanisms such as benevolent religious reappraisal, religious forgiveness and purification, and seeking religious support. "Negative religious coping," in contrast, entails a reappraisal of God's powers, spiritual discontent, and a belief in a punishing deity.[111] For example, a survey of members of the Oregon Army National Guard has revealed that soldiers who reported higher existential well-being prior to deployment were less likely to develop depressive symptoms post-deployment; however, those who employed negative religious coping strategies prior to combat deployment were more likely to develop PTSD symptoms.[112] Parallel studies of U.S. veterans have linked negative religious coping to more severe PTSD as well as to depression and anxiety.[113]

The study of religious practice and its effects on combat effectiveness is still in its infancy. Even within the narrow topic of religion and resilience, the findings remain speculative, in part because the literature remains overly focused on internal states of mind instead of rituals and physical practices. We know all too little about how group rituals differ from individual rituals in their ability to prepare soldiers for battle. We have not mapped the full array of ceremonies that soldiers partake in to gird themselves for battle, express grief, or share difficult experiences. It is not clear who does and does not initiate, lead, and participate in these religious sessions, and we have no good data on the difference that these rituals make. The studies discussed here do suggest, however, that such questions are worth pursuing in full.

War and Religiosity

Another trove of unanswered questions pertains to the inverse of the relationships examined so far: How does war affect religiosity in turn? This question is of significance not only because it reverses the causal arrow of the arguments presented above but also because it allows us to explore the recursive relationship between religion and war. If the religiosity of soldiers does not merely shape war but is also shaped by war in turn, then we can expect both to evolve over time, a development that we would not presume if religiosity were unaffected by the experience of war. Decision makers who are unaware of this feedback loop will misdiagnose the influence of religion across wars. Soldiers, in turn, can experience the exponential effects of this cycle over the course of a single conflict if, for example, battlefield trauma prompts a decline in religiosity that heightens the susceptibility to yet more trauma.

As the brief historical survey in this section shows, the effects of war on religiosity do, indeed, vary across time. The single most important factor affecting this process is not the brief exposure of soldiers to war but the underlying social-religious setting in which the war occurs. It is, however, possible to identify several mechanisms through which combat itself has affected the religiosity of soldiers across history.

Religiosity can increase in times of war if religion can offer soldiers a sense of security and comfort in the face of death. For some soldiers, divine providence means physical protection. If this is so, we should expect religiosity to intensify as soldiers move closer to the front and prepare to encounter danger.[114] For other soldiers, religion provides a sense of meaning, an explanation for the daily challenges of combat that justifies participation.[115] For these soldiers, it is not necessarily combat that produces faith but rather prior religious belief that offers strength during combat and is, in turn, bolstered at times of peril.[116] Soldiers also enjoy the social benefits that group rituals offer: a sense of cohesion, camaraderie, and an emotional outlet. Interactions with chaplains, whether a formal confession or an informal conversation, offer a range of psychological benefits to soldiers seeking to reconcile themselves with death, confront trauma, or overcome the guilt of killing.[117]

Nevertheless, the military environment itself is not conducive to piety. Soldiers without a deep grounding in religious tradition may find it hard to preserve their spiritual life in the absence of a family or church community. The superficial religiosity acquired at times of crisis, "in the foxholes," rarely survives the war because soldiers without a religious background cannot be expected to acquire it on the spot.[118]

The primary mechanism for the loss of faith on the battlefield is the inability to reconcile religious beliefs with the experience of war. Guilt over killing others or the inability to save the wounded often leads to a weakening or even a complete loss of religious faith.[119] The negative effects of battlefield experience on religion are particularly pronounced among individuals who have low initial levels of religiosity and who employ negative religious coping. Trauma can lead to a further deterioration of religiosity because traumatic experiences tend to destabilize religious beliefs, prompting increases or decreases in religiosity.[120] At the individual level, the curve plotting the relationship between religious crisis and war seems to assume an inverse bell shape. Soldiers with particularly high or low levels of religiosity emerge from the test of war with their beliefs (or lack thereof) intact, perhaps even strengthened; in contrast, soldiers whose religious identity is uncertain find their feeble religious foundation shattered by the experience of war.

The record on religiosity in U.S. wars shows a swing from very high levels of religiosity during the Civil War, a decline in World War I, a rise in World War II, and an even greater decline during the Vietnam War. Civil War armies were among the most religious in U.S. history.[121] The figures on battlefield conversions alone paint a startling picture of religious revival in both armies. By contemporary estimates, between 100,000 and 200,000 Union soldiers converted during the war, approximately 5–10 percent of the entire army. The number of spectators or previously converted individuals at religious revivals was even higher. In the South, 7,000 men con-

verted between fall 1863 and spring 1864 alone, accounting for 10 percent
of the men under Robert E. Lee's command in that period.[122] In all, about
150,000 Confederate soldiers, or about 15 percent of the Confederate army,
converted during the war.[123] Some Civil War chaplains recorded that they
preached four to six sermons a day and baptized over two hundred men a
year, often a dozen at a time.[124] This religious revival had a direct effect on
the morale of participants and an indirect effect on the duration of the war.
Some scholars have proposed that it was the primary factor that helped soldiers endure the stress and trauma of the war.[125] Others have gone so far as
to argue that, by sustaining both armies during the terrible carnage of 1864,
religion prolonged the war into 1865.[126]

The primary explanation for this religious enthusiasm lies not in the
nature of the Civil War itself but in the broader social changes occurring in
the United States at the time. The religious revival in both armies in 1862
coincided not only with the heaviest fighting of the early Civil War but
also with a growing religious awakening throughout the country, the Great
Revival of 1862–1863.[127] The religion of the military unit came to replace
the functions of the church back home. It provided community, spiritual
guidance, and moral discipline. Because units with a reputation for religious
fervor were seen as courageous and honorable, their members took pride in
the unit and this, in turn, fostered group cohesion. This was not just a matter
of belief but also practice; group prayer, sermons before battle, and revivals between battles contributed to the discipline and cohesion that allowed
the group to endure crises. Religious ceremonies provided entertainment
as well as opportunities for sociability. Conversion ceremonies provided
soldiers with a means of escaping anxiety and reasserting control over their
destiny.[128]

Soldiers also had individual reasons for embracing religion. If the war
was just, by Christian standards, soldiers could justify their participation,
overcome the inhibition against killing, and rationalize the death of comrades.[129] Some were sobered by the presence of death to recognize God's
direct presence on the battlefield, a religious experience that often occurred
in the midst of battle.[130] Others attributed their survival in battle to divine
protection and believed in the power of prayer to protect against fatal bullets. The idea that no harm would come to them unless God had ordained
it helped soldiers manage their fear of dying and strengthened their resolve
to fight. But the knowledge that there was no escape from this preordained
death could also lead to a dangerous fatalism and despondency. The same
piety that boosted morale early in the war could lead to doubt, a crisis of
faith, resignation, and apathy when the tide of war turned.[131]

Most often, faith and the hope of salvation offered a consolation to the dying and a comfort to those facing death. One soldier, mortally wounded at the Battle of Atlanta, "indicated by signs (he could not talk) that he was going home, pointing upward. His eyes were bright and natural. He appeared to be smiling."[132] A dying Union soldier confessed to his nurse, "I have lived an awful life, and I'm afraid to die. I shall go to hell." But after a Methodist minister encouraged him and sang hymns with him, he said, "It's all right with me chaplain! I trust in Christ! God will forgive me! I can die now!"[133]

The churches entered the First World War with expectations that there would be a similar revival. For the first time in modern history, they sent chaplains to war in an official capacity with the hope that they would play a missionary role. A British chaplain noted, "The padre who spent most of his time in the line could rest assured that he would find little difficulty in preaching to the men when he came out, and for the first time on a big scale the gap which so often exists between the clergy and the people was temporarily bridged."[134] One Canadian chaplain noted the beneficial effect that near-misses had on mass attendance.[135] A Catholic padre expressed similar sentiments: "A couple of well-directed shells help my work immensely by putting the fear of God into the hearts of a few careless boys who might not have troubled about coming near me otherwise."[136] The high number of conversions during the war, 40,000 Catholics on the Western front alone, lent some support to the notion that this war, too, bolstered religious sentiments among participants.[137]

The reality was far more complicated. The First World War led soldiers to religious extremes. Some who suffered the strain of war sought solace in religion; some even converted or joined the priesthood. Others grew disillusioned with organized religion, developed a contempt for religion, or lapsed from the church. Most experienced a faith in flux, shifting from belief to atheism and back, or striving to believe without success.[138]

The churches, particularly in England, emerged from the war with a strong sense of pessimism regarding secularization in the armed forces. An ambitious British survey, *The Army and Religion* (1919), found a decline in organized religion among soldiers but a persistence of religious practices. Soldiers had grown disillusioned with the Churches, lost interest in Christianity, and perceived God as a distant and helpless deity. Yet they were eager to receive communion, particularly on the eve of battle, prayed to God before an assault, and thanked him after their return to the trenches.[139] Even when they rejected religion, soldiers did so with mixed motives, some because they associated its practices with superstition or fatalism, others because they felt unworthy of divine protection or because they considered battlefield prayers to be opportunistic, even cowardly.[140]

Robert Graves's claim that "not one soldier in a hundred was inspired by religious feelings of even the crudest sort" in the Great War is hyperbole.[141] Nonetheless, there were clear obstacles to faith in the trenches, the primary one being the soldiers' inability to reconcile the horrors of war with the precepts of religion. The official war correspondent of the *Daily Telegraph* put it thus, "All this blood and mangled flesh in the fields of France and Flanders seemed to them—to many of them, I know—a certain proof that God did not exist, or if He did exist was not, as they were told, a God of love but a monster glad of the agonies of men."[142]

The most visible symbol of that dissonance were the chaplains, who bore the brunt of the attack against religion. "They prayed for victory and thundered from pulpits for the enemy to be smitten hip and thigh," a soldier noted, "but did not believe in doing any of the smiting themselves."[143] Another fumed, "They tell you it's wrong to hate another man, wrong to kill a man, and that's a commandment, and yet they get up in pulpits and out on church parades and tell you that we're fighting for the Lord and talk as if the Germans were devils, and that it's all right to kill them. Bah—padres, I'm sick of them."[144] For some soldiers, it was the mere presence of chaplains on the battlefield that sullied religion. By sending their representatives into the trenches to encourage fighting, the same churches that had failed to stop the war were now legitimizing the enterprise.[145] What little reverence soldiers displayed toward chaplains was reserved for the few who joined the men in the front lines during assaults and exposed themselves to the same dangers as the soldiers under their care.

Nonetheless, the experience of war had long-term effects on the religious practices of the participating societies. British troops had been exposed to vibrant Catholic practices among their allies and in the landscapes of France and Flanders, including devotional shrines, rosaries, prayers for the dead, and frequent communion. These influences played a significant role in the religious reforms that took place in England after the war.[146] In France, the outpouring of devotion by soldiers and citizens to Marguerite-Marie Alacoque and Joan of Arc during the war hastened the canonization of these saints in 1920.[147]

Sobered by the experience of the First World War, and cognizant of weakening church attendance in the interwar years, religious leaders approached the Second World War with modest expectations.[148] The chaplains, who had learned their lesson from the Great War and who now received professional military training, took care to join troops at the front and avoided inflammatory sermons. They recognized that the men they served with were, by and large, indifferent to religion and would not engage with church services or chaplains on their own initiative, so they reached out to soldiers by providing a range of spiritual and emotional services. The eve of war also saw a surge in the construction of chapels on U.S. Army bases (from seventeen to six hundred in the course of one year) and the distribution of large quantities of religious literature to soldiers.[149]

The resulting "war boom in religion" overwhelmed the chaplains.[150] Attendance at religious services rose from about a million servicemen per month in 1941 to 7 million soldiers attending 131 thousand services throughout the army in September 1944.[151] In all, U.S. chaplains are estimated to have conducted 6.5 million services between 1941 and 1947, attended by a total of 300 million soldiers.[152] Catholic chaplains in the British armed forces reported thousands of converts over the course of the war, and German chaplains noted the presence of hundreds of soldiers at many religious services, accounting for up to 80 percent of troops in some units.[153] At the end of the war, only 18 percent of U.S. soldiers surveyed claimed that the war had decreased their faith and 60 percent attested to an increase in religiosity and prayer as result of the war, a position that characterized men with a fearful combat experience in particular.[154] The effects of the war seem to have persisted: a recent follow-up survey confirmed that those World War II veterans who had described their own combat experience as "negative" were significantly more likely to join and attend a church fifty years later.[155]

The opposite trend was apparent during the Vietnam War, which turned many veterans against religion. Some responded to the war with an active, passionate rejection of faith. Others maintained some semblance of religion but expressed an anger at the God who was "AWOL" (absent without leave) or who had failed to prevent the meaningless carnage. Much of this bitterness was directed at the chaplains, who could not offer moral or religious explanations or guidance during the war. Soldiers accused chaplains of hypocrisy, endorsing the killing and praying for victory while also opposing murder.[156] Robert Jay Lifton, a psychiatrist, observed, "The men felt it was one thing to be ordered by command to commit atrocities on an everyday basis in Vietnam but another to have the spiritual authorities of one's society rationalize and attempt to justify and legitimize that process. They felt it to be a kind of ultimate corruption of the spirit."[157] After the war, 74 percent of soldiers surveyed reported having difficulty reconciling their religious beliefs with the traumatic events they had experienced, and 51 percent reported that they had abandoned their religious faith in the war zone. Only 26 percent said that combat experiences had made their faith stronger.[158]

Such a loss of religion during war causes a double blow: not only do the affected soldiers experience a loss of values and meanings but, as the mental health literature argues, this loss hampers their ability to draw on spiritual resources while managing trauma. When soldiers attribute a religious dimension to war trauma, the experience may produce a spiritual crisis. Those suffering from PTSD often admit to religious doubts, feelings of abandonment by God, and a loss of faith, all of which align with other PTSD symptoms such as isolation and despair.[159] Vietnam veterans who suffered from PTSD also tended to score lower on measures of religiosity and were less likely to use religion as a way of getting social support when they needed it.[160] The greater the loss of religion incurred by the experience of war, the more likely veterans were to seek mental health services but the less likely they were to consult with clergy.[161] Many soldiers justified this reticence by expressing rage at having been deceived or let down by military chaplains in a war zone.[162]

To summarize, the trends in the effects of war on the religiosity of soldiers are anything but straightforward. The religious experience of Western soldiers in the twentieth century exhibited variation across wars, across units in wars, and across different phases of war, but the exact sources of that variation remain to be discovered. We might speculate that the effects of military conflict on the religiosity of soldiers mirror the effects of the conflict on society at large, contingent on the manner in which the military is recruited. We might further hypothesize that the type of war conducted (conquest, liberation, counterinsurgency, etc.), the level of the combatants' commitment to the cause of war, their exposure to particular forms of battlefield trauma, the outcome of the war, and general societal attitudes toward the war all affect the ability of participants to sustain and draw on religious ideas and practices. In the absence of precise data, these question must also go unanswered for now.

The correlation among religious practice, religiosity, and military effectiveness remains far from certain. But if a decline in religion can indeed undermine military effectiveness, military organizations ought to aspire to mitigate those effects, either by training chaplains to support units without endorsing war itself, by supporting the efforts of soldiers to sustain a meaningful religious life in uniform, or by recognizing that soldiers who have undergone religious crises are uniquely vulnerable to the ravages of war.

Open Questions

In July 2014, an Order of the Day penned by the commander of the IDF Givati Brigade to his soldiers sparked a flurry of indignation from secular voices inside Israel and prompted accusations that the military was engaged in a "Holy War." Colonel Ofer Winter had written, "The Lord, the God of Israel, make our path on which we go successful, as we are poised to fight for your people Israel against an enemy that abuses your name. . . . May the verse be fulfilled for us that 'the Lord your God goes with you to fight for you with your enemies to save you.'. . ."[163]

My primary goal in this chapter has been to place statements such as these in a comparative context. Analyzed against the Western record, in which the continuous employment of religious practices in militaries has been the norm, the colonel's religious rhetoric appears far less exceptional. But if these practices offer no cause for alarm, why bother collecting information on miracles, rituals, relics, or prayers in the military in the first place? Do these religious practices really matter? I argue that these practices are worth observing, first and foremost, because they are intrinsically interesting. The religion that soldiers practice on the battlefield is both surprising and fundamentally human. It expresses their deepest anxieties and greatest aspirations in ways that are at once creative, bold, and fragile. The religion of soldiers also tells us a great deal about the religious proclivities of the society represented by the military, its shifting demographics, constitutional challenges, and evolving religious character. It ought to be the duty of social scientists to explore these aspects of war-making to their foundations, regardless of any pragmatic utility that may or may not arise from their analyses.

At the same time, religious practices do have real implications for military units, their opponents, and third parties. As I have argued in the previous chapters, and as the findings from the field of mental health suggest, religious practices can have inhibition and motivation effects on the ability of soldiers to participate effectively in combat and return to combat after experiencing trauma. Overt religious practices may also prompt a provocation effect if these practices run afoul of third parties observing the conflict. Soldiers wearing Psalm 91 "Camo Bandanas" on their helmets or "Shield of Strength" tags around their necks may not attract the attention of Muslim publics in the Middle East. But a more provocative patch worn by European and U.S. soldiers in Iraq and Afghanistan seems designed solely to provoke a virulent response of this sort. It is titled "Pork Eating Crusader" and depicts a knight in armor brandishing a ham hock. For the convenience of viewers, the inflammatory title is reprinted at the bottom of the patch in Arabic.[164]

Scholars have only just begun to scratch the surface in the study of religious practices in the military. I have provided some anecdotal evidence about the prevalence of miracles, amulets, relics, benedictions, and prayers. I have not addressed the use of religiously meaningful clothing and insignia, or the impact of religion on the sexual, hygienic, or culinary habits of soldiers. Nor have I touched on the significance of religious rhetoric and discourse in military speeches, orders, and war cries or on the practice of giving units, weapons, and operations religiously inspired names. Students of religion and war would do well to take on these new themes and analyze the ones I have explored here in far greater depth, seeking the kinds of comprehensive and systematic data that I have been unable to obtain.

Most important among the questions that should motivate future research is the puzzle of religion and unit cohesion. How do religious rituals affect the bonds among members of a military unit and the effectiveness of that unit in battle? This question calls for comparisons both across units that coherently employ many, few, or no religious practices and across units that are divided along religious lines. For example, are groups that partake in bonding rituals, such as group prayers or benedictions, better at coordinating their assaults, performing difficult maneuvers, or overcoming adversarial conditions than groups that seldom or never pray together? Are soldiers that share religious experiences, clothing, food, or rhetoric more disciplined, more capable of supporting one another, and more willing to take risks for one another? If so, we should expect the pressures of the battlefield to produce a certain religious uniformity in turn: members of military units, particularly cohesive battle-tested units, should display a convergence in religious practices over time.

The fissiparous tendencies of religious practices ought to be a major concern driving this research. To what extent might conflicting religious practices, or the participation in practices by some members of the group but not others, cause discord and affect performance? Are soldiers more likely to follow orders fully and enthusiastically if the commander issuing the order has shared in their religious experiences? Will units that exhibit diverging practices encounter greater difficulties in coordinating their efforts? Might informal religious practices shared by combatants, such as the many small-group rituals that soldiers tend to improvise and then institutionalize, suffice to help bridge any differences in formal religious identities? The number of open questions regarding the nature and effects of religious practices dwarfs those already addressed.

CHAPTER 6

Religion on the Battlefield
in Iraq, 2003–2009

My goal in this book has been to illustrate how religious practices have shaped the conduct of war between modern professional militaries. The events of 9/11 and subsequent U.S. involvements in the Middle East have focused attention on the role of religious ideas and identities as causes of war. In previous chapters, I have demonstrated that religion acts as force multiplier even in modern wars in which the parties are not motivated by religious ideas or divided along religious identity lines. Religion is an important feature in the landscape of any conflict, regardless of the cause of war or the identities of the participants. In this chapter, I show that religious practices have an even greater impact in conflicts that *do* include a religious justification.

In conflicts of an implicit religious nature (those we might inaccurately call "secular" conflicts), the force-multiplying effects of religion are involuntary and exogenous. Soldiers, commanders, and their units are motivated and inhibited by religion regardless of whether these effects serve the goals of the military organization as a whole. The best that leaders can hope for is to temper these effects by means of training, discipline, persuasion, or avoidance. Decision makers may seek to exploit the religious sensitivities of their opponents but they do so with caution, concerned over provoking a disproportionate backlash.

In contrast, in conflicts with an explicit religious dimension, these four effects—motivation, inhibition, exploitation, and provocation—are not merely incidental but also purposive and endogenous. Institutions incorporate religion into their organizational design with the intention of motivating and constraining soldiers. They exploit their opponents' religious proclivities, not only to gain a military advantage but with the explicit purpose of inciting outrage. As religious ideas interact with religious practices in these settings, the two categories bolster and amplify one another. Consequently, in sectarian conflicts, insurgencies, and terrorism campaigns that rely on religious justifications, both religious ideas and religious practices yield a greater impact on military operations.

This interaction is easy to observe in one of the most compelling documents to emerge from the September 11 attacks, the instruction manual found in the personal belongings of three of the hijackers. This document encourages the participating terrorists to focus on motivating ideas, such as thinking of God, contemplating specific Surahs from the Qur'an, or considering the rewards of paradise. But the document is no less concerned with the perpetrators' religious practices. It prescribes how the hijackers are to wash and dress ("Shave excess hair from the body and wear cologne. . . . Tighten your clothes. . . ."), the long variety of prayers they are to utter, and what they are to shout when they attack. The twin aspects of the instructions buttress one another: Religious ideas and religious practices offer mutual justification, culminating in violent action: "When the confrontation begins, strike like champions who do not want to go back to this world. Shout, 'Allahu Akbar,' because this strikes fear in the hearts of the non-believers. God said: 'Strike above the neck, and strike at all of their extremities.' Know that the gardens of paradise are waiting for you in all their beauty, and the women of paradise are waiting, calling out, 'Come hither, friend of God.' They have dressed in their most beautiful clothing."[1]

My argument in this chapter is an a fortiori argument: if religious practices inhibit, motivate, can be exploited, or provoke in conflicts that lack an overt religious justification, we should expect them to exert these effects to an even greater degree in conflicts in which religious motivations and identities are explicit. This was true of modern interstate wars that were driven by a strong religious–identity element, such as the Iran-Iraq War and the Indo-Pakistani wars. In the Iran-Iraq War, for example, leaders cast their opponents as "infidels"; presented battlefield deaths as "martyrdoms"; consistently used religious ideas, symbols, rhetoric, and rituals to mobilize troops and to sustain the fighting; and even drew on religious principles to make tactical and strategic decisions.[2] In civil wars that divided communities along religious lines, such as the Russian Civil War, the Turkish War of Independence, the Spanish Civil War, and the War in Yugoslavia, religious leaders sanctioned

Table 6.1   Religious practices in religiously motivated war

PUZZLE	PHENOMENON	PRIMARY EFFECT	PRIMARY ACTORS	NET RESULT
Why	Sacred ideas	Motivation	Individual, unit	Multiplier
When	Sacred time	Inhibition, exploitation, provocation	Individual, unit, command	Mixed
Where	Sacred space	Inhibition, exploitation, provocation	Command	Mixed
Who	Sacred leaders	Motivation, exploitation	Individual, unit	Multiplier
How	Sacred rituals	Motivation, provocation	Individual, unit	Mixed

the killing but also became the primary victims of assault, religious buildings and sacred relics were prominent targets of willful destruction, and public acts of religious desecration were a recurrent motif.[3] Table 6.1 showcases the broad range of effects that religious ideas and practices have in religiously motivated conflicts and makes for a stark contrast with table 1.2.

All these phenomena are apparent in the recent Iraq War, both a sectarian war along religious lines and an insurgency motivated by religious ideologies. The literature on this insurgency and on the U.S. counterinsurgency efforts has been focused on Muslim ideas and identities only, to the exclusion of Iraqi and U.S. religious practices.[4] As I show in this chapter, practices related to sacred time, sacred space, and sacred authority influenced both insurgent and counterinsurgent capabilities and decision making. Unlike the effects in the secular interstate wars examined in the bulk of this volume, these effects were intentional, explicit, and significant. The Muslim religious calendar influenced the levels of violence, sacred places became insurgent strongholds, and chaplains acted as advisors and intermediaries on behalf of U.S. forces.

I conclude this chapter with a discussion of the policy implications of my argument. If religious practices affect combat no less than religious ideas, then it is incumbent on decision makers to equip their armed forces with religious intelligence regarding those practices, be they those of their opponents, of third parties, or of their own soldiers. Put differently, this volume is an invitation to supplement our analyses of the religious ideas of insurgents and terrorists with a study of the religious practices of these actors as well as the practices of the professional militaries confronting them. Obtaining this information poses four challenges: the religious intelligence analyst has to ascertain how prominent a role religion will play in a given conflict, what the relevant sacred phenomena are, how salient they are for the specific religious communities present, and how they will affect a given conflict. The U.S. military has started confronting this challenge with limited success.

Sacred Time

Earlier in this volume, I demonstrate that, in twentieth-century century conflicts between professional armed forces, the primary effects of sacred time were exploitation and provocation. This pattern is amplified in conflicts that include a strong religious component, particularly civil wars and insurgencies. In these settings, the exploitation of sacred time is not merely designed to obtain a military advantage but to provoke outrage and fan the flames of sectarian conflict. Nevertheless, for counterinsurgency forces involved in hearts-and-minds campaigns, the most salient effects of sacred time are its constraining effects. These troops may harbor no intention of timing violence to coincide with the religious calendar, but they must contend with the concern that even a coincidental overlap might be interpreted as a religious offense by the very audiences whose cooperation and support they seek.

Ramadan and U.S. Operations in the Middle East

U.S. decision makers have often expressed reluctance about launching attacks in Muslim countries during the holy month of Ramadan for fear of harming civilians, who are particularly likely to attend public gatherings after nightfall, and thus causing a double offense to Muslim sensibilities.[5] When the First Gulf War was launched, in January 1991, U.S. strategists expressed concern that it would fail to conclude before March, the timing of Ramadan that year.[6] In 1998, U.S. President Bill Clinton justified the urgency in launching Operation Desert Fox, a bombing campaign against military targets in Iraq, because Ramadan was merely two weeks away: "For us to initiate military action during Ramadan would be profoundly offensive to the Muslim world and, therefore, would damage our relations with Arab countries and the progress we have made in the Middle East."[7] At the same time, Defense Secretary William Cohen dismissed as "absurd" a cease-fire proposal by Yugoslav President Slobodan Milosevic in April 1999 to honor the Christian Orthodox observance of Easter. The ensuing bombing campaign caused significant outrage in European states with large Christian Orthodox populations, such as Greece, Bulgaria, and Hungary.[8]

The U.S. policy of exercising military restraint during Ramadan changed in 2001 when the George W. Bush administration decided not to suspend its attacks in Afghanistan during the Muslim holy month, despite appeals by Egypt, Saudi Arabia, Indonesia, and Pakistan.[9] Secretary of Defense Donald Rumsfeld dismissed these concerns out of hand: "Then there was you can't bomb on Ramadan. Of course these folks have fought each other for decades on Ramadan. It never bothered them and the implication that we couldn't was not right."[10] Nonetheless, the coincidence in timing between the U.S.-led assault on Tora Bora in December 2001 and the Muslim observance of Ramadan is rumored to have aided Osama bin Laden in escaping U.S. capture. According to one U.S. commander who participated in the battle, U.S. forces relied heavily on local Afghan soldiers, but these regularly abandoned the battlefield in the evening to break their Ramadan fast. This afforded al Qaeda operatives a chance to regroup, reposition, and escape.[11]

Ramadan and Counterinsurgency in Iraq

In October 2003, in anticipation of the first Iraqi Ramadan under U.S. occupation, commanders ordered a reduction of troop presence in urban areas, a scaling back of patrols, the lifting of curfews, and a general instruction that soldiers "keep a low profile," "keep their distance," and show "increased sensitivity to local traditions" during Ramadan.[12] The outbreak of the Iraqi insurgency on that Ramadan, coupled with observations made in subsequent years, seems to have led U.S. decision makers to the conclusion that the ninth month in the Muslim calendar was characterized by peaks in violent attacks.[13] Consequently, John P. Abizaid, chief of the U.S. Central Command, and George W. Casey, then commanding general of the Multi-National Force in Iraq, ordered troops to brace for an escalation of attacks prior to subsequent Ramadan months.[14]

A superficial look at the number of violent incidents per Muslim month might indeed lead to the conclusion that the Ramadan is characterized by a consistent escalation in violence, with peaks in the ninth Muslim months, preceded and followed by troughs in the eighth and tenth Muslim months (see figure 6.1).[15] A closer look, however, shows similar peak-and-trough patterns throughout the year. U.S. troops were thus correct to detect consistent escalations of sectarian and insurgent attacks during Ramadan, but those escalations were neither statistically significant nor unique to Ramadan. In sum, expectations regarding the significance of Ramadan lead U.S. commanders to misperceive a possible coincidence as a pattern of significance.[16]

A far more dramatic and statistically significant trend seems to have eluded observers, either because it occurred too frequently to stand out as a clear pattern or because it involved reductions in violence: both sectarian attacks and insurgent attacks plummeted on Fridays, the "gathering day" (Yaum al-Jumu'ah), regarded as the Muslim day of rest on which believers congregate for worship in mosques. This finding is startling for three reasons. First, the rate of decline is dramatic; attacks associated with sectarian forces declined

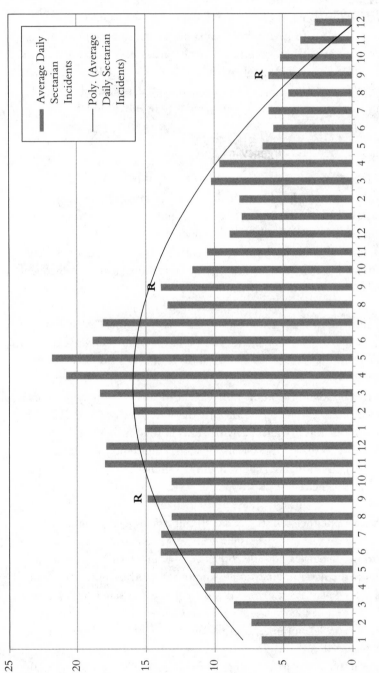

FIGURE 6.1 Average daily sectarian incidents per Muslim month at the peak of the Iraq insurgency for the years 1427–1429 AH, with the ninth month (Ramadan) highlighted

Note: The years 1427–1429 AH correspond to the period January 30, 2006, to December 27, 2008. The numbers along the *x* axis denote the Muslim month in each of the three years covered, starting with 1 (Muharram) and ending in 12 (Dhu al-Hijja). Ramadan is the ninth month of the year. I chose this period, at the height of the insurgency, for illustrative purposes. The analysis that follows covers the entire period between March 20, 2003, and June 30, 2009.

by nearly one-quarter on Fridays compared to other days of the week, and attacks involving insurgent forces declined by more than 40 percent on Fridays. Second, the results are highly significant, statistically speaking.[17] Third, coalition incidents were unaffected by the day of the week, thus confirming that the Friday effect was limited to Muslim combatants. Based on these data, insurgent and sectarian forces in Iraq appeared to be respecting the sanctity of the Muslim day of rest by restraining the initiation of attacks.

Similar declines in the initiation of attacks in Iraq were apparent on the two most significant Sunni holidays: Eid al-Fitr and Eid al-Adha. Eid al-Fitr, a three-day feast that marks the end of Ramadan, was characterized by a significant decline in sectarian (but not insurgent) attacks in 2003–2009. Sectarian attacks were lower by 30 percent in this period compared to the rest of the year.[18] This statistically significant pattern of decline at the end of Ramadan, in contrast to the statistically weaker pattern of escalation during Ramadan, may explain why U.S. leaders perceived that month to be a period of significant variation in violence. In hindsight, what looked like an escalation of violence during Ramadan was in fact a de-escalation of violence in the period after Ramadan.

Eid al-Adha, the feast of sacrifice that occurs on the tenth day of the twelfth Islamic month, constrained both sectarian and insurgent attacks. The former declined by one-quarter during this five-day feast, whereas the latter declined by nearly 70 percent.[19] Both of these holy days thus had a restraining effect on insurgent and sectarian violence, either due to the combatants' preoccupation with celebrating these feasts or because they perceived the significance of the holy day (forgiveness and peace in the case of Eid al-Fitr, sacrifice and submission in the case of Eid al-Adha) to be incompatible with violence.[20]

This statistical exercise is useful not merely for exploring the effects of sacred time on insurgencies but also for demonstrating the utility of quantitative analysis in establishing a correlation between violence and religious practice. Such analyses can be useful in complementing the varieties of qualitative evidence that I have relied on throughout this volume. Yet testing the relationship between sacred time and conflict by statistical means requires precise data on the distribution of conflict over time. It also sets a high bar: establishing this correlation demands that most occurrences of a given sacred day coincide with most occurrences of conflict. An alternative approach, that sets a more modest standard of correspondence, measures the share of violent incidents that coincides with the sacred days of the target community, regardless of the ratio of sacred days in which no violence takes place.

For example, between 2004 and 2009, insurgents executed eighty-eight attacks against Christian individuals and groups for which exact dates are known, including kidnappings, murders, executions, shootings, and bombings.[21] Thirty-three of these incidents (or 37.5 percent) occurred on Sundays. In the same period, insurgents executed forty-five attacks against churches, of which twenty-eight (or 62.2 percent) occurred on Sundays. Sunday attacks on Christians and on churches were thus nearly three and four times higher, respectively, than we might have expected had these attacks been randomly distributed across the week. Iraqi Christians were four times more likely to fall victims to an attack on a Sunday, compared to any other average weekday, unless they attended church, in which case their likelihood of succumbing to an attack was twelve times higher than on any other average day of the week (see figure 6.2).[22]

How can we explain this pattern? These attacks exploited both the vulnerability and the outrage effects of initiating conflict on a sacred date. Insurgents were able to rely on the concentration of large numbers of Christian victims in churches on Sundays and could expect those attacks to elicit the greatest degree of rage given their timing and location. The coordinated nature of many of these attacks lends further credence to the suspicion that the assailants chose the dates for the attacks carefully and with an eye on maximizing casualties and indignation.[23]

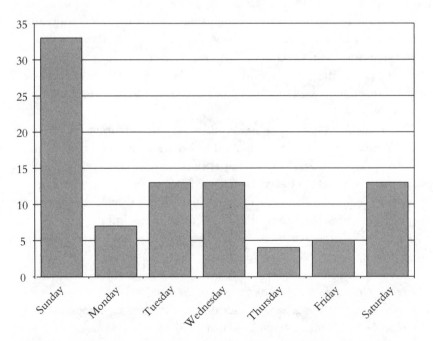

FIGURE 6.2 Insurgent attacks against Christians in Iraq (2004–2009) by day of the week

Sacred Space

Like sacred time, sacred space has had a wide range of effects on U.S. operations in Iraq. In stark contrast with the constraining role of sacred space in conventional interstate war (explored in chapter 3), here it provided opportunities for motivation, exploitation, and provocation. In conflicts that entail an overt religious dimension, parties may intentionally draw sacred space into the fighting, particularly if they are insurgents driven by religious identities and motivations, and more so if they are facing counterinsurgents identified with a foreign religious tradition, as was the case in Iraq. There, insurgents exploited sacred space in the hopes that U.S. actions would provoke Muslim audiences and undermine coalition counterinsurgency efforts.

Religiously Motivated Insurgency and Sacred Space

Religiously motivated combatants can take advantage of both the physical characteristics of sacred sites and the rules imposed on those sites by local communities, thus forcing their opponents to choose between desecration and defeat. This force-multiplying effect of sacred space is particularly effective for insurgents, who can use the location, layout, and presence of unarmed worshippers at sacred sites to level the playing field with counterinsurgency forces. The rules governing access to a shrine and behavior within it enhance that force-multiplying effect even further. Moreover, shrines that constitute visible symbols of particular religious communities offer attractive targets to sectarian insurgents who wish to provoke their opponents and maximize civilian fatalities.[24]

Combatants who occupy a sacred place can expect to find cover among the crowds attending the site, and they can use the constant flow of worshippers, religious rituals, and tacit or explicit consent from the shrine managers as a cover for establishing a permanent base for their operations. The location of many of these shrines in city centers makes for quick and convenient ingress and egress at times of need, sheltered by a dense urban environment that further hampers combat operations. Many older shrines resemble veritable fortresses, surrounded by tall and thick walls with narrow windows and doors. Other shrines are self-sufficient, and include gardens, wells, and stores of provisions. The broader the scope of social functions that the shrine performs, the better the odds that combatants will find food and water at the site, supplies that will prove useful for surviving a prolonged siege. Combatants who know their way around a shrine can shelter in hidden rooms, passageways, and subterranean vaults. Insurgents have also used minarets, guest houses and water towers to snipe at counterinsurgency forces.

The religious rules governing access to the site and behavior in it further advantage the party that shares a religious affiliation with the local community. Some of these rules explicitly discriminate between outsiders and members of the faith, who enjoy a freedom of movement and access that may be unattainable to their adversaries. Other directives, such as those banning weapons or prohibiting the use of force in a sacred place, might apply equally to members of the faith and outsiders. Worshippers are nevertheless likely to show leniency in applying these rules to members of their own religious community, particularly if the insurgents can persuade worshippers that they are acting in defense of the faith and in defense of the sacred site.

As long as insurgents are shooting out and counterinsurgency forces are shooting in, much of the responsibility for the damage to the shrine will be placed squarely on the shoulders of the latter. Insurgents have even willfully desecrated sites in the course of fighting, in the expectation that the counterinsurgency forces would be blamed for the destruction and draw the wrath of religious communities. Even though insurgents are usually complicit in any damage or desecration that occurs at a sacred site by virtue of having drawn the fighting there, counterinsurgency forces must take care to manage media depictions and public perceptions of the conflict, lest they find themselves bearing the brunt of believers' anger.

Finally, sacred sites also become the focus of sectarian violence because these places are potent social symbols of the targeted groups. Their design and ornamentation capture key elements of the religious tradition in a symbolic form that is immediately recognizable to others. This parallelism between the religious group and its sacred space makes that space vulnerable to attack from those seeking to harm the group. By targeting or damaging the shrine most sacred to a group, its rivals hope to strike at the heart of the group's values, heritage, and pride. Such an attack carries unmistakable significance: it is not merely an act of violence but a challenge to the core of the religious group and all it represent. To make matters worse, sacred places are vulnerable because they tend to teem with religious adherents. Rivals striking at these structures can thus expect to exact significant casualties from the target community.

Sacred Space and Counterinsurgency in Iraq

In Iraq, assaults timed to coincide with peak attendance at mosques have resulted in massive casualties, particularly in the attacks of August 2003; March and December 2004; February, March, July, and November 2005;

January, February, April, and July 2006; and January 2008. The most extreme of these attacks, on March 2, 2004, coincided with the observance of the Shi'a holy day of Ashura. Over 180 Shi'a worshipers lost their lives in separate attacks in Baghdad and Karbala that day, making this the deadliest day in Iraq since the U.S. invasion of 2003.[25] The bombing of February 22, 2006, demolished one of the most revered and beautiful shrines in Iraq, the Askari Mosque in Samarra. It ended the lives of over one hundred worshipers and led to a series of revenge attacks on Sunni mosques with mounting casualty figures, leading some analysts to view the attack as the symbolic starting point of the Iraqi civil war.[26]

Despite this pattern of sectarian assaults, counterinsurgency operations near mosques provoked a consistent outcry over the U.S. desecration of Muslim sacred space. Some Iraqis objected to specific U.S. actions taken in or near mosques; others objected to the very presence of non-Muslims in mosques. U.S. troops, in turn, had to contend with widely varying interpretations and perceptions of what constituted an offense, knowing all too well that some clearly offensive actions were entirely unavoidable from an operational standpoint.

For example, it was not surprising that Iraqis and other Muslims around the world were outraged when mosques in Falluja, Kufa, and Samarra were

FIGURE 6.3 A Marine keeps an eye out for snipers from a rooftop overlooking the Imam Ali Shrine in Najaf.
Photo by Carolyn Cole/Los Angeles Times via Getty Images

severely damaged, particularly when these attacks caused significant civilian casualties. Yet Iraqis also erupted in protest in August 2003 when a U.S. helicopter blew away a flag from the minaret of a mosque, an incident that unleashed violent protests and resulted in multiple Iraqi casualties.[27] Sunni clerics also decried the desecration of mosques in Ramadi, where coalition troops found weapons, ammunition, and explosives, even though the searches were conducted by Iraqi soldiers while U.S. forces remained outside the mosques. One prominent Sunni cleric, Sheikh Muhammad Bashar al-Faydi, launched an appeal to Pope John Paul II to condemn the attack. Another, Sheikh Abdullah Abu Omar, exclaimed, "This cowboy behavior cannot be accepted. The Americans seem to have lost their senses and have gone out of control."[28] In the Shi'a city of Najaf, a tense standoff between local residents and a U.S. platoon took place in April 2003 because the residents were under the false impression that the platoon was on its way to the Shrine of Ali. A crowd of two hundred residents blocked the platoon and exclaimed, "In the city, okay. In the mosque, no!" The U.S. soldiers lowered their weapons and knelt down "in a surreal act of submission," before retreating.[29]

Iraqi objections to U.S. behavior toward sacred sites, although genuine, played into the hands of the insurgents in Iraq. The insurgents consistently exploited the U.S. reluctance to execute standard operations near mosques for fear of a public backlash. First and foremost, they turned these sites into centers for rallying public support for the insurgency. Sunni clerics used their podiums at large mosques in Baghdad, such as Abu Hanifa and Umm al-Qura, to exhort the population to join the insurgency and call for a holy war against U.S. soldiers. In the early stages of the war, it was common to hear calls for jihad over mosque loudspeakers, particularly in mosques located in Samarra and Falluja where U.S. forces were conducting particularly intense operations.

The use of mosques to store ammunition posed a more significant challenge. In mosques throughout Baghdad, Karbala, Kufa, and Mosul, U.S. forces found explosives and bomb-making materials, rifles, machine guns, bullets, mortars and rounds, rocket-propelled grenades and launchers, anti-U.S. propaganda, and pro-insurgency documents. Although at times the weapons were well concealed in the mosque, the quantity and quality of the weapons discovered in some cases left no doubt that worshippers were well aware of their presence and location. The storage of weapons in mosques was most apparent in Falluja where, according to one U.S. military report, more than 20 of the 133 mosques in the city contained caches of weapons or were used as bases for insurgency operations.[30] For example, one mosque, headed by Abdullah Janabi, a radical Sunni cleric and insurgent leader, was "packed with bombs, guns, rocket-propelled grenades and ammunition," as well as "an aluminum shed full of mortars and TNT" and even "an ice cream truck, decorated with orange, red, and blue popsicles and packed with rocket-propelled grenades and bomb-making materials." The mosque was also rigged to explode, presumably so that U.S. troops would bear the blame for its destruction.[31]

Enemy fire directed at U.S. troops from inside mosques posed the greatest difficulty for U.S. operations in Iraq. In most cases, insurgents used rifles or rocket-propelled grenades to target soldiers from inside the mosque or from its minarets. Often, conflicts between soldiers and insurgents ended with the latter's retreat into the apparent safety of the mosque.[32]

Moktada al-Sadr, a Shi'a cleric, was particularly adept at exploiting sacred sites for his personal safety and the security of his militia. In April 2004, he successfully avoided capture by U.S. troops by seeking refuge in a mosque in Kufa guarded by militiamen armed with heavy machine guns and rocket-propelled grenades. Al-Sadr then moved to the most sacred Shi'a shrine in Iraq, the Imam Ali Shrine in Najaf. Ignoring calls by Iraq's then prime minister, Ayad Allawi, to leave the mosque, al-Sadr remained in the shrine and continued to call for war against U.S. forces.[33]

The aborted siege of the Imam Ali Shrine in Najaf represents one extreme end of the spectrum of U.S. policy: situations in which U.S. troops abandon operations altogether for fear of harming a mosque. Although U.S. military helicopters and jets targeted houses around the mosque and U.S. Marines conducted intense combat in the adjacent cemetery, the marines received explicit instructions not to fire at the shrine. Predictably, the insurgents eventually withdrew into the shrine itself. After eight days, U.S. forces withdrew completely from the site in response to intense pressure from Arab and Muslim leaders worldwide. They were replaced by Iraqi policemen who, thanks to intervention by Grand Ayatollah Ali al-Sistani, were able to enter the shrine and disarm al-Sadr's men.

In all cases, U.S. soldiers operated under orders that prohibited raids on mosques unless insurgents were using these sites for hostile purposes. As Colin Powell, then secretary of state, explained, "We understand the sacred place in the life of Islam that mosques occupy. . . . [O]ur commanders are extremely sensitive to anything that would violate that concept."[34] Even when insurgents did seek refuge inside mosques, U.S. troops often ceased pursuit for fear of inflaming the local population.[35]

When U.S. soldiers did decide to pursue operations, despite proximity to a mosque, they sought to minimize harm to that site. This was most apparent in the rules governing the targeting of mosques from the air. The military drew up a "no strike" list (NSL) for Iraq in the early planning stages of the war that included mosques, schools, cultural sites, and other sensitive locations. United Nations agencies and nongovernmental organizations provided the input for these lists, which grew to include thousands of targets to be avoided.[36] This NSL was constantly reviewed and updated to reflect changes in the law of armed combat, the rules of engagement, or the reality on the ground. For example, as the 2007 *Joint Fires and Targeting Handbook* explains, "a church that functions as a weapons storage facility or a barracks will lose its protected status and may be legally attacked."[37]

The NSL placed constraints on both air and ground attacks. The presence of a protected facility was a key criterion in calculating the collateral damage likely to result from an attack. Judge advocates advised commanders on the legality of specific strikes guided by the law of armed conflict but cognizant that "lawful military targets located near protected buildings are not immune from attack, but the principle of proportionality must be carefully applied."[38] Sites from the NSL were programed into artillery batteries and could not be fired on without manual override. Forward air controllers, the troops in forward positions responsible for coordinating air and artillery strikes, relied on grid reference guides, maps that numbered and identified all structures in a given location. This allowed commanding officers at the Combat Operations Center to confirm that no strikes were aimed at or near mosques. Decision makers planning air operations were constrained by special instructions (SPINS) regarding the inviolability of sacred shrines.[39]

As the training of Iraqi security forces progressed, U.S. troops gradually transferred responsibility for operations in mosques to their Iraqi counterparts, especially when the shrine was one of particular importance or popularity. During an operation at a Fallujah mosque that served as an insurgent command center, for example, "the Marines opened the doors of the mosque for Iraqi security forces to clear out the interior; it was thought better to let the Iraqis go into the holy place, even though it had been transformed into a kind of barracks. The Iraqis entered, their uniforms crisp and spotless because they had done none of the fighting until then, and fought with the insurgents and won."[40] Yet using Iraqi soldiers to secure the interior of the mosques provided a partial solution at best. Given their inferior training, Iraqi soldiers were no less likely to damage structures or injure innocent civilians inside mosques. Consequently, Iraqi forces were equally hesitant to operate inside shrines and at times even refused outright to do so.[41]

At the other end of the continuum of U.S. responses were cases in which U.S. forces assaulted mosques with full knowledge of the destruction that was likely to result. Although in some instances the damage to the shrines was accidental, at other times it was part of a concerted strategy to occupy or destroy mosques from which terrorists had been expelled. This strategy of positioning troops on the rooftops and minarets of former insurgent hide-outs perversely led to insurgent attacks on those mosques. For example, in November 2004, Marines positioned on the roof of the largest mosque in Ramadi managed to prevent a suicide bomber from driving into the build-ing and destroying the mosque. In April 2005, insurgents blew up the top of the Malwiya minaret, one of the most important Iraqi heritage sites, because U.S. forces were using the 1,000-year-old sandstone tower as a sniper's nest.[42]

All-out attacks by U.S. forces at sacred sites have tended to occur after particularly significant, difficult, or drawn-out battles with insurgents situated inside. In April 2004, for example, U.S. Marines attacked the Abdul Aziz al-Samarrai mosque in Falluja with Hellfire missiles and two 500-pound bombs. Lieutenant Colonel Brennan Byrne claimed that between thirty and forty insurgents had been firing at Marines from the mosque, explaining that, "if they use the mosque as a military machine, then it's no longer a house of worship and we strike."[43] Such destruction came at a tangible cost to the reputation of the United States. A banner on one of the mosques destroyed during the fighting in Fallujah summarized this sentiment succinctly: "Vio-lation of the mosque's sanctuary dishonors the world's Muslims."[44]

Sacred Authority

During the Iraq War, as in all prior U.S. engagements, chaplains accompanied forces to the theater of operations. As before, they encouraged, guided, and motivated soldiers by means of sermons, religious services, and sessions with individual soldiers. General David Petraeus, at the time the commanding general of coalition forces in Iraq, expressed the essence of this pastoral role when he instructed his senior chaplain to "get all over the theater . . . take care of soldiers; tell me what they need and what I need to know."[45] But U.S. chaplains also took on two new sets of responsibilities in the twenty-first century, liaison and advisement, both expressed in a 2009 Joint Publication by the Department of Defense, *Religious Affairs in Joint Operations,*[46] which significantly revised prior religious affairs guidelines from 2004 and 1996.

These new roles were a function of the interreligious nature of the con-flict. There is no need for chaplains to engage in liaison or advisement in wars lacking an overt religious component. In those settings, chaplains are able to focus their attentions on the soldiers in their own armed forces who share their religious affiliation. The occasional encounter with enemy POWs perform no particular operational function because they, too, tend to share the religious affiliation with the ministering chaplain. In wars that cross religious lines, however, chaplains emerge as useful issue area experts who can provide basic information about indigenous religions and perhaps even build bridges with their religious counterparts, a crucial component in sectarian conflicts in which religious cleavages provoke tensions and in which the goodwill of the local population is a key asset.

Chaplains as Liaisons

Religious Affairs in Joint Operations was explicit in assigning chaplains the task of acting as liaisons, particularly between the military, indigenous religious leaders, and local faith-based nongovernmental organizations, a message repeated in the field manuals and handbooks of the individual services.[47] The underlying logic was that chaplains could establish personal relationships with local clergy based on their common vocation, the chaplain's noncombatant status, and his expertise in indigenous religion. These ties of trust and understanding could then form the foundation for bridge-building efforts and even provide an early warning function of sorts as chaplains conveyed local concerns to their commanders.[48]

This was not without precedent. Chaplains had acted as go-betweens with local communities before this, but heretofore they had done so in an ad hoc manner and at their own initiative. Chaplains in the Canadian and South African armed forces had performed mediation and reconciliation functions in Yugoslavia and South Africa, respectively.[49] During North Atlantic Treaty Organization (NATO) operations in Yugoslavia, a U.S. chaplain is said to have elicited the support of a restive Orthodox priest by encouraging his commander to attend religious services in the local parish church.[50] A Jewish chaplain with the Combined Joint Task Force–Horn of Africa sought to counter religious extremism in Uganda by organizing meetings between Christian and Muslim religious organizations in which he acted as "honest broker." He even managed to set up an interfaith medical clinic and persuaded his unit to build a water line for a local mosque; however, his efforts were never integrated into the mission of the task force.[51]

During the Second Gulf War, the liaison task took on a new priority for chaplains, in part due to recommendations by the Iraq Study Group, headed by James Baker and Lee Hamilton. It recommended that the United States encourage dialog between Iraqi sectarian communities and that religious leaders, inside and outside Iraq, take the lead in speaking out on behalf of peace and reconciliation.[52] In part, the participation of chaplains was designed to demonstrate that Americans were not impious infidels but respected their own religious leaders and would treat local religions with the same respect.[53]

Chaplains took on the task of meeting with religious leader with the goal of mitigating conflict and preventing the escalation of minor disputes. They inquired about the needs of local communities and engaged imams in conversations about religious commonalities designed to build trust. For example, when a group of marines accidently killed two Iraqi civilians in Nasiriyah in the early stages of the invasion, the unit commander gave his chaplain, Brian Waite, the task of gathering locals to explain what had happened and to organize an appropriate burial. The chaplain then met on a daily basis with the local leaders to learn about their needs for food, water, and medical care and to coordinate the provision of those needs. Other chaplains helped in the renovation of mosques and the construction of schools, and they facilitated a dialog between local Muslims and Christians.[54] One chaplain, Captain John Stutz, participated in weekly meetings with two religious councils in Mosul, the Council of Imams and the Council of Bishops, and cooperated with religious leaders to address community concerns over matters such as sanitation and crime. He also instructed U.S. soldiers on how to interact with imams in a respectful manner.[55]

In 2007, Colonel Michael Hoyt, the senior chaplain for all U.S. forces in Iraq, assumed a leading role in the Iraq Interreligious Congress (IIRC), one of the pillars of the new counterinsurgency approach, alongside the "surge" and the Sunni "awakening." Hoyt organized and financed religious dialogues, met with religious and political leaders (including Iraqi Prime Minister Nouri Maliki), and coordinated funding and relief efforts with private security contractors, U.S. federal agencies, and international organizations. Hoyt also worked with Canon Andrew White, head of the Foundation for Relief and Reconciliation in the Middle East, to organize peace initiatives among Iraqi religious leaders. Their goal was to encourage religious conversations that could be translated into tangible efforts to prevent terrorism and bolster the new Iraqi government. Their efforts, involving seven hundred of the most influential religious leaders in Iraq, resulted in an accord that pledged nonviolence, cooperation in protecting holy sites, and the support of the government. A subsequent Sunni–Shi'a *fatwa* in 2008 called for an end to all religious violence.[56]

In Afghanistan, the senior chaplain for the International Security Assistance Force (ISAF) organized meetings between multinational chaplains and local mullahs who were recognized as local powerbrokers in the hopes that these would act as trusted partners in state-building efforts. A Muslim U.S. Army chaplain prayed with Afghan co-religionists in a local mosque, relying on a common language and ritual to break down the barriers to communication.[57]

The challenges and risks of interfaith liaison required, according to Hoyt, "a daily deeply personal reliance on piety, theological integrity, submission, and patience."[58] His background allowed him to speak persuasively about charity, forgiveness, sacrifice, social order, and communal support. His unique status, as both unarmed cleric and representative of the U.S. military, provided him access to sensitive locations, and his willingness to take risk and move without an armed escort made a positive impression on his interlocutors.

Yet, like many junior chaplains under his command, Hoyt faced the constant concern that his religion would be exploited for political ends.[59] This warning was echoed in the chaplain handbooks, which warned against participating in operations entailing manipulation or deception and prohibited chaplains from taking the lead in formal negotiations. Several scholars have expressed concerns about the pitfalls of this new liaison task, particularly the exposure of the chaplains to physical danger; the risks to the chaplains' ethical integrity; and the concern that chaplains might become embroiled in religious disputes, perhaps even in proselytizing. But even these critics have recognized that no branch of the officer corps is better positioned to serve this function, despite the dearth in official chaplain liaison training.[60]

Chaplains as Religious Advisors

Chaplains had always been expected to support commanders in their decision making by offering input on moral and religious issues. *Religious Affairs in Joint Operations* expanded and formalized this role, requiring chaplains to advise commanders about the impact of religion on operations and to teach soldiers about religious differences between themselves and the local communities they would be interacting with.[61] This included information on "worship, rituals, customs, and practices of U.S. military personnel, international forces, and the indigenous population. . . ."[62]

The different services of the U.S. military embraced this advisement role with varying degrees of enthusiasm and provided additional instructions to their chaplains. The Army, which received chaplain advisement most enthusiastically, called on its chaplains to report on indigenous religions in the area of operations: "What and where are the places that are considered sacred? What are the significant religious holidays and how are they celebrated? How could this impact the operation or the timing of the operation"?[63] The Marine Corps instructed its chaplains to brief commanders on behavior that was likely to be perceived by the local populace as unduly provocative and profane.[64]

Most surprisingly, the new guidelines relied on chaplains to act as "subject matter experts" who would draw up "religious estimates" analyzing the religious cultural implications of battlefield decisions. These estimates were based on questions such as: "how do US political goals for this situation interface with the religious sensibilities of the host nation concerned and the local communities in the operational area?" and "how does religion [in the host nation] affect the use of force, civilian and military?"[65]

This aspect of advisement required chaplains to strike a tough balance between their pastoral obligations and their noncombatant status, on the one hand, and their new position as "religious intelligence" purveyors, on the other hand. The new guidelines stressed, for example, that, although chaplains had to inform their superiors about the presence of religious structures and monuments of antiquity in specific locations, this obligation could not extend to assisting commanders in drawing up target lists. Their goal, after all, was to "ameliorate suffering and to promote peace and the benevolent expression of religion . . . without employing religion to achieve a military advantage."[66] Chaplains handled this challenge by referring potential informants to the appropriate military authorities and by electing to travel unaccompanied by personnel who might be collecting intelligence.[67]

Religious Intelligence

If chaplains are constrained from collecting information about religion to achieve a military advantage, who should take on that task? I argue that this task requires religious intelligence analysts who are responsible for obtaining and analyzing information about sacred phenomena relevant to a conflict situation.[68] The goals of the religious intelligence analyst should be to predict the effects of religious beliefs and practices on allies, opponents, and third parties and to provide an assessment of how those various effects might constrain or facilitate combat. If the primary claims of this book hold true, and religion has force-multiplying and force-dividing effects even in conflicts involving Western, professional, and ostensibly secular militaries, then the tasks of the religious intelligence analyst are indispensable for the success of combat operations. Thus the primary policy recommendation that arises from this analysis is that religious intelligence analysts be trained and deployed as a precondition for adapting military organizations to the realities of religion on the modern battlefield.

The challenge faced by the religious intelligence analyst is to overcome four common—and false—assumptions about the role of religion in conflict. These are the same misconceptions that I have sought to correct throughout this volume. First, religion is not a dichotomous variable in conflict. Because religious ideas and practices are present in all disputes to differing degrees, conflicts cannot be divided into purely religious and purely secular types. Second, the role of religion is not limited to ideas. Religious symbols, rituals, and authority structures shape conflict as well. Third, these ideas and practices do not always conform to the orthodoxy or orthopraxy of a religious movement as captured in its formal theology or scripture. They are often local, popular, and eclectic variations that reflect the preferences or habits of a religious subgroup. Fourth, combatants do not automatically succumb to religious ideas. Their resilience depends on their religious identities as individuals and on the discipline of their organization.

To guard against these traps, the religious intelligence analyst must ask four questions. First, how prominent are religious ideas and practices in a given conflict? *Prominence* captures the ability of religion to define the cause, the identity of participants, or merely the audience to a dispute. Second, what sacred phenomena are relevant for the execution of combat operations, and what is their formal centrality? *Centrality* is determined by religious ideas. Third, how salient are these factors for the specific religious communities present, given the available information about their idiosyncrasies? *Salience* is determined by religious practices. Fourth, how are the particular symbols and practices that this community associates with the sacred likely to impact combat? *Impact* is determined by military practices. Each of these steps deserves a brief discussion.

Prominence

The sacred is particularly prominent when religion acts as a primary motivator of conflict, as in wars of conversion, disputes over sacred space, or holy wars. In these settings, participants and observers will permit—indeed, rely on—religious symbols and rituals to play a significant role in regulating violence. Such wars of religion are, however, few and far between, particularly in the contemporary era.[69]

A more common setting, in which the sacred plays a less prominent role, is one in which parties are either self-defined or other-defined based on religious indicators, regardless of the cause of the dispute.[70] In these ethnic or sectarian clashes, the parties draw on the sacred, not to define the purpose of conflict but to determine the fault lines separating their camps. Religious rituals and symbols act as identifiers, enhance group cohesion, and provide actors with an auxiliary justifications for joining or abstaining from conflict.

Finally, the sacred will play a smaller role when only third parties organize or determine their stance in the dispute based on religious principles. These are the interstate conflicts that have occupied the bulk of this volume, and even here, as I hope to have persuasively shown, religious intelligence has an important role to play. In all these cases, the influence of the sacred falls along a continuum; it motivates conflict either more or less, and it shapes the identities of one, two, or more parties and bystanders to varying degrees.

The greater the likelihood that religious considerations will affect combat, the more vital the contribution of religious intelligence to decision making. The prominence of religion in a given conflict thus determines the extent to which a faulty or accurate religious analysis can sway conflict outcomes.

Centrality

The centrality of sacred time, space, authority, or ritual depends on their formal ability to provide key religious functions to believers. The more central a factor is in the religious landscape of the community, the greater its ability to provide access to the divine by enhancing communication with the gods, manifesting the presence of the gods, and conveying divine meanings.[71] For example, formal Catholic doctrine suggests that believers can hope for a closer experience of God during Easter, in St. Peter's Basilica in Rome, in the presence of the pope, and during mass. These beliefs and practices are formal by virtue of having been enshrined in sacred scripture, validated through continuous community practice and reverence, and endorsed by the appropriate religious hierarchy.

These sources allow us to rank sacred phenomena by centrality. The more significant the historical or mythical event commemorated on a sacred day, the greater the importance of the holy day. Salient dates tend to occur less frequently in the religious calendar, are often characterized by rules and practices that deviate more significantly from day-to-day behavior, and are accompanied by stricter penalties for transgression.[72] Because of these penalties, as well as the potential favors to be gained on particularly potent sacred days, significant sacred days can often be recognized by the crowds they draw to rituals and sacred sites.

Sacred space can be ranked along similar lines. Formally speaking, sacred sites of primary centrality tend to be those on which some divine revelation or the founding moment of a religious movement has taken place. Sites of secondary importance are located on consecrated ground, chosen by religious leaders, and imbued with significance by tombs and relics. Sites of tertiary importance, such as village mosques, mirror more central shrines in design and orientation. The more central a shrine, the better its utility in providing believers with religious benefits and the more likely believers are to respond vehemently to damage or desecration.[73]

In religious movements characterized by a hierarchical leadership, such as Catholicism, Shi'a Islam, and Mormonism, the centrality of religious actors is determined by their position in that hierarchy, which in turn depends on their seniority, the respect they command among peers, and their technical expertise in matters sacred. In nonhierarchical movements, such as Shintoism, Judaism, or Sunni Islam, centrality is more elusive, often correlating with the ability to attract and lead a religious community. The more central a religious actor, the greater his or her ability to interpret and even manipulate the rules that govern sacred parameters such as time and space.

Finally, the centrality of a sacred ritual depends on its ability to provide salvation, blessing, healing, or protection. Minor rituals are often individualist and eclectic practices that consist of some variation on a group ritual of greater significance. The more central the ritual, the more likely it is to draw crowds of worshippers and the greater the chance that it will occur in a sacred place, at a sacred time, and under the guidance of a religious authority figure.

Salience

These heuristics notwithstanding, common practice can elevate seemingly inferior sacred times, places, authorities, and rituals to a higher status depending on their salience to a particular religious community. Believers do not practice religion in its "pure" form. Religions do not consist of sacred precepts locked in ancient scriptures; they are lived and dynamic, displaying local idiosyncrasies. These practices are not deviations from true religion because no such absolute standard exists. Rather, they are variants that believers accept as valid and meaningful.[74]

To further complicate matters, believers will place a higher value on religious factors if they perceive those to be under threat. Conflict during a sacred day, at a sacred site, involving a religious leader, or during a religious ritual can thus serve to enhance the significance of each of those phenomena. This means that recognizing the relevance of a religious factor in a particular social and political setting requires a contextualized understanding of local biases, practices, superstitions, and preferences and of how those shift the official centrality of a given factor.

Impact

Finally, the analyst must translate findings from the religious to the military sphere to assess the impact of religious beliefs and practices on combat operations. An understanding of salience may suffice to ascertain how *civilian observers* will react to conflict at sacred times, in sacred space, involving sacred authority, or entailing sacred rituals, but it will provide inadequate information about how *combatants* will act in these circumstances. Determining the military impact of combat involving sacred factors will require taking into account the distribution of religious identities among the combatants (and, hence, prevailing perceptions of centrality and salience), the prevalence of practices, and the extent to which military discipline mitigates or amplifies religious proclivities.

By extension, military organizations can improve the resilience of their troops to the impact of religious practices by recognizing their own religious vulnerabilities and by compensating for those weaknesses. Such training would require identifying exogenous sources of religious motivation, to ensure that soldiers are not unduly influenced in the use of force, as well as pinpointing potential sources of religious constraint. Decision makers will want to train military forces to identify and exploit their opponents' religious vulnerabilities while remaining within the bounds of the law of armed combat and under the threshold of religious provocation. All these precautions are untenable in the absence of appropriate religious intelligence.

Policy Implications

If, as I have argued throughout this book, religious practices have a force-multiplying effect in all wars, who ought to be assigned the task of providing accurate religious intelligence? Should scholars of religion, anthropologists, military chaplains, or soldiers perform these tasks? The difficulty posed by the subject matter requires an analyst who can brave the four challenges discussed in the previous section, evaluating the prominence, centrality, salience, and impact of the sacred in a given conflict. In the absence of individuals who are proficient in religion, politics, anthropology, and military affairs at one and the same time, decision makers will have to rely on teams of specialists who can complement one another's abilities.

Scholars trained in religion and politics are often adept at overcoming the first two obstacles. Armed with information about a conflict and the relevant religious traditions, they can offer careful speculation about the religious ideas and practices at play in a dispute and the degree to which they might shape motivations and identities. The third hurdle, estimating salience, requires supplementing these hypotheticals with in-depth knowledge of local traditions, practices, and biases. The detailed ethnographic familiarity required for understanding how a specific religious subgroup perceives and implements the formal symbols and ceremonies of a broader religious movement suggests the need for anthropological training and experience.

The U.S. military has engaged in several efforts to recruit anthropologists as advisors on cultural issues. This practice is part of a larger move toward "culture-centric warfare" in the U.S. military.[75] In the 2006 U.S. Army counterinsurgency field manual, two contributing anthropologists, Montgomery McFate and David Kilcullen, detail the cultural expert's skill set, including the ability to decipher social structures, language, power, authority, and interests. Cultural knowledge, they argue, involves information about local notions of rationality, appropriate behaviors, levels of religious devotion, norms concerning gender, rituals, symbols, myths, narratives, ancient grievances, and more.[76]

The deployment of anthropologists in support of combat troops raises several difficulties. For one, a vocal majority in the American Anthropological Association (AAA) is vehemently opposed to cooperation with the military. Rather than developing tools to maintain high levels of professional integrity in times of war, many anthropologists have abandoned the task entirely and have decried the "military-anthropology complex" as a "grave breach of the AAA's code of ethics."[77] The use of anthropological observation and analysis as a source of intelligence, some argue, endangers informants, other anthropologists, and the integrity of the discipline. These critics have branded colleagues who advise armed forces as "warrior-intellectuals" who are providing "a manual for indirect colonial rule."[78] Whereas the Department of Defense has teamed up with the National Science Foundation to launch Minerva, an initiative to fund social science research on culture in regions of concern, alarmed scholars have formed the Network of Concerned Anthropologists to counter the "militarization" of their discipline.[79] This network has asked its members to sign a pledge affirming that they would not engage in research that contributes to counterinsurgency. The underlying logic seems to be that a military ignorant of anthropology is preferable to a military that might misuse the insights that anthropologists provide.

A second problem with the use of anthropologists as military contractors is that their ability to analyze the salience of religious factors is not matched with the skills needed to interpret their impact on military operations. Social scientists who specialize in local cultural practices are unlikely to have an expertise in military affairs. Even those few who are capable of working alongside military forces in a combat zone are thus unlikely to be able to translate their findings from the religious to the military sphere unaided. It was this need to understand both religion and military operations prior to analyzing the tactical and strategic impact of practices that prompted the U.S. military to assign chaplains this role. But chaplains receive no formal training in the gathering or analyzing of religious intelligence, and the expectation that they will act as unarmed battlefield spies endangers their status as non-combatants.[80]

Aware of this conflict of interest and the potential danger to chaplains, the U.S. military moved to explore a new option. The Human Terrain System (HTS), launched in fall 2006, was a program to create embedded teams to provide "direct social-science support in the form of ethnographic and social research, cultural information research, and social data analysis."[81] Each team consisted of two civilian social scientists to analyze the region and its culture, and two military personnel with a background in tactical intelligence to act as research manager and analyst. An officer, acting as leader, formed the link between the Human Terrain Team (HTT) and the unit to which it was attached, usually a forward-deployed brigade. The team's goal was to create a database covering social, economic, and cultural information that could be used by its brigade. Other teams worked at the division or corps level to collate information gathered by HTT's, form a more complete picture of the operational environment, and relay that information to a larger team of social scientists located in the Foreign Military Studies Office in Fort Leavenworth.[82] This Reachback Research Center (RRC) was part of a larger organization that acted as a clearinghouse for cultural knowledge, providing on-the-ground ethnographic research, performing secondary source research on-demand, and conducting predeployment cultural training on specific countries.[83]

In 2009, at the peak of the HTS experiment, the project consisted of 700 people and operated 42 teams. It was "essentially an experiment on how to conduct social science in support of the military in combat."[84] The focus of HTS was not on religion. Its emphasis was on understanding tribal networks, social structures, authority figures, emergent political groups, political ideologies, economic indicators, and grievances. Moreover, its focus was on the civilians that formed the "human terrain," not on insurgents and their faith. Yet even within this limited purview, the teams provided occasional information on religious practices that proved useful to military operations. For example, one team offered the elementary but prudent suggestion that their brigade reschedule its weapon search in a local mosques so as to avoid the Friday prayer time.[85]

The strength of the HTS approach, a reliance on a combination of academic and military resources, also proved to be its primary weakness.[86] Despite integration training, members of HTS teams found communication and cooperation across the academic–military divide to be a significant challenge. Just as scholars were not always attuned to operational needs, so soldiers did not make research requirements their top priority. On the academic side of that divide, social scientists in the front lines encountered time, resource, and security obstacles to conducting professional analyses. Basic social science techniques, from controlled sampling to participant observation, proved unfeasible in combat zones. Given the significant opposition to the HTS program among social scientists, the military encountered difficulties in locating qualified PhDs (in suitable physical condition) for the program. It did not consult HTS program directors prior to hiring civilian contractors and it did not permit the program to fire unqualified personnel at will. Commanders encountered similar difficulties recruiting and training soldiers who had an adequate academic background to support the research needs of their academic counterparts and exploit their findings in an optimal manner. Some in the military expressed skepticism about the "touchy-feely" information that HTS provided. Others were resentful of the fact that HTS was drawing funding away from other cultural programs in the military. Yet even those military units that complained about how HTS executed particular tasks or managed its personnel expressed support for the program as a whole and embraced the utility of cultural analysis.[87]

The drawdown of troops from Iraq and Afghanistan ended the HTS program. Despite the difficulties that HTS faced during its short tenure, similar programs are likely to grow in prominence as actors identified in religious terms and motivated by religion become increasingly involved in asymmetric conflicts. This projected growth in the prominence of religion should prompt decision makers to draw on the combined expertise of religion scholars, political scientists, ethnographers, and military specialists for religious intelligence analysis. Political scientists who are interested in supporting such efforts should broaden their outlook on religion and conflict from an exclusive focus on the sacred as an idea that generates religious disputes to the sacred as a constellation of practices that pervade all disputes. By studying the manifold ways in which the sacred shapes combat, beyond the analysis of sacred time, space, authority, and ritual, political scientists can play their part in unravelling the role of religion on the battlefield.

ACKNOWLEDGMENTS

I thank my family for their enthusiasm, support, and patience throughout the writing of this book. My daughter, Annie, and my son, Mikey, supplied the laughter, chaos, and ultimate purpose that I needed to see the project through. Laura, to whom I dedicate this book, removed all obstacles and provided peace, intellectual stimulation, and love.

Many, many friends and colleagues read rough copies of chapters, conference papers, and article drafts that later became parts of this book. I thank them for their diligent reading; for many hours spent in animated conversation; and for their gentle prodding, poignant critiques, bold suggestions, and creative ideas. Their list includes, but is not limited to, Dima Adamsky, Leila Austin, Uri Bar-Joseph, Michael Barnett, Matthias Basedau, David Benson, Stephen Biddle, Risa Brooks, David Buckley, Daniel Byman, Erica Chenoweth, Stuart Cohen, Jeff Colgan, Christopher Clary, Michael Desch, Charles Doran, Alex Downes, Yoav Duman, David Edelstein, Asif Efrat, Ehud Eiran, Jeffrey Engel, Tanisha Fazal, Jonathan Fine, Taylor Fravel, Marty Finnemore, Scott Gartner, Mark George, Eugene Gholz, Tony Gill, James Goldgeier, Jessica Gottlieb, John Hall, Bernard Harcourt, Kirstin Hasler, Mike Hayden, Peter Henne, James Hollifield, Reyko Huang, Valeria Hudson, Piki Ish-Shalom, Joshua Itzkowitz-Shifrinson, Amaney Jamal, Patrick James, Mujeeb Khan, Noa Levanon Klein, Jason Klocek, Dan Lindley, Jason Lyall, Cecilia Lynch, John Mearsheimer, Dan Miodownik, Assaf Moghadam, Larry Napper, Andrew Natsios, Abe Newman, Daniel Nexon, Robert Pape, T. V. Paul, Krzysztof Pelc, Arie Perliger, Roger Petersen, Daniel Philpott, Bryan Price, Brian Rathbun, Lorinc Redei, Sebastian Rosato, Joshua Rovner, Scott Sagan, Richard Samuels, Arieh Saposnik, Thomas Scherer, Jacquelyn Schneider, Tanya Schwarz, Jacob Shapiro, Joshua Shifrinson, Brad Simpson, Jack Snyder, Paul Staniland, Jeremy Suri, Hiroki Takeuchi, Stephen Van Evera, Carolyn Warner, and Marie-Joelle Zahar.

I am grateful to the audiences at the various academic institutions at which I presented ideas from this book for their constructive questions and incisive comments. They include (by longitude west of the center of the universe): the faculty and students of the International Relations Department at Hebrew University in Jerusalem, the Political Science Department at the University of Haifa, the Faculty Seminar of the Lauder School at the Interdisciplinary Center (IDC) Herzliya, the Security Studies Program at the Massachusetts Institute of Technology (MIT), the Center for International Peace and Security Studies co-sponsored by McGill and the University of Montreal, the Combating Terrorism Center at West Point, the Institute for International and Regional Studies at Princeton University, the Global Politics and Religion Initiative at the Paul H. Nitze School of Advanced International Studies (SAIS), the Institute for Security and Conflict Studies at George Washington University, the Mortara Center for International Studies at Georgetown University, the International Security Program at Notre Dame, the Program on International Security Policy at the University of Chicago, the Josef Korbel School of International Studies, the Luce Foundation Program on Religion and International Affairs at Arizona State University, the International Studies Public Forum at the University of California–Irvine, the Center for International Studies at the University of Southern California (USC), the Nazarian Center for Israel Studies at the University of California–Los Angeles (UCLA), the International Relations Program at the University of California–Davis, and the International Security Colloquium at the University of Washington. The students and faculty at the illustrious University of California–Berkeley Monday International Relations Seminar (aka MIRTH) proved particularly supportive and insightful, as they always do.

I am particularly grateful to the organizers of the Lone Star National Security Forum for corralling faculty from across the University of Texas system for a focused discussion of several of my chapter drafts that offered invaluable feedback. I had the unique privilege of completing this manuscript at the International Institute for Counter-Terrorism (ICT) in the Interdisciplinary Center in Herzliya, an exceptionally collegial and intellectually stimulating research center. I am deeply grateful to my host, Dean Boaz Ganor, for his hospitality and encouragement. I thank the scholars and staff at the ICT, in particular Stevie Weinberg and Devorah Margolin, for creating a welcoming and productive working environment.

I owe a great debt to the many research assistants who contributed to the empirical foundations of this book, often combing through large swaths of history with only the vaguest notion of what they were looking for. They did so without demurring, took welcome initiatives, and proposed fruitful research trajectories of their own. Among the undergraduates, Alex Dubin and Christina Anecito helped with chapter 3, and Courtney Tran helped with chapter 5. Zuzanna Gruca diligently edited multiple chapters. Among the graduate students, Andrius Galisanka, Melissa McAdam, and Rengyee Lee toiled on chapter 2. Jason Klocek and Alice Ciciora, brilliant scholars in their own right, supported the entire project with relentless patience, wisdom, and drive, particularly during the archival work underpinning chapter 3.

Others conclude with thanks to their nearest and dearest, but I will end with my gratitude to the staff at Cornell University Press. Christopher Way and two anonymous reviewers offered careful and constructive suggestions that boosted the quality of the book considerably. Julie Nemer performed exceptionally thorough copyediting on the volume and Karen Laun expertly guided it through the production process. Most of all, I am grateful to Roger Haydon, an editor of exceptional kindness, wit, and energy, who strikes the perfect balance between confident counsel and professional deference. His faith in this volume was essential to its fruition.

NOTES

1. Why? Religion as a Cause of War

1. Constitutive effects produce meaning and significance. Regulative effects constrain action. John Searle, *The Construction of Social Reality* (New York: Free Press, 1995).

2. On the relationship between religion and international conflict, see Daniel Philpott, "Has the Study of Global Politics Found Religion?" *Annual Review of Political Science.* 12 (2009): 183–202; Nukhet A. Sandal and Patrick James, "Religion and International Relations Theory: Towards a Mutual Understanding," *European Journal of International Relations* 17, no. 1 (2011): 3–25; Michael Barnett, "Another Great Awakening? International Relations Theory and Religion," in *Religion and International Relations Theory,* edited by Jack Snyder, 91–114 (New York: Columbia University Press, 2012); Scott Thomas, "Religion and International Conflict," in *Religion and International Relations,* edited by Ken R. Dark, 1–23 (Basingstoke, UK: Macmillan, 2000); Andreas Hasenclever and Volker Rittberger, "Does Religion Make a Difference? Theoretical Approaches to the Impact of Faith on Political Conflict," *Millennium: Journal of International Studies* 29, no. 3 (2000): 641–74; Daniel Philpott, "Explaining the Political Ambivalence of Religion," *American Political Science Review* 101, no. 3 (2007): 505–25; Jonathan Fox, "Religion as an Overlooked Element of International Relations," *International Studies Review* 3, no. 3 (2001): 53–73; Nukhet Sandal and Jonathan Fox, *Religion in International Relations Theory: Concepts, Tools, and Debates* (London: Routledge, 2013).

3. Ron E. Hassner, "Religion and International Affairs: The State of the Art," in *Religion, Identity and Global Governance: Ideas, Evidence and Practice,* edited by Patrick James, 37–56 (Toronto: University of Toronto Press, 2010).

4. Ron E. Hassner, "Correspondence: Debating the Role of Religion in War," *International Security* 35, no. 1 (2010): 202–6.

5. Samuel Huntington, *The Clash of Civilizations and the Remaking of the World Order* (New York: Simon and Schuster, 1996).

6. Ibid., 210, 263. Huntington asserts that Christianity is distinct from Islam because it recognizes the separation of Church and State; Islam is an absolutist religion of the sword; both Christianity and Islam are monotheistic (so they "cannot easily assimilate additional deities," 210); universalistic, missionary, and teleological religions that espoused crusades and jihad, respectively. See also 70, 211, 264.

7. Ron E. Hassner, *War on Sacred Grounds* (Ithaca: Cornell University Press, 2009); Ron E. Hassner, "The Pessimist's Guide to Religious Cooperation," in *Holy Places in the Israeli-Palestinian Conflict: Confrontation and Co-Existence,* edited by Marshall J. Breger, Yitzhak Reiter, and Leonard Hamme, 145–57 (London: Routledge, 2010);

Ron E. Hassner, "Fighting Insurgency on Sacred Ground," *Washington Quarterly* 29, no. 2 (2006): 149–66.

8. See, for example, Roland H. Bainton, *Christian Attitudes towards War and Peace* (Nashville: Abingdon, 1960); John Kelsay and James Turner Johnson, eds., *Just War and Jihad: Historical and Theoretical Perspectives on War and Peace in Western and Islamic Traditions* (New York: Greenwood, 1991); James Turner Johnson and John Kelsay, *Cross, Crescent and Sword: The Justification and Limitation of War in Western and Islamic Tradition* (New York: Greenwood, 1990); Paul Ramsey, *The Just War: Force and Political Responsibility* (Rowman & Littlefield, 2002). Note the telling exception of Michael Walzer, who combines an acute interest in the practice of just war theory with an effort to sever the theory from its religious roots. *Just and Unjust Wars: A Moral Argument with Historical Illustrations* (New York, Basic Books, 1977).

9. See, for example, Robert Pape, *Dying to Win: The Strategic Logic of Suicide Terrorism* (New York: Ramdon House, 2006); Pippa Norris and Ronald Inglehart, *Sacred and Secular: Religion and Politics Worldwide* (Cambridge, MA: Cambridge University Press, 2004); Monica Duffy Toft, "Getting Religion? The Puzzling Case of Islam and Civil War," *International Security* 31, no. 4 (2007): 97–131. For a discussion of religion and rationalism in political science, see Joshua Mitchell, "Religion Is Not a Preference," *Journal of Politics* 69, no. 2 (May 2007): 351–62; Clyde Wilcox, Kenneth D. Wald, and Tedd G. Jelen, "Religious Preferences and Social Science: A Second Look," *Journal of Politics* 70, no. 3 (July 2008): 874–79; Joshua Mitchell, "A Reply to My Critics," *Journal of Politics* 70, no. 3 (July 2008): 880–83; J. Ann Tickner, "On Taking Religious Worldviews Seriously," in *Power, Interdependence, and Nonstate Actors in World Politics,* edited by Helen Milner and Andrew Moravcsik, 223–42 (Princeton: Princeton University Press, 2009).

10. Huntington, *Clash of Civilizations*, 67–68, 129–30, 245, 292.

11. Contrast one side—Bruce M. Russett, John R. Oneal, and Michaelene Cox, "Clash of Civilizations, or Realism and Liberalism Deja Vu? Some Evidence," *Journal of Peace Research* 37, no. 5 (September 2000): 583–608; Errol A. Henderson and Richard Tucker, "Clear and Present Strangers: The Clash of Civilizations and International Politics," *International Studies Quarterly* 45, no. 2 (2001): 317–38; Giacomo Chiozza, "Is There a Clash of Civilizations? Evidence from Patterns of International Conflict Involvement, 1946–97," *Journal of Peace Research* 39, no. 6 (2002): 711–34, with Philip G. Roeder, "Clash of Civilizations and Escalation of Domestic Ethnopolitical Conflicts," *Comparative Political Studies* 36, no. 5 (2003): 509–40.

12. Contrast Jonathan Fox, "The Increasing Role of Religion in State Failure: 1960 to 2004," *Terrorism and Political Violence* 19, no. 3 (2007): 395–414, with James Fearon and David Laitin, "Ethnicity, Insurgency, and Civil War," *American Political Science Review* 97, no. 11 (2003): 75–90.

13. Contrast one side—Andrej Tusicisny, "Civilizational Conflicts: More Frequent, Longer, and Bloodier?" *Journal of Peace Research* 41, no. 4 (2004): 485–98; Susanna Pearce, "Religious Rage: A Quantitative Analysis of the Intensity of Religious Conflicts," *Terrorism and Political Violence* 17, no. 3 (2005): 333–52; Jonathan Fox, "Religion and State Failure: An Examination of the Extent and Magnitude

of Religious Conflict from 1950 to 1996," *International Political Science Review* 25, no. 1 (2004): 55–76—with Bethany A. Lacina, " Explaining the Severity of Civil Wars," *Journal of Conflict Resolution* 50, no. 2 (2006): 276–89; Ragnhild Nordas, "Gunning for God? Religion and Conflict Severity," paper presented at the International Studies Association 55th Annual Conference, Toronto, March 26–29, 2014.

14. Contrast one side—Toft, "Getting Religion?"; Nordas, "Gunning for God?—with Jonathan Fox, "Is Islam More Conflict Prone than Other Religions? A Cross-Sectional Study of Ethnoreligious Conflict," *Nationalism and Ethnic Politics* 6, no. 2 (2000): 1–23; Roeder, "Clash of Civilizations"; Pearce (2005).

15. For a discussion, see, for example, Brian Lia, "An Empirical Examination of Religion and Conflict in the Middle East, 1950–1992," *Foreign Policy Analysis* 2, no. 1 (2006): 21–36.

16. See, for example, Errol A. Henderson, "Culture or Contiguity: Ethnic Conflict, the Similarity of States, and the Onset of War, 1820–1989," *Journal of Conflict Resolution* 41, no. 5 (1997), 661; Fox, "Religion and State Failure."

17. This point is made eloquently in William T. Cavanaugh, *The Myth of Religious Violence: Secular Ideology and the Roots of Modern Conflict* (Oxford: Oxford University Press, 2009). See also Meic Pearse, *The Gods of War: Is Religion the Primary Cause of Violent Conflict?* (Downers Grove, IL: InterVarsity Press, 2007); Rodney Stark, *God's Battalions: The Case for the Crusades* (New York: HarperCollins, 2009); Karen Armstrong, *Fields of Blood: Religion and the History of Violence* (New York: Knopf, 2014).

18. Hassner, "Correspondence"; Hassner, "Religion and International Affairs."

19. See for example Monica Duffy Toft, "Issue Indivisibility and Time Horizons as Rationalist Explanations for War," *Security Studies* 15, no. 1 (2006): 34–69; Isak Svensson, "Fighting with Faith: Religion and Conflict Resolution in Civil Wars," *Journal of Conflict Resolution* 51, no. 6 (2007): 930–49; Pearce, "Religious Rage"; Michael Horowitz, "Long Time Going: Religion and the Duration of Crusading," *International Security* 34, no. 2 (2009): 162–93; Monica Duffy Toft and Yuri M. Zhukov, "Islamists and Nationalists: Rebel Motivation and Counterinsurgency in Russia's North Caucasus" *American Political Science Review* 109, 02 (2015): 222–38; Jason Klocek, "State Repression and Religious Disorder," paper presented at the 2013 Annual Meeting of the American Political Science Association, Chicago, August 31, 2013; Jason Klocek and Lionel Beehner, "Divine Intervention: Foreign Military Involvement in Religious Civil Wars," paper presented at the International Studies Association 55th Annual Conference, Toronto, March 26–29, 2014.

20. For reviews of this literature, see, for example, J. Ann Tickner, *Gender in International Relations: Feminist Perspectives in Achieving Global Security* (New York: Columbia University Press, 1992); Joshua S. Goldstein, *War and Gender: How Gender Shapes the War System and Vice Versa* (Cambridge, UK: Cambridge University Press, 2003); J. Ann Tickner, "Feminist Responses to International Security Studies," *Peace Review* 16, no. 1 (2004): 43–48; Helen Kinsella, *The Image before the Weapon: A Critical History of the Distinction between Combatant and Civilian* (Ithaca: Cornell University Press, 2011).

21. See, for example, Brent Nongbri, *Before Religion: A History of a Modern Concept* (New Haven: Yale University Press, 2012); Elizabeth Shakman Hurd, *The Politics of Secularism in International Relations* (Princeton: Princeton University Press, 2009); Robert M. Bosco, "Persistent Orientalisms: The Concept of Religion in International Relations," *Journal of International Relations and Development* 12, no. 1 (2009): 90–111; Bruce Lincoln, "The Study of Religion in the Current Political Moment," in *Holy Terrors: Thinking about Religion after September 11* (Chicago: University of Chicago Press, 2003), 1–18; Cavanaugh, *Myth of Religious Violence*. These scholars were influenced, in part, by Talal Asad, "The Construction of Religion as an Anthropological Category," in *Genealogies of Religion: Discipline and Reasons of Power in Christianity and Islam* (Baltimore: Johns Hopkins University Press, 1993), 27–54.

22. Martin Riesebrodt, *The Promise of Salvation: A Theory of Religion*, translated by Steven Rendall (Chicago: University of Chicago Press, 2010), 12, 128.

23. Riesebrodt, *Promise of Salvation*.

24. Ibid., xxi, 18. Riesebrodt distinguishes between religions and religious traditions, such as Judaism and Buddhism, that contain religious practices as well as cultural or ethnic systems and symbols. This distinction allows Riesebrodt to sidestep the question of whether these religious traditions are of a kind (xxi, 14).

25. Ibid., esp. 21, 90.

26. For religion as practice, see Karen Armstrong, *The Case for God* (New York: Knopf, 2009); Gracie Davie, *Religion in Britain since 1945* (Oxford: Blackwell, 1994).

27. Riesebrodt, *Promise of Salvation*, xii–xiii.

28. Ivan Strenski, "On 'Religion' and Its Despisers," in *What Is Religion? Origins, Definitions and Explanations,* edited by Thomas Idinopulos and Brian C. Wilson (Leiden: E. J. Brill, 1998), 116.

29. Ludwig Wittgenstein, *Philosophical Investigations,* edited by G.E.M. Anscombe and R. Rhees (New York: Macmillan, 1953), Aphorism 38.

30. Riesebrodt, *Promise of Salvation*, 91, 112.

31. Ibid., 173.

32. Ibid., 5–6, 16.

33. Riesebrodt argues persuasively that non-Western cultures show consistent historical awareness of the concept of religion. Far from being the passive recipients of the concept, as post-colonial scholars make them out to be, non-Western practitioners recognize the differences between local religions and contrast these with those of outsiders, often in competitive terms. This was as true of Confucians or Daoists describing Buddhist others as it was of Christians describing Muslim others (ibid., 21–45).

34. Its interpretivism and the primacy of the sacred distinguishes this approach from contemporary work on practice in sociology and international relations. My emphasis is on the role that salvation plays as a motivator for action, not on the role that text, repetition, and performance play in fixing meaning. For alternative approaches to practice, see Emanuel Adler and Vincent Pouliot, *International Practices* (Cambridge, UK: Cambridge University Press, 2011); Iver B. Neumann, "Returning Practice to the Linguistic Turn: The Case of Diplomacy," *Millennium: Journal of*

International Studies 31, no. 3 (2002): 627–51; Theodore R Schatzki, K. Knorr-Cetina, and Eike von Savigny, eds., *The Practice Turn in Contemporary Theory* (New York: Routledge, 2001).

35. Precise figures are hard to come by given the discrepancy between the number of chaplains officially assigned to the war effort and the number who were actually deployed. Moreover, constant fluctuations in the arrival and departure of chaplains make it hard to estimate how many chaplains were actually at the front at any given time. Casualty figures, and particularly the subset of "killed in action" (as distinct from "died of wounds" or "died in service"), are equally difficult to establish given the ambiguity of the terms. For discussions, sources, and estimates see Michael Snape, *The Royal Army Chaplains' Department 1796–1953: Clergy under Fire* (Woodbridge, UK: Boydell Press, 2008), esp. 194, 225, 280. Snape is relying in part on War Office, *Statistics of the Military Effort of the British Empire during the Great War* (London: HMSO, 1922, reprinted by the London Stamp Exchange), 190. Alternative figures appear in Tom Johnstone and James Hagerty, *The Cross on the Sword: Catholic Chaplains in the Forces* (London: Geoffrey Chapman, 1996); Edward Madigan, *Faith under Fire: Anglican Army Chaplains and the Great War* (New York: Palgrave Macmillan, 2011), 142, 269.

36. I am grateful to Michael Allbrook and Peter Howson for corresponding with me and for providing me with precise information about the identities of British chaplains who died in the Great War. Allbrook, who maintains the website "They Gave Their Today," www.theygavetheirtoday.com, relied on data from the Commonwealth War Graves Commission, the *Times* death notices, and the Memorial to the Royal Army Chaplains Department at Aldershot to compile his data. Peter Howson is the author of "Deaths among Army Chaplains, 1914–20," *Journal of the Society for Army Historical Research*, 83 (2005): 63–77, and *Muddling Through: The Organisation of British Army Chaplaincy in World War One* (Solihull, UK: Helion & Company, 2013). I matched these names and dates with information about the denomination and manner of death for each chaplain from David T. Youngson, *Greater Love: A Directory of Chaplains of the British Army, Australian, Canadian, East African, New Zealand and South African Forces and Ministers of Religion Who Gave Their Lives in the Period 1914–1922* (Hartlepool, UK: Printability Publishing, 2008).

37. Early in the war, Anglican chaplains made up 76 percent of the British chaplains deployed to the front, whereas Catholic chaplains amounted to a mere 15 percent. After June 1915, and for the duration of the war, this disparity declined somewhat to an average of 57 percent Anglican chaplains to 19 percent Catholic chaplains. These denominational ratios, too, are hard to assess. See Michael Snape, *God and the British Soldier: Religion and the British Army in the First and Second World Wars* (New York: Routledge, 2005), 102–3, citing LPL, Davidson Papers, Vol. 344, Great War: Clergy 1915–1917, 218, 228; and LPL, Davidson Papers, Vol. 345, Great War: Clergy 1917–1919, 4; Haidee Blackburne, *Trooper to Dean* (Bristol, UK: J. W. Arrowsmith, 1955), 59–60; see also sources listed in note 35.

38. In the U.S. Civil War, Irish-Catholic and German-Catholic units suffered disproportionately high casualty rates, in part because they were assigned to the deadliest battles. Most notorious of all was the Irish Brigade that participated in the First Battle of Bull Run (Manassas), the Seven Days Battles, the Battle of Antietam

(60 percent casualties), the Battle of Fredericksburg (84 percent casualties), and Gettysburg. Randall M. Miller, "Catholic Religion, Irish Ethnicity, and the Civil War," in *Religion and the American Civil War,* edited by Randall M. Miller, Harry S. Stout, and Charles Reagan Wilson (New York: Oxford University Press, 1998), 265, 272.

39. There is some debate about the existence of this order. Michael Snape cites the order verbatim and reports the date on which it was lifted, January 15, 1916. *God and the British Soldier,* 97; *Royal Army Chaplains' Department,* 223, citing Liddle Collection, University of Leeds, GS 0531, M. S. Evers. Further evidence about this order appears in Albert Marrin, *The Last Crusade: The Church of England in the First World War* (Durham: Duke University Press, 1974), 208; Alan Wilkinson, *The Church of England and the First World War* (Southampton, UK: Camelot Press, 1978), 129–30, citing Frank R. Barry, *Period of My Life* (1970), 54, 60–61; P. Middleton Brumwell, *The Army Chaplain: The Royal Army Chaplains' Department, the Duties of Chaplains and Morale* (London: Adam & Charles Black. 1943), 37; Stephen H. Louden, *Chaplains in Conflict: The Role of Army Chaplains since 1914* (London: Avon Books, 1996), 51. Peter Howson is skeptical about the existence of a formal order of this sort (private correspondence, February 2013). The Reverend E. C. Crosse suggested that it caused outrage and was widely ignored; he noted that the Fifth Army order of battle, issued by General Hubert Gough, permitted chaplains to go wherever they liked. Linda Parker, *The Whole Armour of God: Anglican Chaplains in the Great War* (Solihull, UK: Helion & Company, 2009), 28, 43, citing E. C. Cross Papers, IWM (80/22/1), 69.

40. Duff Crerar, *Padres in No Man's Land: Canadian Chaplains and the Great War* (Montreal: McGill-Queen's University Press, 1995), 111–12, 348n. 16; Parker, *Whole Armour of God,* 24–28.

41. Snape, *God and the British Soldier,* 103.

42. Ibid.; Parker, *Whole Armour of God,* 34, 82, citing William Drury, *Camp Followers: A Padre's Recollections of the Nile, Somme and Tigris during the First World War* (Dublin: Exchequer Printers, 1968), 127.

43. Oliver Rafferty, "Catholic Chaplains to the British Forces in the First World War," *Religion, State & Society* 39, no. 1 (2011): 33–62.

44. Johnstone and Hagerty, 88, citing *Catholic Herald,* October 21, 1914.

45. Indeed, it may well be that many of the seventy-six chaplains (whose precise manner of death in action was not recorded) were Anglicans; however, there is no sound reason to assume that British authorities were systematically careless in collecting data on the deaths of Anglican chaplains compared to their Catholic counterparts. If anything, the pattern regarding recognition of acts of bravery in citations for medals suggests the opposite bias.

46. It is worth noting that a similar pattern seems apparent in the Crimean War. There, six Anglican and six Catholic chaplains perished, not due to enemy action but due to disease contracted in primitive field hospitals. Because here, too, the total number of Anglican chaplains exceeded that of Catholics threefold, some scholars have argued that differences in the nature of denominational ministration to the sick explain the higher proportional death rates of Catholic chaplains. Whereas Anglican chaplains preached, held services, read, and prayed with the sick, their Catholic counterparts also heard confessions and physically anointed the dying, which required

close and recurring contact with patients suffering from contagious diseases. James Hagerty and Tom Johnstone, "Catholic Military Chaplains in the Crimean War," *Recusant History* 27, no. 3 (2005), 430–31; Snape, *Royal Army Chaplains' Department,* 91–94.

47. Youngson, *Greater Love,* 23, citing John Henry Patterson, *With the Zionists in Gallipoli* (New York: George H. Doran, 1916), 100.

48. Martin Purdy, "Roman Catholic Army Chaplains during the First World War: Roles, Experiences and Dilemmas" (MA thesis, University of Central Lancashire, 2012), 44, citing *Daily Express,* August 22, 1917.

49. Johnstone and Hagerty, 112–13, 198. Similarly, Snape confirms "their tendency to be at hand in order to administer the sacraments to the wounded and dying." *Royal Army Chaplains' Department,* 169.

50. On nationalism, culture, and combat motivation see Omer Bartov, *The Eastern Front, 1941–45: German Troops and the Barbarization of Warfare* (New York: St. Martin's Press, 1985); Stephen Biddle and Stephen Long. "Democracy and Military Effectiveness," *Journal of Conflict Resolution* 48, no. 4 (2004): 525–46; Morriss Janowitz and Stephen D. Wesbrook, eds., *The Political Education of Soldiers* (Beverly Hills: Sage Publications, 1983); Paul Stern, "Why Do People Sacrifice for Their Nations?" *Political Psychology* 16, no. 2 (1995): 22–65.

51. Robert M. Edsel, *Saving Italy: The Race to Rescue a Nation's Treasures from the Nazis* (New York: W. W. Norton, 2013), 97, citing John North, ed., *The Memoirs of Field-Marshal Earl Alexander of Tunis: 1940–1945* (London: Cassell and Co., 2000), 90.

52. David Hapgood and David Richardson, *Monte Cassino* (New York: Congdon and Weed, 1984), 76–77, citing Howard McGraw Smyth, "German Use of the Abbey of Monte Cassino Prior to Allied Aerial Bombardment of 15 February 1944," undated memorandum, Office of the Chief of Military History, U.S. Army, 5.

53. Matthew Parker, *Monte Cassino: The Hardest-Fought Battle of World War II* (New York: Doubleday, 2004), 37; David Fraser, *Wars and Shadows: Memoirs of General Sir David Fraser* (London: Allen Lane, 2002), 184–85; Hapgood and Richardson, *Monte Cassino,* 36–37, 42, 58, 73, 77, 79, 89, 94, 108, 222, 238.

54. Hapgood and Richardson, *Monte Cassino,* 110, 139; Edsel, *Saving Italy,* 45–46; Lynn H. Nicholas, *The Rape of Europa: The Fate of Europe's Treasures in the Third Reich and the Second World War* (New York: Alfred A. Knopf, 1994), 240.

55. Edsel, *Saving Italy,* 45–47, citing Fred Majdalany, *The Battle of Cassino* (Boston: Houghton Mifflin, 1957), 122.

56. Hapgood and Richardson, *Monte Cassino,* 153–54, citing the private papers of Major-General Donald R. Bateman, Imperial War Museum, London.

57. Parker, *Monte Cassino,* 163.

58. Hapgood and Richardson, *Monte Cassino,* 165, 170–71. No source or date is provided.

59. Ibid., 167, citing records of II Corps and 34th Division, Fifth Army History, part IV, 92, National Archives (NARA).

60. Hapgood and Richardson, *Monte Cassino,* 199, citing Intelligence annex to Operations Order 341, signed by Arthur M. Clark, Lieutenant-Colonel, Air Corps.

61. Hapgood and Richardson, *Monte Cassino*, 161–64; Nicholas, *Rape of Europa*, 246.

62. Hapgood and Richardson, *Monte Cassino*, 30, 53, 63–64, citing F. Jones, "Report on the Events Leading to the Bombing of the Abbey of Monte Cassino on 15 February 1944," Public Records Office, London (1949), 49.

63. Hapgood and Richardson, *Monte Cassino*, 158–59; Parker, *Monte Cassino*, 161.

64. John Ellis, *Cassino: The Hollow Victory: The Battle for Rome, January–June 1944* (New York: McGraw-Hill, 1984), 169–70; Parker, *Monte Cassino*, 163–64; Martin Blumenson, "The Bombing of Monte Cassino," *American Heritage* 19, no. 5 (1968), 20.

65. In those five weeks, the British Corps lost 4,000 men among their three divisions. The French Corps suffered 2,500 casualties. The U.S. 36th Division lost 2,000 men, and the 34th Division lost around 2,200. Majdalani, *Battle of Cassino*, 103–4; North, *Memoirs*, 90.

66. In Edsel, *Saving Italy*, 63–64.

67. Hapgood and Richardson, *Monte Cassino*, 199.

68. Ibid., 211.

69. Message from the Harold H. Tittmann, Assistant to the Personal Representative of President Roosevelt to Pope Pius XII, to the Cardinal of State (Maglione), May 23, 1944, *Foreign Relations of the United States*, 1944, Vol. IV, 1308; Hapgood and Richardson, *Monte Cassino*, 227.

70. Message from the Apostolic Delegate at Washington to President Roosevelt, March 13, 1944, *Foreign Relations of the United States*, 1944, Vol. IV, 1283; Hapgood and Richardson, *Monte Cassino*, 241.

71. Hapgood and Richardson, *Monte Cassino*, 81, 169, citing the diary of Eusebio Grossetti and Martino Matronola, two monks, December 19, 1943.

72. Hapgood and Richardson, *Monte Cassino*, 213, 221–24, citing "U.S. Intelligence Comments," Magic summary no. 700, February 24, 1944, Records of the National Security Agency; Parker, *Monte Cassino*, 173, 177; Majdalany, *Battle of Cassino*, 158.

73. In Majdalany, *Battle of Cassino*, 181.

74. Hapgood and Richardson, *Monte Cassino*, 81, 169, citing from the diary of Grossetti and Matronola, December 19, 1943.

75. Hapgood and Richardson, *Monte Cassino*, 164, 199.

76. In North, *Memoirs*, 119.

77. Johnstone and Hagerty, *Cross on the Sword*, 216, citing Rev. Dom Rudesind Brookes, *Father Dolly: The Guardsman Monk* (London: Melland, 1983), 155.

78. I thank Peter Henne and Michael Barnett for discussing some of these issues with me. See Peter S. Henne, "Never Waste a Religious Crisis: Do States Benefit from Global Religious Contention?" paper prepared for the International Studies Association 55th Annual Meeting, Toronto, March 26–29, 2014; Michael Barnett and Janice Stein, *Sacred Aid: Faith and Humanitarianism* (Oxford: Oxford University Press, 2012); Colin Elman, "Explanatory Typologies in Qualitative Studies of International Politics," *International Organization* 59, no. 2 (2005): 293–326; Andrew Bennett, "Causal Mechanisms and Typological Theories in the Study of Civil Conflict," in *Transnational Dynamics of Civil War*, edited by Jeffrey T. Checkel, 205–31 (Cambridge, UK: Cambridge University Press, 2013); Jeff D. Colgan, "Fueling the Fire: Pathways from Oil to War," *International Security* 38, no. 2 (2013): 147–80.

2. When? Sacred Time and War

1. An early version of this chapter appeared as "Sacred Time and Conflict Initiation," *Security Studies* 20, no. 4 (2011): 491–520.

2. Gerardus van der Leeuw, *Religion in Essence and Manifestation* (Princeton: Princeton University Press, 1986), 386.

3. Other conceptions of sacred time, including metaphysical, eschatological, and mythical sacred time, may have effects of their own on international security, but these are beyond the scope of this chapter. For example, on the relationship between belief in the afterlife and violence, see Monica Duffy Toft, "Issue Indivisibility and Time Horizons as Rationalist Explanations for War," *Security Studies* 15, no. 1 (2006): 34–69. On eschatological time and terrorism, see Mark Juergensmeyer, *Terror in the Mind of God* (Berkeley: University of California Press, 2000). James A. Aho, *Religious Mythology and the Art of War: Comparative Religious Symbolisms of Military Violence* (Westport, CT: Praeger, 1981) examines the relationship between mythical time and warfare. For quantitative analyses of religion and war, see also Errol A. Henderson, "Culture or Contiguity: Ethnic Conflict, the Similarity of States, and the Onset of War, 1820–1989," Journal of Conflict Resolution 41, no. 5 (1997): 649–68; Jonathan Fox, "Is Islam More Conflict Prone than Other Religions? A Cross-Sectional Study of Ethnoreligious Conflict," *Nationalism and Ethnic Politics* 6, no. 2 (2000): 1–23; Jonathan Fox, *Religion, Civilization, and Civil War: 1945 through the New Millennium* (Lanham, MD: Lexington Books, 2005).

4. On the relationship between sacred space and sacred time, see Mircea Eliade, *The Sacred and the Profane: The Nature of Religion* (New York: Harcourt, Brace, 1959), 73–76, citing Hermann Usener, *Götternamen*, 2nd ed. (Bonn: Cohen, 1920), 191.

5. On military effectiveness, see Stephen Biddle, *Military Power: Explaining Victory and Defeat in Modern Battle* (Princeton: Princeton University Press, 2004); Stephen Peter Rosen, *Societies and Military Power: India and Its Armies* (Ithaca: Cornell University Press, 1996); Dan Reiter and Alan C. Stam, *Democracies at War* (Princeton: Princeton University Press, 2002); Stephen Biddle and Robert Zirkle, "Technology, Civil-Military Relations, and Warfare in the Developing World," *Journal of Strategic Studies* 19, no. 2 (1996): 171–212; Kenneth Pollack, *Arabs at War: Military Effectiveness, 1948–1991* (Lincoln: University of Nebraska Press, 2002); Allan R. Millett and Williamson Murray, eds., *Military Effectiveness* (Boston: Allen and Unwin, 1988).

6. Risa A. Brooks and Elizabeth A. Stanley, ed., *Creating Military Power: The Sources of Military Effectiveness* (Stanford: Stanford University Press, 2007), 1–26.

7. Ibid., 11–12.

8. *Yediot Aharonot* (Israeli daily newspaper), quoted in "Secrecy Preceded Onslaught," Agence France Presse, December 28, 2008, http://www.asiaone.com/News/AsiaOne%2BNews/World/Story/A1Story20081228-110844.html. This logic may also have been at work during Operation Opera, the 1981 Israeli strike against the Iraqi reactor at Osirak. It took place during the Jewish holy day of Shavuot, when pilots would have been expected to be on leave, and on a Sunday, when foreign workers were expected to be absent from the site. Peter Scott Ford, "Israel's Attack on Osiraq: A Model for Future Preventive Strikes?" (MA thesis, Naval Postgraduate School, 2004), 36. A similar calculation may have motivated an Israeli attack on the Jewish Sabbath during the Lebanon War; see Glenn Frankel, "Israeli Raid Kills 40 in Lebanon; Rare Attack on Sabbath Uses Element of Surprise," *Washington Post*,

September 6, 1987. Israel also launched its largest airstrike during Operation Cast Lead on a day that was both a Jewish Sabbath and in the midst of Hanukkah; see Shay Fogelman, "Shock and Awe," *Ha'aretz*, December 31, 2010; Todd Venezia, "Hell Fire Rains on Gaza; Massive Israeli Airstrike; Bloodiest Hit in 60 Years; Just the 'Opening Stage,'" *New York Post*, December 28, 2008, 4. I thank Stuart Cohen and Noa Levanon Klein for drawing my attention to the timing of these attacks.

9. In William M. Lamers, *The Edge of Glory: A Biography of General William S. Rosecrans* (New York: Harcourt, Brace & World, 1961), 189; Roy J. Honeywell, *Chaplains of the United States Army* (Washington, DC: Office of the Chief of Chaplains, Department of the Army, 1958), 130–31.

10. In Steven E. Woodworth, *While God Is Marching On: The Religious World of Civil War Soldiers* (Lawrence: University of Kansas Press, 2001), 83, citing Tracy J. Power, *Lee's Miserables: Life in the Army of Northern Virginia from the Wilderness to Appomattox* (Chapel Hill: University of North Carolina Press, 1998), 4–5.

11. Herman A. Norton, *Struggling for Recognition: The United States Army Chaplaincy: 1791–1865* (Honolulu: University Press of the Pacific, 2004), 145–46.

12. Woodworth, *While God Is Marching On*, 83.

13. Lamers, *Edge of Glory*, 189.

14. Ibid., 188, 242, 338; James Lee McDonough, *Chattanooga: A Death Grip of the Confederacy* (Knoxville, University of Tennessee Press, 1984), 45.

15. Lamers, *Edge of Glory*, citing Rosecrans to Henry Halleck, telegraph of January 3, 1863.

16. Woodworth, *While God Is Marching On*, 78–79.

17. Ibid., 83, citing William McCarter, *My Life in the Irish Brigade: The Civil War Memoirs of Private William McCarter, 116th Pennsylvania Infantry*, edited by Kevin E. O'Brien (Campbell, CA: Savas, 1996), 71–72.

18. Gardiner H. Shattuck, *A Shield and Hiding Place: The Religious Life of the Civil War Armies* (Macon, GA: Mercer University Press 1987), 76, citing George B. McClellan, *McClellan's Own Story: The War for the Union* (New York: Charles L. Webster and Co., 1887), 355, 395, 402, 445; Oliver O. Howard, *Autobiography of Oliver Otis Howard, Major General United States Army*, Vol. 1 (Freeport, NY: Books for Libraries Press, 1971), 164–65.

19. Woodworth, *While God Is Marching On*, 80, citing Cyrus F. Boyd, *The Civil War Diary of Cyrus F. Boyd, Fifteenth Iowa Infantry, 1861–1863*, edited by Mildred Thorne (Millwood, NY: Kraus, 1977), 47.

20. Woodworth, *While God Is Marching On*, 80, citing Alfred Tyler Fielder, *The Civil War Diaries of Captain Alfred Tyler Fielder, 12th Tennessee Regiment Infantry, Company B, 1861–1865*, edited by Ann York Franklin (Louisville: self-published, 1996), 70.

21. Michael Snape, *The Royal Army Chaplains' Department 1796–1953: Clergy under Fire* (Woodbridge, UK: Boydell Press, 2008), 183, 194; Edward Madigan, *Faith under Fire: Anglican Army Chaplains and the Great War* (New York: Palgrave Macmillan, 2011), 172; William D. Cleary, "The Ministry of the Chaplain," in *Religion of Soldier and Sailor*, edited by Willard L. Sperry (Cambridge: Harvard University Press, 1945), 74.

22. Stephen Nissenbaum, *The Battle for Christmas* (New York: Alfred A. Knopf, 1996).

23. Malcolm Brown, "The Christmas Truce 1914: The British Story," in *Meetings in No Man's Land: Christmas Fraternization in the Great War*, edited by Mac Ferro, Malcolm Brown, Rémy Cazals, and Olaf Mueller (London: Constable & Robinson, 2007), 21.

24. Stanley Weintraub, *Silent Night: The Story of the World War I Christmas Truce* (New York: The Free Press, 2001), 5–7. Robert Axelrod devotes an entire chapter of *The Evolution of Cooperation* (New York: Basic Books, 2006), chap. 4, 73–87, to analyzing how these arrangements evolved.

25. Weintraub, Silent Night, 14–15, 25; Brown, "Christmas Truce 1914," 25.

26. As cited in Brown, "Christmas Truce 1914," 29.

27. Ibid., 32, 44–45, 51; Weintraub, Silent Night, 42, 61.

28. These include sporadic fraternization during Christmas in 1915 and, on the Eastern front, during Easter in 1916; Brown, "Christmas Truce 1914," 73.

29. I thank Jacob Shapiro for bringing these cases to my attention.

30. Duncan McLeod, "Operation Christmas," June 22, 2011, http://theinspirationroom.com/daily/2011/operation-christmas/.

31. Duncan McLeod, "Rivers of Light," June 25, 2012, http://theinspirationroom.com/daily/2012/rivers-of-light/; Laurel Wentz, "Columbia's 'Operation Bethlehem' Guides Guerrilla Fighters Out of Jungle," December 12, 2012, http://adage.com/article/global-news/colombia-s-op-bethlehem-guides-insurgents-jungle/238739/; Laurel Wentz, "This Christmas, Colombia Enlists Moms in Anti-Guerrilla Campaign," December 17, 2013, http://adage.com/article/global-news/christmas-colombia-enlists-moms-guerrilla-campaign/245691/.

32. Norman Davies, *Europe: A History* (New York: HarperCollins, 1998), 875–76.

33. Ivo Banac, *The National Question in Yugoslavia: Origins, History, Politics* (Ithaca: Cornell University Press, 1988), 403.

34. Mitja Velikonja, *Religious Separation and Political Intolerance in Bosnia-Herzegovina* (College Station: Texas A&M Press, 2003), 99–100.

35. Michael Tierney, *Eoin MacNeill: Scholar and Man of Action, 1867–1945* (Oxford: Clarendon Press, 1980), 199–214; Jonathan Githens-Mazer, *Myths and Memories of the Easter Rising: Cultural and Political Nationalism in Ireland* (Portland, OR: Irish Academic Press, 2006), 113; William J. Brennan-Whitmore, *Dublin Burning: The Easter Rising from behind the Barricades* (Dublin: Gill & Macmillan, 1996), 13.

36. Jeffrey Halverson, Harold L. Goodall Jr., and Steven R. Corman, *Master Narratives of Islamic Extremism* (New York: Palgrave Macmillan, 2011), 81–94.

37. Fouad Ibrahim, "*Al-Shahada:* A Centre of the Shiite System of Belief," in *Dying for Faith: Religiously Motivated Violence in the Contemporary World*, edited by Madawi Al-Rasheed and Marat Shterin (London: I. B. Tauris, 2009), 117; Manochehr Dorraj, "Symbolic and Utilitarian Political Value of a Tradition: Martyrdom in the Iranian Political Culture," *Review of Politics* 59, no. 3 (1997): 502–53; Chibli Mallat, "Religious Militancy in Contemporary Iraq: Muhammad Baqer as-Sadr and the Sunni-Shia Paradigm," *Third World Quarterly* 10, no. 2 (1988), 724.

38. As a direct consequence, Ireland is the only country that does not commemorate its independence day on a fixed date in the calendar but moves the commemoration in conjunction with the religious calendar; the proclamation of the Irish Republic is commemorated on Easter Monday every year, regardless of whether this coincides with April 25, the date on which the Easter Rising occurred in 1916.

39. I thank Gideon Aran for drawing my attention to these ambivalent connotations. Israeli Defense Minister Moshe Dayan observed, "Henceforth, Yom Kippur would take on added solemnity." *Story of My Life* (New York: William Morrow, 1976), 473. See also Charles S. Liebman and Eliezer Don-Yehiya, *Civil Religion in Israel* (Berkeley: University of California Press, 1983), 168–69.

40. At the extremes, the civil-religious significance of war can overshadow and even subsume the initial religious significance of the date. We might call this the "Crispin Effect": although initially the occasion of St. Crispin's Day may have lent some significance to the Battle of Agincourt, in English narratives the sacred day now derives its significance from the battle.

41. Qur'an, Surah 3, verses 13, 123–25; Surah 8.

42. Taha El Magdoub Hassan El Badri and Mohammed Dia El Din Zohdy, *The Ramadan War, 1973* (Dunn Loring, VA: T. N. Dupuy, 1978), 48; Insight Team of the London Sunday Times, *The Yom Kippur War* (Garden City, NY: Doubleday, 1974), 75.

43. For example, the terrorists mounted a fake license plate to the vehicle used in the attack with the number AZ H 314 to commemorate the 314 warriors who fought alongside Muhammad at the Battle of Badr. Madawi Al-Rasheed, "Rituals of Life and Death: The Politics and Poetics of *Jihad* in Saudi Arabia," in *Dying for Faith: Religiously Motivated Violence in the Contemporary World*, edited by Madawi Al-Rasheed and Marat Shterin (London: I. B. Tauris, 2009), 82–83.

44. Jubin M. Goodzari, *Syria and Iran: Diplomatic Alliance and Power Politics in the Middle East* (London: I. B. Tauris, 2006), 69–70; Joana Dodds and Benjamin Wilson, "The Iran-Iraq War: Will without Means," in *Conflict and Insurgency in the Contemporary Middle East*, edited by Barry Rubin (New York: Routledge, 2009), 56.

45. Elliott Horowitz, "The Rite to Be Reckless: On the Perpetration and Interpretation of Purim Violence," *Poetics Today* 15, no. 1 (1994): 9–54.

46. Elliott Horowitz, *Reckless Rites: Purim and the Legacy of Jewish Violence* (Princeton: Princeton University Press, 2006); Jerold Auerbach, *Hebron Jews: Memory and Conflict in the Land of Israel* (Lanham, MD: Rowman and Littlefield, 2009), 137–38.

47. Mike Guzofsky, quoted in Geoffrey Paul and Jenni Frazer, "From Brooklyn to Kirya Arba," *Jewish Chronicle* (London), March 4, 1994.

48. In Josephus Flavius, *Against Apion*, translated by John M. G. Barclay (Leiden: Brill, 2007), Book 1, Part 22.

49. First Maccabees 2:41 (King James Version).

50. A *pa* is a Maori fortification. Tom Brooking, *Milestones—Turning Points in New Zealand History* (Wellington: Mills Publications, 1988), 69; Tim Ryan and Bill Parham, *The Colonial New Zealand Wars* (Wellington: Grantham House Publishing, 1986), 27. Along similar lines, Native American leaders are said to have exploited the routine Sunday observance of seventeenth-century colonial settlers to attack their families on the way to church or destroy their properties while they were attending services; Parker C. Thompson, *From Its European Antecedents to 1791: The United States Army Chaplaincy* (Honolulu: University Press of the Pacific, 2004), 18.

51. Thomas Schelling, "Foreword," in Roberta Wohlstetter, *Pearl Harbor: Warning and Decision* (Stanford: Stanford University Press, 1962), vii.

52. James William Morley, ed., *Japan's Road to the Pacific War, vol. 5: The Final Confrontation: Japan's Negotiations with the United States, 1941,* translated by David Anson Titus (New York: Columbia University Press, 1994), 322–23. See also Ian Kershaw,

Fateful Choices: Ten Decisions That Changed the World, 1940–1941 (New York: Penguin Group, 2007), 372; John Toland, *The Rising Sun: The Decline and Fall of the Japanese Empire, 1936–1945* (New York: Modern Library, 2003), 183.

53. Mitsuo Fuchida, "I Led the Air Attack on Pearl Harbor," *Reader's Digest* 64, February 1954, 944, quoted in Roberta Wohlstetter, *Pearl Harbor: Warning and Decision* (Stanford: Stanford University Press, 1962), 378.

54. Nathan Miller, *War at Sea: A Naval History of World War II* (Oxford: Oxford University Press, 1997), 198.

55. In Dorothy Perkins, *Japan Goes to War: A Chronology of Japanese Military Expansion from the Meiji Era to the Attack on Pearl Harbor, 1868–1941* (Collingdale, PA: Diane Publishing, 1997), 168.

56. Robert L. Gushwa, *The Best and Worst of Times: The United States Army Chaplaincy 1920–1945* (Honolulu: University Press of the Pacific, 2004), 102.

57. Edwin T. Layton, Roger Pineau, and John Costello, *I Was There: Pearl Harbor and Midway: Breaking the Secrets* (New York: William Morrow, 1985), 309.

58. Carl Smith and Adam Hook, *Pearl Harbor, 1941: The Day of Infamy* (Sterling Heights, MI: Osprey Publishing, 1999), 21–22.

59. Cecil B. Currey, *Victory at Any Cost: The Genius of Viet Nam's Gen. Vo Nguyen Giap* (Washington, DC: Brassey's, 1997). For dissenting opinions that emphasize a political rationale for the choice of date, see Ronnie E. Ford, *Tet 1968: Understanding the Surprise* (London: Frank Cass, 1995), 126; Ang Cheng Guan, "Decision-Making Leading to the Tet Offensive (1968)—The Vietnamese Communist Perspective," *Journal of Contemporary History* 33, no. 3 (1998): 341–53.

60. In James J. Wirtz, *The Tet Offensive* (Ithaca: Cornell University Press, 1991), 110.

61. William C. Westmoreland, *A Soldier Reports* (New York: Dell Publishing, 1976), 106–7.

62. Ibid., 424; Wirtz, *Tet Offensive*, 221; James H. Willbanks, *The Tet Offensive: A Concise History* (New York: Columbia University Press, 2007), 32; Pham Van Son, ed., *The Viet Cong "Tet" Offensive 1968* (Saigon: Republic of Vietnam Armed Forces Printing and Publication Center, 1968), 387, 419; Ford, *Tet 1968*, 103.

63. Wirtz, *Tet Offensive*, 221.

64. Willbanks, *Tet Offensive*, 26; Son, *Viet Cong "Tet" Offensive 1968*, 53.

65. Pham, *Viet Cong "Tet" Offensive 1968*, 362.

66. Muhamed Borogovac, *The War in Bosnia 1992–1995* (Boston: Bosnian Congress, 1995), Pt. 5, Chap. 6.

67. Carl Savich, "Srebrenica: The Untold Story," September 4, 2005, http://www.serbianna.com/columns/savich/051.shtml.

68. Franklin D. Roosevelt, "Day of Infamy Speech," delivered to a joint session of Congress, December 8, 1941.

69. Emily S Rosenberg, *A Date Which Will Live: Pearl Harbor in American Memory* (Durham: Duke University Press, 2003), 31, 33.

70. Hilary Conroy and Harry Wray, *Pearl Harbor Reexamined: Prologue to the Pacific War* (Honolulu: University of Hawaii Press, 1990), 123.

71. The executive officer of the *U.S.S. Enterprise*, for example, accompanied the first raids against the Japanese Navy in the central Pacific with the verse "an eye for an eye, a tooth for a tooth, this Sunday it's our turn to shoot." Miller, *War at Sea,*

233–34; John B. Lundstrom, *The First Team: Pacific Naval Air Combat from Pearl Harbor to Midway* (Annapolis: Naval Institute Press, 2005), 63.

72. Pham, *Viet Cong "Tet" Offensive 1968*, 13–14.

73. Abba Eban, *An Autobiography* (New York: Random House, 1977), 504. See also Linda Greenhouse "News of Conflict Given at Yom Kippur Prayers," *New York Times*, October 7, 1973.

74. Daniel J. Elazar, "United States of America: Overview," in *The Yom Kippur War: Israel and the Jewish People*, edited by Moshe Davis (New York: Arno Press, 1974), 11.

75. Yoram Hazony, "Israel's Right and Left Converge," *New York Times*, April 26, 2002, 29.

76. In Joel Brinkley, "Mideast Turmoil: Mideast; Bomb Kills at Least 19 in Israel as Arabs Meet over Peace Plan," *New York Times*, March 28, 2002, 1.

77. Joel Brinkley and Serge Schmemann, "Mideast Turmoil: The Fighting; Sharon Calls Arafat an Enemy and Sends Tanks to Isolate Him at Headquarters in Ramallah," *New York Times*, March 29, 2002, 1; Michael R. Gordon, "Mideast Turmoil: Strategy; Limits of Force: Superior Israeli Firepower Isn't Likely to End Terror," *New York Times*, April 14, 2002, 16; Matt Rees, "The Battle of Jenin," *Time Magazine*, May 13, 2002.

78. Noam Dvir, "Four People Killed in Terror Attack at Jerusalem Synagogue," *Yedioth Ahronoth*, November 18, 2014, http://www.ynetnews.com/articles/0,7340,L-4593099,00.html, accessed November 18, 2014.

79. Ron E. Hassner, "Fighting Insurgency on Sacred Ground," *Washington Quarterly* 29, no. 2 (2006), 158–59; C. Christine Fair, "The Golden Temple: A Tale of Two Sieges," in *Treading on Sacred Ground*, edited by Sumit Ganguly and C. Christine Fair, 37–65 (Oxford: Oxford University Press, 2008).

80. Mark Tully and Satish Jacob, *Amritsar: Mrs. Gandhi's Last Battle* (London: Jonathan Cape, 1985).

81. For example, Jews can observe up to fifty-five primary holy days a year in addition to the weekly Sabbath; some Muslims venerate as many as thirty-six holy days (including the month-long Ramadan fast) in addition to attending congregational prayers on Fridays; and according to some Catholic and Orthodox Christian calendars, nearly every day of the year is associated with a saint, above and beyond Sunday observance and the veneration of major holy days. See Cyril Glassé, *The New Encyclopedia of Islam* (Lanham, MD: Rowman & Littlefield, 2008), 109–10; Leo Trepp, *The Complete Book of Jewish Observances* (New York: Behrman House, 1980), 88–90; Catholic Church, International Committee on English in the Liturgy, *General Instruction of the Roman Missal* (Washington, D.C.: United States Conference of Bishops, 2003); Archbishop Dmitri Royster, trans., *The Priest's Service Book* (Dallas: Diocese of the South Orthodox Church in America, 2003).

82. William Manchester, *Goodbye, Darkness: A Memoir of the Pacific War* (Boston: Back Bay, 2002), 355. See also George Feifer, *The Battle of Okinawa: The Blood and the Bomb* (Guilford, CT: Globe Pequot, 2001), 106.

83. A historical precedent that may have inspired Giap, the successful attack by the Vietnamese General Quang Trung against the Chinese during Tet in 1789, and the decision by the North Vietnamese leaders to advance their celebration of Tet by one day lend further credence to the claim that Giap intentionally exploited the sacred

day; Clark Dougan and Stephen Weiss, eds., *Nineteen Sixty-Eight* (Boston: Boston Publishing, 1983), 11.

84. Currey, *Victory at Any Cost*, xix–xx.

85. Anwar el-Sadat, *In Search of Identity: An Autobiography* (New York: Harper & Row, 1977), 241.

86. Mohammed Abdel Ghani El-Gamasy, *The October War: Memoirs of Field Marshal El-Gamasy of Egypt* (Cairo: American University in Cairo Press, 1993), 181.

87. Saad el Shazly, *The Crossing of the Suez* (San Francisco: American Mideast Research, 2003), 36.

88. On concerns that a mobilization on Yom Kippur would lead to panic, see Uri Bar-Joseph, *The Angel: Ashraf Marwan, the Mossad, and the Yom Kippur War* [in Hebrew] (Or Yehuda, Israel: Kinneret, Zmaora-Bitan, Dvir, 2010), 242, 246.

89. In Eli Zeira, *The October 73 War: Myth against Reality* [in Hebrew] (Tel Aviv: Yedi'oth Ahronot, 1993), 141, my translation.

90. D. K. Palit, *Return to Sinai: The Arab Offensive, October 1973* (New Delhi: Lancer Publishers & Distributors, 2002),77; Chaim Herzog, *The War of Atonement* (Jerusalem: Steimatzky's Agency, 1975), 64–65, 72, 172; A. J. Barker, *Yom Kippur War* (New York: Ballantine's, 1974), 42, 69, 93; Abraham Rabinovich, *The Yom Kippur War: The Epic Encounter That Transformed the Middle East* (New York: Schocken Books, 2004), 97–99.

91. Golda Meir, *My Life* (Jerusalem: Steimatzky's Agency, 1975), 355; Insight Team of the London Sunday Times, *Yom Kippur War,* 115, 136.

92. Rabinovich, *The Yom Kippur War*, 100; Barker, *Yom Kippur War*, 43.

93. Walter Laqueur, *Confrontation: The Middle East and World Politics* (New York: Quadrangle/New York Times Books, 1974), 89; Ariel Sharon and David Chanoff, *Warrior: The Autobiography of Ariel Sharon* (New York: Simon and Schuster, 1989), 289; Insight Team of the London Sunday Times, *Yom Kippur War,* 76; Rabinovich, *The Yom Kippur War*, 46, 99.

94. Eban, *Autobiography* (New York: Random House, 1977), 504; Insight Team of the London Sunday Times, *Yom Kippur War,* 76; Rabinovich, *The Yom Kippur War*, 46. Donald Neff, *Warriors against Israel: How Israel Won the Battle to Become America's Ally* (Brattleboro, Vt.: Amana Books, 1988), 164.

95. Rabinovich, *The Yom Kippur War*, 129; Herzog, *The War of Atonement*, 54, 85–88, 98; Sharon and Chanoff, *Warrior*, 303; Michael I. Handel, "Crisis and Surprise in Three Arab-Israeli Wars," in *Strategic Military Surprise: Incentives and Opportunities,* edited by Klaus Knorr and Patrick Morgan (New Brunswick: Transaction Books, 1983), 137, 145n. 62.

96. El-Gamasy, *October War,* 181. See also Handel, "Crisis and Surprise," 137.

97. Uri Bar-Joseph, *The Watchman Fell Asleep: The Surprise of Yom Kippur and Its Sources* (Albany: SUNY Press, 2005), 167, 247, citing Research Department report of 11 a.m. on October 5, 1973, par. 26f.

98. Qur'an, Surah 3, verses 13, 123–25; Surah 8.

99. Henry Kissinger and Muhammad Hassanain Haikal, "Kissinger Meets Haikal," *Journal of Palestine Studies* 3, no. 2 (1974), 219–20; El-Gamasy, *October War,* 181.

100. Such a misreading of Ramadan was not without parallel. During the Iran-Iraq War, Saddam Hussein approached Ayatollah Khomeini with a proposal to cease fighting during Ramadan. His suggestion was greeted with jeers from the Iranian

mullahs, who pointed out that Ramadan was not one of the three sacred (*haram*) months in which fighting was prohibited but a blessed (*mubarak*) month in which Muslims had a particular inspiration and incentive to fight. Akbar Hashemi Rafsanjani, *Dar maktab-i jum'a: Majmu'a-yi khutbaha-yi namaz-i jum'a-yi Tehran*, Vol. 3, 12/4/60 (Tehran: Ministry of Islamic Guidance, 1365/1987), 274, cited in Saskia Gieling, *Religion and War in Revolutionary Iran* (London: I. B. Tauris, 1999), 165.

101. Bar-Joseph, *Watchman Fell Asleep,* 165–70, citing Research Department report of 11 a.m. on October 5, 1973, pars. 20 and 39.

3. Where? Sacred Space and War

1. The Protocols of the Geneva Convention, adopted in 1977, long after the events analyzed in this chapter, made additional demands on how armies should treat such sites in case of doubt and prohibited reprisals against cultural objects and places of worship.

2. Ron E. Hassner, "At the Horns of the Altar: Counterinsurgency and the Roots of the Sanctuary Practice," *Civil Wars*. 61, no. 1 (2007): 131–52.

3. Ron E. Hassner, *War on Sacred Grounds* (Ithaca: Cornell University Press, 2009).

4. Tom Johnstone and James Hagerty, *The Cross on the Sword: Catholic Chaplains in the Forces* (London: Geoffrey Chapman, 1996), 152–53.

5. Simon Sebag Montefiore, *Jerusalem: The Biography* (New York: Alfred Knopf, 2011), 434, 436, citing John Grigg, *Lloyd George: War Leader* (London: Penguin, 2002), 339–43; Ronald Storrs, *Orientations* (London: I. Nicholson & Watson, 1943), 303–5.

6. Montefiore, *Jerusalem,* 517–19, citing Queen Noor, *Leap of Faith: Memoirs of an Unexpected Life* (New York: Miramax Books, 2005), 75–77.

7. Annette Becker, *War and Faith: The Religious Imagination in France, 1914–1930*, translated by Helen Mc Phail (Oxford: Berg Publishers, 1998), 63.

8. Peter Liddle, John Bourne, and Ian Whitehead, eds., *The Great World War: 1914–1945, vol. 2: The People's Experience* (London: HarperCollins, 2001), 401, 414; Edward Madigan, *Faith under Fire: Anglican Army Chaplains and the Great War* (New York: Palgrave Macmillan, 2011), 187; Michael Snape, *God and the British Soldier: Religion and the British Army in the First and Second World Wars* (London: Routledge, 2005), 43.

9. Snape, *God and the British Soldier*, 44–45; Paul Fussell, *The Great War and Modern Memory* (Oxford: Oxford University Press, 2000), 40, 132–34.

10. Liddle, Bourne, and Whitehead, *Great World War,* 414, citing the *Daily Mail*, December 31, 1940, 3, and Peter Donnelly, ed., *Mrs. Milburn's Diaries: An Englishwoman's Day-to-Day Reflections, 1939–45* (Glasgow, UK: Fontana, 1980), 80.

11. Helen Jones, *British Civilians in the Front Line: Air Raids, Productivity and Wartime Culture, 1939–45* (Manchester: Manchester University Press, 2006), 67; Vere Hodgson, *Few Eggs and No Oranges: Vere Hodgson's Diary, 1940–45* (London: Persephone, 1976), 250.

12. In Susan Briggs, *The Home Front: War Years in Britain 1939–1945* (London: George Weidenfeld and Nicolson, 1975), 68.

13. In Max Hastings, "The Blitz's Iconic Image," *Daily Mail* (London), December 31, 2010, http://www.dailymail.co.uk/news/article-1342305/The-Blitzs-iconic-image-On-70th-anniversary-The-Mail-tells-story-picture-St-Pauls.html, accessed March 2014.

14. In Constantine FitzGibbon, *Winter of the Bombs: The Story of the Blitz in London* (New York: W. W. Norton, 1957), 214.

15. Terry Ashwood, "Guardians of St. Paul's" British Pathé, film 1578.23 (August 7, 1944), http://www.britishpathe.com/video/guardians-of-st-pauls-aka-guardians-of-st-pauls.

16. Vanessa Chambers, "'Defend Us from All Perils and Dangers of This Night': Coping with Bombing in Britain during the Second World War," in *Bombing, States, and Peoples in Western Europe 1940–1945,* edited by Claudia Baldoli, Andrew Knapp, and Richard Overy (London: Continuum, 2011), 157–58.

17. Richard Overy, *The Bombers and the Bombed: Allied Air War over Europe: 1940–1945* (New York: Viking, 2014), 436.

18. George Washington enforced such orders in Canada, as did Wellington during the Peninsular Wars; Parker C. Thompson, *From Its European Antecedents to 1791: The United States Army Chaplaincy* (Honolulu: University Press of the Pacific, 2004), 122; Michael Snape, *The Redcoat and Religion: The Forgotten History of the British Soldier from the Age of Marlborough to the Eve of the First World War* (London: Routledge, 2005), 214–15, citing Philip Guedalla, *The Duke* (Ware, UK: Wordsworth Editions, 1997), 163; Richard Holmes, *Redcoat* (London: HarperCollins, 2001), 355–56.

19. Michael Snape, *The Royal Army Chaplains' Department 1796–1953: Clergy under Fire* (Woodbridge, UK: Boydell Press, 2008), 233, 334; Duff Crerar, *Padres in No Man's Land: Canadian Chaplains and the Great War* (Montreal: McGill-Queen's University Press, 1995), 111, 139; and Albrecht Schuebel, *300 Jahre Evangelische Soldatenseelsorge* (Munich: Evangelischer Pressverband, 1964), 103.

20. American Commission for the Protection and Salvage of Artistic and Historic Monuments in War Areas, *Report of the American Commission for the Protection and Salvage of Artistic and Historic Monuments in War Areas* (Washington, D.C.: U.S. Government Historical Reports on War Administration, 1946), [henceforth: REAC], 62–63, 104.

21. Snape, *God and the British Soldier,* 36–37; Donald F. Crosby, *Battlefield Chaplains: Catholic Priests in World War II* (Lawrence: University Press of Kansas 1994), 180.

22. David Hapgood and David Richardson, *Monte Cassino* (New York: Congdon and Weed, 1984), 199, citing Intelligence annex to Operations Order 341, signed by Arthur M. Clark, lieutenant-colonel, Air Corps.

23. U.S. artillery missed its target but set the roof of the Camposanto cemetery ablaze, destroying its early Renaissance frescoes; Robert M. Edsel, *Saving Italy: The Race to Rescue a Nation's Treasures from the Nazis* (New York: W. W. Norton, 2013), 179–83.

24. The card files of the American Commission for the Protection and Salvage of Artistic and Historical Monuments in War Areas contain detailed records of churches exploited in this manner, as well as structures spared despite their use by the enemy. See, for example, files for Echtz (Germany), Muenchen-Gladbach (Germany), Wuerzburg (Germany), all in the Records of the American Commission

for the Protection and Salvage of Artistic and Historical Monuments in War Areas (The Roberts Commission), 1943–1946 [henceforth: RAC], Control Card File for Borrowed Photographs of Cultural Institutions and Artwork in Europe and Other War Areas, National Archives (NARA), A1, Entry 64A, http://www.archives.gov/research/holocaust/finding-aid/civilian/rg-239.html; REAC, 72, 100; Hapgood and Richardson, *Monte Cassino*, 30.

25. REAC, 117; RAC, Memoranda, Commission Memoranda, "Memo from Webb, Office of War Information," n.d., 4; Robert M. Edsel, *The Monuments Men: Allied Heros, Nazi Thieves, and the Greatest Treasure Hunt in History* (New York: Center Street, 2009), 79, 84, 107, 109.

26. Anthony C. Grayling, *Among the Dead Cities: The History and Moral Legacy of the WWII Bombing of Civilians in Germany and Japan* (New York: Walker, 2006), 46; Richard Overy, *Bombers and the Bombed*, 103–6; Randall Hansen, *Fire and Fury: The Allied Bombing of Germany, 1942–1945* (London: NAL Caliber, 2009), 22.

27. Hansen, *Fire and Fury*, esp. 66, 70, 110, 115, 148–49.

28. Ibid., 23, citing Portal papers, "Memorandum from Portal to Churchill," written September 21, 1940, and sent September 25, 1940.

29. Max Hastings, *Bomber Command: The Myths and Realities of the Strategic Bombing Offensive, 1939–1945* (New York: The Dial Press, 1979), 127–28, citing Memorandum by Professor Frederick Lindemann, later Baron Cherwell.

30. Stephen A. Garrett, *Ethics and Airpower in World War II: The British Bombing of German Cities* (New York: St. Martin's, 1993), 96–97.

31. Hansen, *Fire and Fury*, 161, 166, citing PRO AIR 2/7852, Letter to the Undersecretary of State, Air Ministry, October 25, 1943, and PRO AIR 2/7852, Letter from Air Ministry to Harris, n.d.

32. Bryce Committee, "Report of the Committee on Alleged German Outrages," http://www.firstworldwar.com/source/brycereport.htm, accessed March 2014.

33. From Frank A. Mumby, ed., *The Great World War: A History*, Vol. 1 (London: Gresham Publishing, 1915), esp. 93–94, 128.

34. Albert Marrin, *The Last Crusade: The Church of England in the First World War* (Durham: Duke University Press, 1974), 89, citing Harkwicke D. Rawnsley, "Louvain, August 25, 1914," in *The European War, 1914–1915: Poems* (1915), 50; Alan Wilkinson, *The Church of England and the First World War* (Southampton, UK: Camelot Press, 1978), 46.

35. Becker, *War and Faith*, 15, 78; Mumby, *Great World War*, 146–47; Philip Jenkins, *The Great and Holy War: How World War I Became a Religious Crusade* (New York: HarperCollins, 2014), 91.

36. Andy Rooney, *My War* (New York: Public Affairs, 2008), 249.

37. Stephan Glienke, "The Allied Air War and German Society," in *Bombing, States, and Peoples in Western Europe 1940–1945,* edited by Claudia Baldoli, Andrew Knapp, and Richard Overy (London: Continuum, 2011), 193.

38. Edsel, *Monuments Men*, 33; Lynn H. Nicholas, *The Rape of Europa: The Fate of Europe's Treasures in the Third Reich and the Second World War* (New York: Alfred A. Knopf, 1994), 248.

39. Edsel, *Saving Italy*, 53.

40. Hadley Cantril, ed., *Public Opinion: 1935–1946* (Princeton: Princeton University Press), 1069, question 37.

41. Richard T. Howard, "Yes, It's Worth It," *Sunday Express* (London), January 5, 1941, 6.

42. In "Vicar's 'Blood Up,'" *Daily Mirror* (London), January 2, 1941, 3.

43. In Russel Jones and John H. Swanson, eds., *Dear Helen: Wartime Letters from a Londoner to Her American Pen Pal* (Columbia: University of Missouri Press, 2009), 145–47.

44. In Godfrey Winn, *Sunday Express* (London), November 17, 1940.

45. Edsel, *Saving Italy,* 34, citing Arthur Harris, *Bomber Offensive* (Barnsley, UK: Pen & Sword Military Classics, 2005), 51, and *Air Marshal Arthur Harris Speaks about RAF Bomber Command's Strategic Offensive against Germany*, 35 mm film Imperial War Museum, London, RAF Film Production Unit, June 3, 1942.

46. Rooney, *My War,* 85–87.

47. In Grayling, *Among the Dead Cities*, 53, 173.

48. Garrett, *Ethics and Airpower,* 12, citing Churchill's speech to the House of Commons, October 8, 1940.

49. Grayling, *Among the Dead Cities*, p.45, citing Charles K. Webster and Noble Frankland, *The Strategic Air Offensive against Germany, 1939–1945* (London: H. M. Stationery Off., 1961), no page number listed.

50. Garrett, *Ethics and Airpower,* 11.

51. Grayling, *Among the Dead Cities*, 43, 45, 192; Overy, *Bombers and the Bombed,* 58; Garrett, ibid., 11, 103.

52. Raleigh Trevelyan, *Rome '44: The Battle for the Eternal City* (New York: Viking Press, 1982), 24–25; Robert Katz, *The Battle for Rome* (New York: Simon & Schuster, 2003), 14–16.

53. "Memorandum by Ray Atherton, Acting Chief of the Division of European Affairs, to the Under Secretary of State Welles, March 8, 1943," 916, in *Foreign Relations of the United States* [henceforth: *FRUS*], *1943, vol. II: Europe* (Washington, DC: U.S. Government Printing Office); Overy, *Bombers and the Bombed,* 335, citing British National Archives, AIR 19/215, RAF Delegation, Washington, DC, to Air Ministry, June 26, 1943.

54. In Grayling, *Among the Dead Cities*, 51.

55. Todd Leventhal, *Iraqi Propaganda and Disinformation during the Gulf War: Lessons from the Future* (Abu Dhabi: The Emirates Center for Strategic Studies and Research, 1999).

56. David E. Sanger and Helene Cooper, "Iran Confirms Existence of Nuclear Plant," *New York Times*, September 25, 2009.

57. Hapgood and Richardson, *Monte Cassino*, 26.

58. See for example "'Memorandum of Conversation' between Sumner Welles and the British Ambassador to the United States, Viscount Halifax, February 18, 1942," 791–92; "Message from U.S. Secretary of State, Cordell Hull to President Franklin Roosevelt, December 3, 1942," 793; "Message from the U.S. Ambassador in the United Kingdom, John Gilbert Winant, to the Secretary of State, Cordell Hull, December 8, 1942," 794; and "Message from the British Ambassador in the United States, Viscount Halifax, to the U.S. Secretary of State, Cordell Hull, December 22, 1942," 798–99, in *FRUS, 1942, vol. III: Europe* (Washington, DC: U.S. Government Printing Office).

59. Overy, *Bombers and the Bombed,* 333–35, citing British National Archives, Air 8/436, Portal to Cardogan, Permanent Secretary, Foreign Office, October 26, 1941;

citing British National Archives, Air 19/215, Sinclair marginalia on "Bombing of Targets in Rome," December 1942; and citing British National Archives, AIR 9/215, Sinclair to Temple, July 17, 1943.

60. Ronald Schaffer, *Wings of Judgment: American Bombing in World War II* (New York: Oxford University Press, 1985), 44–45, citing Minutes of Meeting, 99th Meeting of the Combined Chiefs of Staff, June 25, 1943, file CCS 373.11 Rome (6-10-43), sec. 1, RG 218, NARA.

61. "Message from Titmann to the U.S. Secretary of State, Cordell Hull, January 5, 1943," 911, in *FRUS, 1943, vol. II.*

62. Cantril, *Public Opinion,* 1068–69, questions 31, 32, 35.

63. See for example "Messages of Amleto Cicognani, Apostolic Delegate to the United States, to Myron C. Taylor, Personal Representative of President Roosevelt to Pope Pius XII, June 25, 1943 and June 28, 1943," 920–23; "Message from Amleto Cicognani, Apostolic Delegate to the United States, to Myron C. Taylor, Personal Representative of President Roosevelt to Pope Pius XII, July 15, 1943," 928; "Memorandum from the Apostolic Delegation at Washington to the Department of State, August 18, 1943," 944–45; and "Memorandum from the Apostolic Delegation at Washington to the Department of State, August 20, 1943," 945–46, in *FRUS, 1943, vol. II.*

64. "Message from Pope Pius XII to President Roosevelt, May 19, 1943," 917, in *FRUS, 1943, vol. II.*

65. Overy, *Bombers and the Bombed,* 334; Quentin Reynolds, *The Amazing Mr. Doolittle: A Biography of Lieutenant General James H. Doolittle* (New York: Appleton-Century-Crofts, 1953), 262–63.

66. Message from Churchill to Roosevelt, C-302, June 10, 1943, in *Churchill & Roosevelt: The Complete Correspondence,* Vol. 2, edited by Warren F. Kimball (Princeton: Princeton University Press, 1984), 234.

67. Message from Roosevelt to Churchill, R-285, June 14, 1943, in *Churchill & Roosevelt: The Complete Correspondence,* Vol. 2, edited by Warren F. Kimball (Princeton: Princeton University Press, 1984), 250–51.

68. "Message from President Roosevelt to pope Pius XII, June 16, 1943," 919–20, in *FRUS, 1943, vol. II.*

69. Message from Roosevelt to Churchill, R-287, June 15, 1943, in *Churchill & Roosevelt: The Complete Correspondence,* Vol. 2, edited by Warren F. Kimball (Princeton: Princeton University Press, 1984), 250–51.

70. Message from Churchill to Roosevelt, C-321, June 19, 1943 in *Churchill & Roosevelt: The Complete Correspondence,* Vol. 2, edited by Warren F. Kimball (Princeton: Princeton University Press, 1984), 265.

71. "Message of Amleto Cicognani, Apostolic Delegate to the United States, to Myron C. Taylor, Personal Representative of President Roosevelt to Pope Pius XII, June 25, 1943," 921, in *FRUS, 1943, vol. II.*

72. "Memorandum by President Franklin D. Roosevelt to the Secretary of State, June 28, 1943," 923, in *FRUS, 1943, vol. II.*

73. Message from Roosevelt to Churchill, R-313, July 9, 1943, in *Churchill & Roosevelt: The Complete Correspondence,* Vol. 2, edited by Warren F. Kimball (Princeton: Princeton University Press, 1984), 319–20.

74. Reynolds, *Amazing Mr. Doolittle*, 263–64; Gordon C. Zahn, *Chaplains in the RAF: A Study in Role Tension* (Manchester: University of Manchester Press, 1969), 127–28, 191n. 4.

75. Edsel, *Saving Italy*, 33, citing Conrad Crane, *Bombs, Cities, and Civilians: American Airpower Strategy in World War II* (Lawrence: University Press of Kansas, 1993), 94.

76. "Rome: Precision Bombing Problem Was What to Hit Also What Not to Hit," in *Impact: The Army Air Forces' Confidential Picture History of World War II*, Vol. 2 (New York: James Parton, 1980), 43–44.

77. REAC, 68–69.

78. Richard McMillan, *Twenty Angels over Rome: The Story of Fascist Italy's Fall* (London: Jarrolds, 1944), 23.

79. Cyrus L. Sulzberger, "Clark Order Prohibits 5th Army from Attacking Church Property," *New York Times*, January 29, 1944.

80. Reynolds, *Amazing Mr. Doolittle*, 263–64.

81. In Hapgood and Richardson, *Monte Cassino*, 85.

82. Schaffer, *Wings of* Judgment, 46.

83. Edsel, *Saving Italy*, 40, citing Report on Conversation with Herbert Matthews, NARA, M1944, Roll 57.

84. Schaffer, *Wings of Judgment*, 46; Trevelyan, *Rome '44*, 11; REAC, 68–69.

85. Edsel, *Saving Italy*, 12–15.

86. "Message from Pope Pius XII to President Roosevelt, July 20, 1943," 931–33, in *FRUS*, 1943, vol. II.

87. "Message from the Cardinal Secretary of State, Luigi Maglione, to Harold H. Tittmann, Assistant to the Personal Representative of President Roosevelt to Pope Pius XII, August 15, 1943," 942, in *FRUS, 1943, vol. II.*

88. "Message from Tittmann to the Secretary of State, Cordell Hull, July 27 and 31, 1943," 934, 937, in *FRUS, 1943, vol. II.*

89. "Message from the Combined Chiefs of Staff to the Commander in Chief of the Allied Forces in North Africa, December 15, 1943," 952–53, in *FRUS, 1943, vol. II.*

90. Schaffer, *Wings of Judgement*, 45–46; Reynolds, *Amazing Mr. Doolittle*, 264.

91. Crane, *Bombs, Cities, and Civilians*, 59–61; "Rome," 43–44.

92. Trevelyan, *Rome '44*, 142.

93. Overy, *Bombers and the Bombed*, 336.

94. Dan Kurzman, *The Race for Rome* (Garden City, NY: Doubleday, 1975), 83–84, 94.

95. Bishop of Chichester, UK Parliamentary Debate, House of Lords, February 9, 1944.

96. U.K. Parliamentary Debate, House of Lords, February 16, 1944.

97. Edsel, *Saving Italy*, 49, 88–89, 135, citing Karl Wolff, "Niederschrift über meine Besprechungen mit Adolf Hitler," Munich, March 28, 1972, http://www.ptwf.org.

98. Nicholas, *Rape of Europa*, 247, citing the *New York Times*, March 13, 1944.

99. See, for example, "Message from the Secretary of State to Diplomatic Representatives in the American Republics, March 18, 1944," 1988, in *FRUS, 1944, vol. IV: Europe* (Washington, DC: U.S. Government Printing Office); Trevelyan, *Rome '44*, 179.

100. "Message from the Secretary of State to Mr. Harrold Tittmann, Assistant to the Personal Representative of President Roosevelt to Pope Pius XII, March 17, 1944," 1287, *FRUS, 1944, vol. IV.*

101. Cantril, *Public Opinion*, 1069, question 41.

102. In Edsel, *Saving Italy,* 135.

103. Nicholas, *Rape of Europa*, 248.

104. Similar commissions functioned, on a smaller scale, in Britain, France, and Belgium. The most significant of these was the British Committee for the Preservation and Restitution of Works of Art, Archives, and Other Material in Enemy Hands, also known as the MacMillan Committee. The primary focus of these committees, unlike the Roberts Commission, was on restitution and reparation. They left the question of protecting monuments to military authorities. A liaison committee, the Vaucher Committee, founded by the Conference of Allied Ministers in Education, coordinated the efforts of the Roberts and MacMillan commissions in matters of restitution. The German Abteilung Denkmalschutz was responsible for protecting monuments and cultural treasures, but it did so inconsistently, often assisting in the systematic looting and expropriation of art. German efforts to protect monuments relied in large part on the discretion of individual commanders. See Edsel, *Saving Italy* 78, 114–15, 142–44; REAC, 92.

105. Schaffer, *Wings of Judgment*, 47–48.

106. REAC, 34.

107. William L. M. Burke, "Full Draft Text for the Office of War Information," May 26, 1945, NARA M1944, RAC, Miscellaneous Records, 14–15, 26; REAC, 19–20; Edsel, *Saving Italy*, 61, 104; Schaffer, *Wings of Judgment*, 48.

108. REAC, 19, 35; Burke, "Full Draft Text," 13.

109. REAC, 27, 57; "Carpet Bombing & Resolution Thereon," n.d., and "Draft minutes of the 2nd Meeting of the Committee held at 3 Hanover Street, W1, on Saturday, April 29 [1944] at 11 o'clock" RAC, Memoranda, Commission Memoranda; Colonel Henry C. Newton, "Report on Status of Monuments, Fine Arts and Archives in the European Theater," June, 13, 1944 [AMG-18], RAC, MFAA Field Reports, 107.

110. A. W. Pence, "Historical Monuments and Works of Art in Italy," order of January 9, 1944, RAC, Materials Concerning the Subcommission for Monuments, Fine Arts, and Archives (Italy), Commission—Subcommission for Monuments, Fine Arts, and Archives Reports, 106.

111. Burke, "Full Draft Text"; RAC, Miscellaneous Records, 13; and REAC, 36.

112. "Minutes of a Special Meeting of the American Commission for the Protection and Salvage of Artistic and Historic Monuments in Europe," October 8, 1943, 16, RAC.

113. These are sites that received one, two, or three stars in the country handbooks. I was unable to locate the handbooks for Italy and Germany, and relied on the atlases that accompanied the handbooks instead. The handbooks and atlases covered the same monuments, but the atlases listed them in a slightly more condensed form: monuments within monuments (e.g., an important chapel inside an important cathedral) appear as single entries. The numbers for Germany and Italy are thus probably underinflated, as is the proportion of religious sites to other sites.

114. Introduction to "Czechoslovakia" list, n.d., 1; "Civil Affairs Handbook, Norway, Section 17: Cultural Institutions," vii; and "Civil Affairs Handbook, Denmark, Section 17: Cultural Institutions," RAC.

115. "Civil Affairs Handbook, France, Section 17C: Cultural Institutions Central and Southern France," viii, RAC.

116. Introduction to "Italy" list, 2, June 1943, 2, and "Civil Affairs Handbook, Italy, Section 17A: Cultural Institutions Central Italy," 7, RAC.

117. Introduction to "France" list, n.d., 8, and Introduction to "Italy" list, June 1943, 1, RAC.

118. "Civil Affairs Handbook, Japan, Section 17: Cultural Institutions," n.d., vii, RAC.

119. The word *simple* is crossed out in the document draft; Introduction to "Japan" lists, n.d., 1, 4, RAC.

120. Introduction to "Tunisia" lists, n.d., n.p., RAC.

121. Introduction to "Indo-China" list, n.d., 1, RAC.

122. Introduction to "Siam (Thailand)" list, n.d., n.p., RAC.

123. Introduction to "Holland" list, n.d., 3, RAC.

124. In Edsel, *Monuments Men,* 23.

125. "Minutes of a Special Meeting of the American Commission for the Protection and Salvage of Artistic and Historic Monuments in Europe," October 8, 1943, 10, RAC.

126. "Outline of the Commissions Accomplishments and Future Activities for the House Committee on Appropriations," n.d., 3, RAC.

127. "Remarks by David E. Finley, Vice Chairman of RC at Hearing of the Appropriations Committee, House of Representatives," September 6, 1945, 3, RAC.

128. REAC, 37.

129. "Statement Regarding the Establishment, Organization, and Activities of the Commission," June 2, 1944, 7, RAC.

130. Introduction to "Greece" list, n.d., 2; Introduction to "Hungary" list, n.d., 2; Civil Affairs Handbook, "France," Section 17C: "Cultural Institutions Central and Southern France," xiv–xv.; and Civil Affairs Handbook, "The Netherlands," Section 17: "Cultural Institutions," 1, RAC.

131. REAC, 123, citing unnamed MFA&A report of January 1945.

132. See Edsel, *Monuments Men*; Nicholas, *Rape of Europa; The Rape of Europa,* film, written and directed by Richard Berge and Bonni Cohen (Menemsha Films, 2006); *The Monuments Men,* film, screenplay by George Clooney and Grant Heslov, directed by George Clooney (Columbia Pictures, 2014).

133. "Report of Activities to November 1943," 243, RAC.

134. Colonel Henry C. Newton, "Field Report: Florence," June 13, 1944, 16, RAC.

135. Overy, *Bombers and the Bombed,* 345, citing British National Archives, AIR 19/215, Slessor to Air Ministry, February 29, 1944.

136. Benjamin C. McCartney, "Return to Florence," *National Geographic* 87, no. 3 (March 1945): 257–96.

137. Accuracy assessments from July 1942 claimed that bombers in daylight raids using the Norden bombsight successfully placed 90 percent of bombs within

a 1-mile radius of the aiming point and almost 50 percent within 500 yards—ten times more accurate than RAF night bombing; Overy, *Bombers and the Bombed,* 101.

138. Edsel, *Saving Italy,* 108–9.

139. Schaffer,*Wings of Judgment,* 48–49.

140. Burke, "Full Draft Text," 19.

141. Edsel, *Saving Italy,* 104–9, 179–81, 202.

142. "Minutes of a Special Meeting of the American Commission for the Protection and Salvage of Artistic and Historic Monuments in Europe," October 8, 1943, RAC.

143. Edsel, *Monuments Men,* 64.

144. "Letter from Justice Roberts to Henry L. Stimson, Secretary of War," August 10, 1944, and "Draft Minutes of the 5th Meeting of the Committee," June 19, 1944, 2–3, RAC.

145. Burke, "Full Draft Text," 27.

146. "Memo from Webb, Office of War Information," n.d., 3, RAC.

147. REAC, 98–99.

148. Burke, "Full Draft Text," 26.

149. "Magdeburg," Control Card File for Borrowed Photographs of Cultural Institutions and Artwork in Europe and Other War Areas, April 19, 1945, RAC.

150. "Memo from Webb, Office of War Information," n.d., 3, RAC.

151. Jay Nordlinger, "A Colonel at Chartres," *National Review Online,* May 10, 2011, http://www.nationalreview.com/corner/266849/colonel-chartres-jay-nordlinger, accessed March 2014; "Distinguished Service Cross Citation for Colonel Welborn Barton Griffith, Jr.," http://projects.militarytimes.com/citations-medals-awards/recipient.php?recipientid=6100, accessed March 2014.

152. Edsel, *Monuments Men,* 79, 84, 107; Keri Douglas, "Monuments Men: Is Art Worth Dying For?" May 23, 2013, http://9musesnews.com/2013/05/23/monuments-men-is-art-worth-dying-for, accessed March 2014.

153. Burke, "Full Draft Text," 33; Hansen, *Fire and Fury,* 277.

154. Hansen, *Fire and Fury,* 267.

155. REAC, 128, 151.

156. Edsel, *Monuments Men,* 260; Burke, "Full Draft Text," 16.

157. Edsel, *Monuments Men,* 40.

158. Nicholas, *Rape of Europa,* 250, 263.

159. REAC, 49–50, 59, 83, 97–99.

160. Edsel, *Monuments Men,* 312.

4. Who? Sacred Leaders and War

1. For example, on Catholic support for the Crimean War as a function of the number of Catholic chaplains, see Michael Snape, *The Royal Army Chaplains' Department 1796–1953: Clergy under Fire* (Woodbridge, UK: Boydell Press, 2008), 67. On Irish-Catholic support for the First World War, see Oliver Rafferty, "Catholic Chaplains to the British Forces in the First World War," *Religion, State & Society* 39, no. 1 (2011), 40.

2. Snape, *Royal Army Chaplains' Department 1796–1953,* 228, citing I. W. M. Documents, E. C. Crosse.

3. See Dale R. Herspring, *Soldiers, Commissars and Chaplains* (Lanham, MD: Rowman & Littlefield, 2001); Albrecht Schuebel, *300 Jahre Evangelische Soldatenseelsorge* (Munich: Evangelischer Pressverband, 1964), 83, 101–11; Josef Perau, *Priester im Heere Hitlers: Errinerungen 1940–1945* (Essen: Ludgerus, 1962), 43.

4. Stephen H. Louden, *Chaplains in Conflict: The Role of Army Chaplains since 1914* (London: Avon Books, 1996), 71–72, citing Roger R. Venzke, *Confidence in Battle, Inspiration in Peace: The United States Army Chaplaincy 1945–1975* (Washington, DC: U.S. Government Printing Office, 1977), 37.

5. In Louden, *Chaplains in Conflict,* 13; John W. Brinsfield, *Encouraging Faith, Supporting Soldiers: The United States Army Chaplaincy, 1975–1996, Part I* (Washington, DC: Department of the Army, 1997), 3.

6. See for example David S. Bachrach, "The Medieval Military Chaplain and His Duties," in *The Sword of the Lord: Military Chaplains from the First to the Twenty-First Century,* edited by Doris L. Bergen (Notre Dame: University of Notre Dame Press, 2004), 55–56; Herman A. Norton, *Struggling for Recognition: The United States Army Chaplaincy: 1791–1865* (Honolulu: University Press of the Pacific, 2004).

7. Deuteronomy 20:2–4 (King James Authorized Version).

8. Snape, *Royal Army Chaplains' Department 1796–1953,* 212, citing Public Record office, War Office, Registered File, General Series, 32/5636.

9. Snape, *Royal Army Chaplains' Department 1796–1953,* 303.

10. William D. Cleary, "The Ministry of the Chaplain," in *Religion of Soldier and Sailor,* edited by Willard L. Sperry (Cambridge, MA: Harvard University Press, 1945), 89.

11. P. Middleton Brumwell, *The Army Chaplain: The Royal Army Chaplains' Department: The Duties of Chaplains and Morale* (London: Adam & Charles Black, 1943), 37, 51.

12. Anne C. Loveland, "From Morale Builders to Moral Advocates," in *The Sword of the Lord: Military Chaplains from the First to the Twenty-First Century,* edited by Doris L. Bergen (Notre Dame: University of Notre Dame Press, 2004), 241–43, citing Headquarters, Department of the Army, *The Chaplain and Chaplain Assistant in Combat Operations,* FM 16-5 (Washington, DC: Government Printing Office, Dec. 1984), 12, 21–22, and Headquarters, Department of the Army, *Religious Support Doctrine: The Chaplain and Chaplain Assistant,* FM 16-1 (Final Coordinating Draft, April 1989), 3–14.

13. Robert L. Gushwa, *The Best and Worst of Times: The United States Army Chaplaincy 1920–1945* (Honolulu: University Press of the Pacific, 2004), 9, 21; Edward Madigan, *Faith under Fire: Anglican Army Chaplains and the Great War* (New York: Palgrave Macmillan, 2011), 119.

14. Louden, *Chaplains in Conflict,* 38–39.

15. Snape, *Royal Army Chaplains' Department 1796–1953,* 17, citing Edward Ward, *Mars Stript of his Armour: or the Army Displayed in all its True Colours* (London: 1756), 35, and Bennett Cuthberson, *A System for the Compleat Interior Management and Oeconomy of a Battalion of Infantry* (Dublin: Boulter Grierson, 1768), 156–57.

16. Snape, *Royal Army Chaplains' Department 1796–1953,* 79–81.

17. Earl F. Stover, *Up from Handymen: The United States Army Chaplaincy 1865–1920* (Honolulu: University Press of the Pacific, 2004), 75.

18. Norton, *Struggling for Recognition,* 154.

19. Gardiner H. Shattuck, *A Shield and Hiding Place: The Religious Life of the Civil War Armies* (Macon, GA: Mercer University Press, 1987), 52, 57; Steven E. Woodworth, *While God Is Marching On: The Religious World of Civil War Soldiers* (Lawrence: University Press of Kansas, 2001), 149; both Shattuck and Woodworth are citing Union War Department's General Order Numbers 15 and 16, issued May 1861.

20. Snape, *Royal Army Chaplains' Department 1796–1953,* 38, 44, citing Royal Army Chaplains Department Archive, Gleig-Letters, 1845–1846.

21. *The Military Chaplaincy: A Report to the President by the President's Committee on Religion and Welfare in the Armed Forces* (Washington, DC: Government Printing Office, October 1, 1950), 18

22. Michael Snape, *God and the British Soldier: Religion and the British Army in the First and Second World Wars* (New York: Routledge, 2005), 94–96.

23. Snape, *Royal Army Chaplains' Department 1796–1953,* 308, citing Nigel Hamilton, *Monty: The Field Marshal 1944–1976* (London: David & Charles, 1986), 803–4.

24. Loveland, "From Morale Builders to Moral Advocates," 235, citing Headquarters, Department of the Army, *Chaplain and Chaplain Assistant,* 1.

25. U.S. Navy, *Religious Ministry in the U.S. Navy,* Navy Warfare Publication (NWP) 1-05 (Newport, RI: Department of the Navy, August 2003), 5–4, 6–3.

26. Madigan, *Faith under Fire,* 100; Stover, *Up from Handymen,* 239; Snape, *Royal Army Chaplains' Department 1796–1953,* 322, 338.

27. Shattuck, *Shield and Hiding Place,* 86.

28. Ibid., 62; Randall M. Miller, "Catholic Religion, Irish Ethnicity, and the Civil War," in *Religion and the American Civil War,* edited by Randall M. Miller, Harry S. Stout, and Charles Reagan Wilson (New York: Oxford University Press, 1998), 268; Woodworth, *While God Is Marching On,* 156; Herspring, *Soldiers, Commissars and Chaplains,* 31.

29. Madigan, *Faith under Fire,* 105–12; Stover, *Up from Handymen,* 5, 44, 47, 75, 113, 116, 166; Alan Wilkinson, *The Church of England and the First World War* (Southampton, UK: Camelot Press, 1978), 148; Linda Parker, *The Whole Armour of God: Anglican Chaplains in the Great War* (Solihull, UK: Helion & Company, 2009), 40.

30. Stover, *Up from Handymen,* 174–75.

31. Gushwa, *Best and Worst of Times,* 9, 21.

32. Ibid., 23–26, 124–27.

33. Herspring, *Soldiers, Commissars and Chaplains,* 45.

34. Snape, *Royal Army Chaplains' Department 1796–1953,* 226, citing Church Missionary Society Archives, University of Birmingham, XACC/18/Z/1 Army Book.

35. Tom Johnstone and James Hagerty, *The Cross on the Sword: Catholic Chaplains in the Forces* (London: Geoffrey Chapman, 1996), 233; Parker, *Whole Armour of God,* 40.

36. Madigan, *Faith under Fire,* 102–3; Snape, *God and the British Soldier,* 104–5; Duff Crerar, *Padres in No Man's Land: Canadian Chaplains and the Great War* (Montreal: McGill-Queen's University Press, 1995), 127; Johnstone and Hagerty, *Cross on the Sword,* 207.

37. Joanna Bourke, *An Intimate History of Killing: Face to Face Killing in 20th Century Warfare* (New York: Basic Books, 2000), 242–43, citing Scott H. Nelson and

E. Fuller Torrey, "The Religious Functions of Psychiatry," *American Journal of Ortho-psychiatry* 43, no. 3 (April 1973): 262–67.

38. Stover, *Up from Handymen,* 5, 44, 47, 75, 113, 116, 166; Edward Gregory, "The Chaplain and Mental Hygiene," *Journal of Sociology* 52, no. 5 (1947): 420–23; Rachel L. Seddon, Edgar Jones, and Neil Greenberg, "The Role of Chaplains in Maintaining the Psychological Health of Military Personnel: An Historical and Contemporary Perspective," *Military Medicine* 176, no. 12 (2011): 1357–61. According to one source, Air Force chaplains in the late 1990s spent 60–80 percent of their time providing marital counseling to soldiers; Seddon, Jones, and Greenberg, "Role of Chaplains," 1358, citing F. C. Budd, "An Air Force Model of Psychologist-Chaplain Collaboration," *Professional Psychology Research and Practice* 30, no. 6 (1999): 552–56.

39. Snape, *Royal Army Chaplains' Department 1796–1953,* 321, 329, 337–38.

40. Gushwa, *Best and Worst of Times,* 124–27; *Military Chaplaincy,* 15; Herspring, *Soldiers, Commissars and Chaplains,* 40.

41. Crerar, *Padres in No Man's Land,* 143, citing Frederick George Scott, *The Great War as I Saw It* (Toronto: McClelland and Goodchild, 1922), 151–52.

42. Bourke, *Intimate History of Killing,* 279, citing A. Irving Davidson, *A Padre's Reminiscences,* 12, Australian War Memorial.

43. Gordon H. Zahn, *Chaplains in the RAF: A Study in Role Tension* (Manchester: Manchester University Press, 1969). 114.

44. Seddon, Jones, and Greenberg, "Role of Chaplains," 1358–59, citing Glen Milstein, Amy Manierre, Virginia L. Susman, and Martha L. Bruce, "Implementation of a Program to Improve the Continuity of Mental Health Care through Clergy Outreach and Professional Engagement (COPE)," *Professional Psychology: Research and Practice* 39, no. 2 (2008), 218; Nelson and Torrey, "Religious Functions of Psychiatry."

45. Louden, *Chaplains in Conflict,* 99; Brinsfield, *Encouraging Faith, Supporting Soldiers,* 90.

46. Seddon, Jones, and Greenberg, "Role of Chaplains," 1360.

47. Stover, *Up from Handymen,* 173, 202; Snape, *Royal Army Chaplains' Department 1796–1953,* 240, 346; *Military Chaplaincy,* 15–16.

48. Snape, *Royal Army Chaplains' Department 1796–1953,* 327.

49. Gushwa, *Best and Worst of Times,* 23, 26; ibid., 326.

50. Loveland, "From Morale Builders to Moral Advocates," 235.

51. John Smyth, *In This Sign Conquer: The Story of the Army Chaplains* (London: A. R. Mowbray, 1968), 244, 343; Seddon, Jones, and Greenberg, "Role of Chaplains," 1358, citing *Time Magazine,* "Religion: Padre's Hour," March 8, 1943.

52. Loveland, "From Morale Builders to Moral Advocates," 233–35, citing *The Army Character Guidance Program,* ST 16-151 (Carlisle Barracks, PA: Chaplain School, March 1, 1950), 4, 14–15.

53. Loveland, "From Morale Builders to Moral Advocates," 237–39.

54. Bachrach, "Medieval Military Chaplain," 78–80.

55. Crerar, *Padres in No Man's Land,* 147.

56. Ibid., 151, citing National Archives of Canada, Series IIIc, Chaplain Service Records, Vol. 4664, "Reports," A.D.C.S., France, file 2, Beausoleil report, n.d.

57. Stuart A. Cohen, "Israel," in *Religion in the Military Worldwide,* edited by Ron E. Hassner (Cambridge, UK: Cambridge University Press, 2014), 131, citing

Menachem Michaelson, "The Military Rabbinate " [in Hebrew] in *Tzahal be-Cheilov* [The IDF and Its Arms], Vol. 16, edited by Ilan Kfir and Ya'akov Erez, 83–132 (Tel Aviv: Revivim, 1982).

58. Brinsfield, *Encouraging Faith, Supporting Soldiers,* 123–24.

59. Loveland, "From Morale Builders to Moral Advocates," 249n. 41.

60. Louden, *Chaplains in Conflict,* 58, citing Zahn, *Chaplains in the RAF,* 112.

61. Zahn, *Chaplains in the RAF,* 110, citing anonymous, *For the Front: Prayers and Considerations for Catholic Soldiers* (Market Weighton, UK: St. Williams Press, 1918), 23.

62. Snape, *Royal Army Chaplains' Department 1796–1953,* 304, citing Ronald Selby Wright, *Front Line Religion: The Padre Preaches* (London: Hodder and Stoughton, 1941), 133.

63. Snape, *God and the British Soldier,* 224; Kurt O. Berends, "Wholesome Reading Purified and Elevates the Man: The Religious Military Press in the Confederacy," in *Religion and the American Civil War,* edited by Randall M. Miller, Harry S. Stout, and Charles Reagan Wilson, 261–96 (New York: Oxford University Press, 1998), 44; Hartmut Lehmann, "In the Service of Two Kings," in *The Sword of the Lord: Military Chaplains from the First to the Twenty-First Century,* edited by Doris L. Bergen (Notre Dame: University of Notre Dame Press, 2004), 130–33.

64. Crerar, *Padres in No Man's Land,* 149.

65. Michael F. Snape and Stephen G. Parker. "Keeping Faith and Coping: Belief, Popular Religiosity and the British People," in *The Great World War: 1914–1945, vol. 2: The People's Experience,* edited by Peter Liddle, John Bourne, and Ian Whitehead (London: HarperCollins, 2001), 401; Bryan Cooper, *The Tenth (Irish) Division in Gallipoli* (London: Herbert Jenkins Limited, 1918), 189; Albert Marrin, *The Last Crusade: The Church of England in the First World War* (Durham: Duke University Press, 1974), 126, 129, 140, 169.

66. Bourke, *Intimate History of Killing,* citing F. L. Hughes, "The Chaplains Duty in Battle," *Chaplains' Magazine, Middle East* 1, no. 2 (1943), 65–66.

67. Jonathan H. Ebel, *Faith in the Fight: Religion and the American Soldier in the Great War* (Princeton: Princeton University Press, 2010), 76–104; Paul Fussell, *The Great War and Modern Memory* (Oxford: Oxford University Press, 2000), 117, 120; Marrin, *Last Crusade,* 184–85, 212–13; Wilkinson, *Church of England,* 95, 191.

68. Snape, *Royal Army Chaplains' Department 1796–1953,* 222, citing Church Missionary Society Archives, University of Birmingham, XACC 18/F/4, "Notebooks Containing Sermons and Addresses Delivered by L. H. Gwynne," "Sermons from September 1916," December 2, 1917.

69. Crerar, *Padres in No Man's Land,* 113.

70. Donald F. Crosby, *Battlefield Chaplains: Catholic Priests in World War II* (Lawrence: University Press of Kansas 1994), 15.

71. Brinsfield, *Encouraging Faith, Supporting Soldiers,* 25–26.

72. Martin Purdy, "Roman Catholic Army Chaplains during the First World War: Roles, Experiences and Dilemmas" (MA thesis, University of Central Lancashire, 2012), 4.

73. Marrin, *Last Crusade,* 169–72; Wilkinson, *Church of England,* 99–101, 175, 195; Conrad C. Crane, *Bombs, Cities, and Civilians: American Airpower Strategy in World War II* (Lawrence: University Press of Kansas, 1993), 29–30; Anthony C. Grayling,

Among the Dead Cities: The History and Moral Legacy of the WWII Bombing of Civilians in Germany and Japan (New York: Walker & Co., 2006), 179–81, 201.

74. See, for example, Douglas Johnston and Cynthia Sampson, *Religion, the Missing Dimension of Statecraft* (Oxford: Oxford University Press, 1995); Douglas Johnston, *Faith-Based Diplomacy: Trumping Realpolitik* (Oxford: Oxford University Press, 2002); Daniel Philpott, *Just and Unjust Peace: An Ethic of Political Reconciliation* (Oxford: Oxford University Press, 2012).

75. George H. Williams, "The Chaplaincy of the Armed Forces of the United States of America in Historical and Ecclesiastical Perspective," in *Military Chaplains: From a Religious Military to a Military Religion,* edited by Harvey G. Cox (New York: American Report Press, 1972), 56; Gordon C. Zahn, "Sociological Impressions of the Chaplaincy," in *Military Chaplains: From a Religious Military to a Military Religion,* edited by Harvey G. Cox (New York: American Report Press, 1972), 84.

76. Peter Berger and Daniel Pinard, "Military Religion: An Analysis of Educational Materials Disseminated by Chaplains," in *Military Chaplains: From a Religious Military to a Military Religion,* edited by Harvey G. Cox (New York: American Report Press, 1972), 88–89.

77. Alan Wilkinson, "The Paradox of the Military Chaplain," *Theology* 84 (1981): 249–57; Herspring, *Soldiers, Commissars and Chaplains,* 39. For a critical discussion, see Snape, *Royal Army Chaplains' Department 1796–1953,* 6–7.

78. Loveland, "From Morale Builders to Moral Advocates," 241–43, citing Headquarters, Department of the Army, *Chaplain and Chaplain Assistant,* 12, 21–22, and Headquarters, Department of the Army, *Religious Support Doctrine,* 3–14.

79. Crosby, *Battlefield Chaplains,* xxiii, 112, 246, citing his own "Chaplains Questionnaires" from December 1983.

80. In Zahn, *Chaplains in the RAF,* 112.

81. Zahn, "Sociological Impressions of the Chaplaincy," 82, 185.

82. Robert McAfee Brown, "Military Chaplaincy as Ministry," in in *Military Chaplains: From a Religious Military to a Military Religion,* edited by Harvey G. Cox (New York: American Report Press, 1972), 145, citing untitled article by Ralph Blumenthal, *San Francisco Chronicle,* June 26, 1971, 38; Zahn, *Chaplains in the RAF,* 135, 201.

83. Waldo W. Burchard, "Role Conflicts of Military Chaplains," *American Sociological Review* 19, no. 5 (October 1954): 528–35.

84. Ibid., 534.

85. Zahn, "Sociological Impressions of the Chaplaincy," 79; Zahn, *Chaplains in the RAF,* 263, citing Norman MacFarlane, "Navy Chaplaincy: Muzzled Ministry," *Christian Century,* November 2, 1966, 1338.

86. Zahn, *Chaplains in the RAF,* 185, 241.

87. Ibid., esp. 32, 116.

88. Ibid., 157–59.

89. Stephen Louden, "Chaplains as Whistle-Blowers? You're Having a Laugh!" *Journal of the Royal Army Chaplains' Department* (2006), 12–16.

90. Wilkinson, "Paradox of the Military Chaplain," 253.

91. Snape, *Royal Army Chaplains' Department 1796–1953,* 241, citing A. B. A., FHD/A3, letter to army bishop, December 14, 1918.

92. Snape, *God and the British Soldier,* 130, citing Imperial War Museum sound archive, 10660/4, John William Steele.

93. Loveland, "From Morale Builders to Moral Advocates," 244, citing Kermit D. Johnson, *Realism and Hope in a Nuclear Age* (Atlanta: John Knox Press, 1988), 12–14, 108–14; Kermit D. Johnson, "A New Stage: Beyond 'In-House' Ethical Issues," *Military Chaplains' Review* (1982): v; Brinsfield, *Encouraging Faith, Supporting Soldiers,* 15.

94. Stephen A. Garrett, *Ethics and Airpower in World War II: The British Bombing of German Cities* (New York: St. Martin's Press, 1993), 97.

95. Perau, *Priester im Heere Hitlers,* 8, my translation.

96. Bourke, *Intimate History of Killing,* 283.

97. Christine R. Barker and Ines-Jacqueline Werkner, "Military Chaplaincy in International Operations: A Comparison of Two Different Traditions," *Journal of Contemporary Religion* 23, no. 1 (2008), 58.

98. Wilkinson, *Church of England,* 127, citing George Simpson Duncan, *Douglas Haig as I Knew Him* (London: Allen & Unwin, 1966), 21.

99. Snape, *Royal Army Chaplains' Department 1796–1953,* 219, citing Douglas Haig, *Haig's Autograph Great War Diary* [microfilm] (Brighton, 1987), January 15, 1916.

100. Marrin, *Last Crusade,* 209, citing Caroline E. Payne, *Society at War* (Boston: Houghton Mifflin, 1931), 31.

101. Snape, *Royal Army Chaplains' Department 1796–1953,* 221, citing Edward A. Forbes, *Vermelles: Notes on the Western Front* (Edinburgh: Scottish Chronicle Press, 1918), 44–45.

102. Wilkinson, "Paradox of the Military Chaplain," 252.

103. Snape, *Royal Army Chaplains' Department 1796–1953,* 221, citing Lyn Mac-Donald and Shirley Seaton, *1914–1918: Voices and Images of the Great War* (London: Joseph, 1991), 200.

104. Schuebel, *300 Jahre Evangelische Soldatenseelsorge,* 314–15, my translation.

105. Ibid., 145, my translation.

106. Crerar, *Padres in No Man's Land,* 121; Snape, *Royal Army Chaplains' Department 1796–1953,*19, 236; Smyth, *In This Sign Conquer,* 291–94; Crosby, *Battlefield Chaplains,* 45, 126, 132, 134, 138; Bourke, *Intimate History of Killing,* 275; Perau, *Priester im Heere Hitlers,* 27; Schuebel, *300 Jahre Evangelische Soldatenseelsorge.* 154.

107. Smyth, *In This Sign Conquer,* 166, citing Kenneth T. Henderson, *Khaki and Cassock* (Melbourne, Australia: Melville and Mullen, 1919).

108. Smyth, *In This Sign Conquer,* 243, citing Richard Royds.

109. Smyth, *In This Sign Conquer,* 336, citing citation for military cross awarded to Rev. Robin Roe.

110. Gardiner H. Shattuck, "Faith, Morale, and the Army Chaplain in the American Civil War," in *The Sword of the Lord: Military Chaplains from the First to the Twenty-First Century,* edited by Doris L. Bergen (Notre Dame: University of Notre Dame Press, 2004), 112–13.

111. See, for example, Shattuck, *Shield and Hiding Place,* 51; Ebel, *Faith in the Fight,* 73; Gushwa, *Best and Worst of Times,* 149–151, 159; Woodworth, *While God Is Marching On,* 157.

112. See, for example, Johnstone and Hagerty, *Cross on the Sword,* 236.

113. Norton, *Struggling for Recognition,* 105–6, 157; Doris L. Bergen, "German Military Chaplains in the Second World War and the Dilemmas of Legitimacy,"

in *The Sword of the Lord: Military Chaplains from the First to the Twenty-First Century,* edited by Doris L. Bergen (Notre Dame: University of Notre Dame Press, 2004), 171; Woodworth, *While God Is Marching On,* 158; Miller, "Catholic Religion," 289n. 19; Crerar, *Padres in No Man's Land,* 131–32; Crosby, *Battlefield Chaplains,* 48, 227–33.

114. Brinsfield, *Encouraging Faith, Supporting Soldiers,* 141.

115. Michael Snape, "Church of England Army Chaplains in the First World War: Goodbye to 'Goodbye to All That,'" *Journal of Ecclesiastical History* 62, no. 2 (2011), 322; Gushwa, *Best and Worst of Times,* 192; Roy J. Honeywell, *Chaplains of the United States Army* (Washington, DC: Office of the Chief of Chaplains, Department of the Army, 1958), 196, 294.

116. Snape, "Church of England Army Chaplains," 321, citing Peter Howson, "Deaths among Army Chaplains, 1914–20," *Journal of the Society for Army Historical Research* 83 (2005); Stover, *Up from Handymen,* apps. 2, 4; Smyth, *In This Sign Conquer,* 220; Gushwa, *Best and Worst of Times,* 141; Henderson, *Khaki and Cassock,* 196, 294.

117. Gushwa, *Best and Worst of Times,* 141.

118. Bergen, "German Military Chaplains," 174. For an exception among Canadian units in 1917, see Crerar, *Padres in No Man's Land,* 124.

119. Parker, *Whole Armour of God,* 25, 28, citing Revd. F. R. Barry, *Proud of My Life* (London: Holder & Stoughton, 1970), 60.

120. Parker C. Thompson, *From Its European Antecedents to 1791: The United States Army Chaplaincy* (Honolulu: University Press of the Pacific, 2004), 145; Dom H. Alban Boultwood, "With an Armoured Brigade in North Africa and Central Mediterranean," in *The Priest among the Soldiers,* edited by Martin Dempsey (London: Burns, Oates, 1947), 103, citing James C. Dunn, *The War the Infantry Knew 1914–1919* (London: Abacus, 1994), 556. For martyrdom as a motivation, see Purdy, "Roman Catholic Army Chaplains," 40, 44.

121. Snape, *Royal Army Chaplains' Department 1796–1953,* 301, citing Bernard Egan, "Parachutist Chaplains: Training," in *The Priest among the Soldiers,* edited by Martin Dempsey (London: Burns, Oates, 1947), 143.

122. Parker, *Whole Armour of God,* 43, citing Oswin Creighton, *With the 29th Division in Gallipoli* (New York: Longmans, Green, 1916), 121. See Purdy, "Roman Catholic Army Chaplains," 39.

123. Snape, *Royal Army Chaplains' Department 1796–1953,* 226, citing Church Missionary Society Archives, University of Birmingham, XACC/18/Z/1 Army Book.

124. Schuebel, *300 Jahre Evangelische Soldatenseelsorge,* 55, my translation.

125. Madigan, *Faith under Fire,* 115, citing Harry W. Blackburne, "A Chaplain's Duties," in *Chaplains in Council* (London: Edward Arnold, 1917).

126. Purdy, "Roman Catholic Army Chaplains," 44, citing Rene Gaell, *Priests in the Firing Line* (London: Longmans, Green, 1916), 165.

127. Rafferty, "Catholic Chaplains," 44, citing James McCann, "A Catholic Chaplain in the Great War," *Irish Monthly,* July/August 1940, 416; Purdy, "Roman Catholic Army Chaplains," 45, citing Alfred O'Rahilly, *The Padre of Trench Street: Father William Doyle* (London: Longmans, Green and Company, 1920), 37.

128. In Crosby, *Battlefield Chaplains,* 129.

129. Snape, *Royal Army Chaplains' Department 1796–1953,* 300–301.

130. Ibid., 1.

131. Gushwa, *Best and Worst of Times,* 141–42.

132. Parker,*Whole Armour of God,* 36, citing Imperial War Museum, E. C. Crosse Papers, IWM (80/22/1), 68, 70.

133. Schuebel, *300 Jahre Evangelische Soldatenseelsorge,* 162, my translation.

134. Parker, *Whole Armour of God,* 34, 82, citing William Drury, *Camp Followers: A Padre's Recollections of Nile, Somme and Tigris during the First World War* (Dublin: Exchequer Printers, 1968), 127.

135. Parker, *Whole Armour of God,* 84; Wilkinson, *Church of England,* 137–38; both Parker and Wilkinson are citing David Raw, *It's Only Me, Life of Theodore Bayley Hardy* (Blackpool, UK: Peters, 1988), 21.

136. Smyth, *In This Sign Conquer,* 199.

137. Johnstone and Haggerty, *Cross on the Sword,* 112–13, 198.

138. Purdy, "Roman Catholic Army Chaplains," 6, citing Robert Graves, *Goodbye to All That* (1929), 158; Marrin, *Last Crusade,* 208; Wilkinson, *Church of England,* 11, citing Guy Chapman, *A Passionate Prodigality: Fragments of an Autobiography* (London, 1933).

139. See chapters in Ron E. Hassner, ed., *Religion in the Military Worldwide* (New York: Cambridge University Press, 2014); Joanne Benham Rennick, "Canada," in Hassner, *Religion in the Military Worldwide,* 53, citing Department of National Defence, *Canadian Forces Chaplain Branch Manual* (Ottawa: Chief of Defense Staff, Department of National Defence, 2003), par. 6.4; Stuart Cohen, *Divine Service? Judaism and Israel's Armed Forces* (Franham, UK: Ashgate, 2014), 15; Cohen, "Israel," 131, citing Ethan Bronner, "A Religious War in Israel's Army," *New York Times,* March 22, 2009, WK1; "The Rabbis and the Army," April 7, 2011, http://www.ynetnews.com/articles/0,7340,L-4091047,00.html.

140. Bourke, *Intimate History of Killing,* 280, citing Michael McKernan, *Australian Churches at War: Attitudes and Activities of the Major Churches, 1914–1918* (Sydney: Australian War Memorial, 1980), 2.

141. Smyth, *In This Sign Conquer,* 225, citing Rev. John McKie Hunter.

142. Smyth, *In This Sign Conquer,* 291–92; Herspring, *Soldiers, Commissars and Chaplains,* 43.

143. Rudolph Peters, *Islam and Colonialism: The Doctrine of Jihad in Modern History* (The Hague: Mouton, 1979), 92–93.

144. Snape, *Royal Army Chaplains' Department 1796–1953,*316–18; Johnstone and Hagerty, *Cross on the Sword,* 267; Smyth, *In This Sign Conquer,* 227, 289–90; Honeywell, *Chaplains of the United States Army,* 278; Schuebel, *300 Jahre Evangelische Soldatenseelsorge,* 136.

145. Smyth, *In This Sign Conquer,* 226, citing Rev. John McKie Hunter.

146. Snape, *Royal Army Chaplains' Department 1796–1953,* 2–3; Smyth, *In This Sign Conquer,* 321.

147. Herspring, *Soldiers, Commissars and Chaplains,* 44; and Johnstone and Haggerty, *Cross on the Sword,* 295. Neither source provides documentation for the claim that defections to communism were lower among the British Gloucestershire Regiment due to its strong religious faith.

148. Honeywell, *Chaplains of the United States Army,* 103, citing James Russell Trumbull, *History of Northampton, Massachusetts* (Northampton, 1898), 107.

149. Madigan, *Faith under Fire,* 115, citing Blackburne, "Chaplain's Duties."

150. Johnstone and Haggerty, *Cross on the Sword,* 215.

151. Smyth, *In This Sign Conquer,* 38.

152. Madigan, *Faith under Fire,* 227, citing Bishop Llewellyn Gwynne's *War Book,* Gwynne Papers, C. M. S. Archive, University of Birmingham, Acc 18/21.

153. Nigel Cave, "Haig and Religion," in *Haig: A Reappraisal 70 Years On,* edited by Brian Bond and Nigel Cave (Barnsley, UK: Leo Cooper, 1999), 242–43; Wilkinson, *Church of England,* 127.

154. Parker, *Whole Armour of God,* 65; Louden, *Chaplains in Conflict,* 48; Snape, *Royal Army Chaplains' Department 1796–1953,* 220, citing Royal Army Chaplains Department Archive, Blackburne Papers, "Conference of A.C.G.s of Armies Held at D.C.G.'s office, August 17, 1917."

155. Snape, "Church of England Army Chaplains," 336, citing Henry C. Jackson, *Pastor on the Nile: Being Some Account of the Life and Letters of Llewellyn H. Gwynne* (London, 1960), 169.

156. Madigan, *Faith under Fire,* 122–23, citing Randall Davidson Papers, Vol. 344: Great War: Clergy, 1915–17, Lambeth Palace Library, f.146.

157. In *Military Chaplaincy,* 13.

158. Snape, *Royal Army Chaplains' Department 1796–1953,* 308, citing Hamilton, *Monty,* 803–4.

159. In *Military Chaplaincy,* 13.

160. Ibid.

161. Schuebel, *300 Jahre Evangelische Soldatenseelsorge,* 126.

162. Snape, *God and the British Soldier,* 180, citing J. H. A Sparrow, *Morale,* War Office Monograph PRO, WO 277/16 (1949).

5. How? Sacred Rituals and War

1. See *Gesta Francorum et Aliorum Hierosolymytanorum* [The Deeds of the Franks], chaps. 10–15, and Raymond d'Aguilers, *Historia Francorum qui Ceperint Jerusalem* [The History of the Franks Who Captured Jerusalem], chaps. 4–9, both quoted in August C. Krey, *The First Crusade: The Accounts of Eyewitnesses and Participants* (Princeton: Princeton University Press, 1921), 174–82; Ron E. Hassner and Michael C. Horowitz. "Debating the Role of Religion in War," *International Security* 35, no. 1 (2010): 201–8.

2. James H. O'Neill, "The True Story of the Patton Prayer," *Review of the News,* October 6, 1971, reprinted at http://www.pattonhq.com/prayer.html, accessed July 2014; Donald F. Crosby, *Battlefield Chaplains: Catholic Priests in World War II* (Lawrence: University Press of Kansas 1994), 155.

3. Albert Marrin, *The Last Crusade: The Church of England in the First World War* (Durham: Duke University Press, 1974), 136–37, citing Geoffrey Gorer, *Exploring English Character* (New York: Criterion Books, 1955), 263–66; Alan Wilkinson, *The Church of England and the First World War* (Southampton, UK: Camelot Press, 1978), 149, 153, 195, citing Alban H. Baverstock, *The Unscathed Crucifix* (London: Faith Press, 1916) and Rev. Alexander Alfred Boddy, *The Real Angels of Mons* (1915).

4. Paul Fussell, *The Great War and Modern Memory* (Oxford: Oxford University Press, 2000), 118, 132.

5. Philip Jenkins, *The Great and Holy War: How World War I Became a Religious Crusade* (New York: HarperCollins, 2014), 15, 145.

6. Annette Becker, *War and Faith: The Religious Imagination in France, 1914–1930*, translated by Helen McPhail (Oxford: Berg Publishers, 1998), 97.

7. Ibid., citing *Pluie de Roses: Interventions de Soeur Therese de l'Enfant-Jesus pendant la Guerre* (Bayeux : Pour le Carmel de Lisieux, 1920), 4.

8. Kobi Nahshoni, "Rabbi Yosef Describes Rachel's 'Manifestation' in Gaza," *Yedioth Aharonot,* January 25, 2009, http://www.ynetnews.com/articles/0,7340,L-3661283,00.html; Kobi Nahshoni, "Rabbi Eliyahu: I Sent Mother Rachel to Gaza," *Yedioth Aharonot,* January 21, 2009, http://www.ynetnews.com/articles/0,7340,L-3659308,00.html, accessed April 2013. I thank Noa Levanon Klein for pointing me to these reports.

9. "Personal Testimonies: The Miracles of Operation Cast Lead," June 22, 2012 [in Hebrew], http://www.yahadoot.net/item.asp?id=574&cid=15, accessed April 2013.

10. Stuart Winer, "Senior Infantry Officer Describes Divine Protection in Gaza," *Times of Israel*, July 31, 2014, http://www.timesofisrael.com/senior-infantry-officer-describes-divine-protection-in-gaza/, accessed July 2014. The biblical verse quoted by the officer is Deuteronomy 20:4.

11. Becker, *War and Faith,* 75; Jenkins, *Great and Holy War,* 90.

12. Gerard J. de Groot, "'We Are Safe Whatever Happens,'—Douglas Haig, the Reverend George Duncan, and the Conduct of War, 1916–1918," in *Scotland and War: AD 79–1918,* edited by Norman McDougall (Edinburgh: John Donald Publishers, 1991), 193–204, citing Haig to Lady Haig, November 17, 1918, Haig MSS, No.141.

13. Robert L. Gushwa, *The Best and Worst of Times: The United States Army Chaplaincy 1920–1945* (Honolulu: University Press of the Pacific, 2004), 173, citing Francis Joseph Spellman, *Action This Day* (New York: Scribners Sons, 1943); Stephen Mansfield, *The Faith of the American Soldier* (Lake Mary, FL: FrontLine, 2005), 38, citing Winston Churchill, *My Early Life* (New York: Scribner, 1977).

14. On religious practices on the medieval battlefield, see, for example, David S. Bachrach, *Religion and the Conduct of War c.300—c.1215* (Woodbridge, UK: Boydell Press, 2003); David S. Bachrach, "The Medieval Military Chaplain and His Duties," in *The Sword of the Lord: Military Chaplains from the First to the Twenty-First Century,* edited by Doris L. Bergen, 69–88 (Notre Dame: University of Notre Dame Press, 2004); Michael McCormick, "The Liturgy of War from Antiquity to the Crusades," in *The Sword of the Lord: Military Chaplains from the First to the Twenty-First Century,* edited by Doris L. Bergen, 45–67 (Notre Dame: University of Notre Dame Press, 2004).

15. Becker, *War and Faith,* 3, citing Alphonse Dupront, *Du Sacre* (Gallimard, 1987).

16. Samuel E. Stouffer, Arthur A. Lumsdaine, Marion Harper Lumsdaine, Robin M. Williams Jr., M. Brewster Smith, Irving L. Janis, Shirley A. Star, and Leonard S. Cottrell Jr., *The American Soldier, vol. 2: Combat and Its Aftermath* (Princeton: Princeton University Press, 1949), 188.

17. Becker, *War and Faith*, 87, 99–100; Marrin, *Last Crusade*, 136–37, citing Gorer, *Exploring English Character*, 263–66; Wilkinson, *Church of England*, 149, 153, 95, citing Baverstock, *Unscathed Crucifix* and Body, *Real Angels of Mons*.

18. Fussell, *Great War and Modern Memory*, 124.

19. Jenkins, *Great and Holy War*, 123–24.

20. Ibid., 124, citing Hanns Bächtold-Stäubli, *Deutscher Soldatenbrauch und Soldatenglaube* (Strasbourg: K. J. Trübner, 1917).

21. Michael F. Snape and Stephen G. Parker. "Keeping Faith and Coping: Belief, Popular Religiosity and the British People," in *The Great World War: 1914–1945, vol. 2: The People's Experience*, edited by Peter Liddle, John Bourne, and Ian Whitehead (London: HarperCollins, 2001), 401 and 414.

22. Becker, *War and Faith*, 65–66, 83.

23. Stouffer et al., *American Soldier, vol. 2*, 188.

24. John Keegan and Richard Holmes, *Soldiers: A History of Men in Battle* (London: H. Hamilton, 1985), 52; Michael Snape, *God and the British Soldier: Religion and the British Army in the First and Second World Wars* (London: Routledge, 2005), 234, citing Spike Milligan, *Monty: His Part in My Victory* (London: Penguin, 1978), 43.

25. Father Walter Finn, "In Italy," in *The Priest among the Soldiers*, edited by Martin Dempsey (London: Burns Oates, 1947), 105; John Smyth, *In This Sign Conquer: The Story of the Army Chaplains* (London: A. R. Mowbray, 1968), 237.

26. Snape, *God and the British Soldier*, 185, 234, citing John Coghlan, *Memorandum for Catholic Army Chaplains and Officiating Chaplains to the Forces* (London: United Services Catholic Association, 1942), 10–11.

27. Gushwa, *Best and Worst of Times*, 168–171; Roy J. Honeywell, *Chaplains of the United States Army* (Washington, DC: Office of the Chief of Chaplains, Department of the Army, 1958), 260.

28. John W. Brinsfield, *Encouraging Faith, Supporting Soldiers: The United States Army Chaplaincy, 1975–1996*, Pt. II (Washington, DC: Department of the Army, 1997), 59, 80, 85, 174.

29. Mansfield, *Faith of the American Soldier*, 43–48; "Point 27 with Shields of Strength," https://point27.org/about-2/, accessed June 2014. The text is a paraphrase in the first person of Joshua 1:9.

30. Bachrach, "Medieval Military Chaplain," 85n. 12, citing Aleksandr S. Senin, "Russian Army Chaplains during World War I," *Russian Studies in History* 32 (1993): 43–52.

31. Amit Ahuja, "India," in *Religion in the Military Worldwide*, edited by Ron E. Hassner (Cambridge, UK: Cambridge University Press, 2014), 162.

32. Tom Johnstone and James Hagerty, *The Cross on the Sword: Catholic Chaplains in the Forces* (London: Geoffrey Chapman, 1996), 303.

33. Aaron Skabelund and Akito Ishikawa, "Japan," in *Religion in the Military Worldwide*, edited by Ron E. Hassner (Cambridge, UK: Cambridge University Press, 2014), 34–35.

34. Oliver Rafferty, "Catholic Chaplains to the British Forces in the First World War," *Religion, State & Society* 39, no. 1 (2011), 49.

35. John Nagy, "Father John Jenkins' Gettysburg Address," *Notre Dame Magazine* (autumn 2013), 13.

36. Crosby, *Battlefield Chaplains,* 239–40; Father R. Lester Guilly, "In N.W. Europe," in *The Priest among the Soldiers,* edited by Martin Dempsey (London: Burns Oates, 1947), 131.

37. Crosby, *Battlefield Chaplains,* 214–22.

38. Ibid., 124.

39. Adrian Blomfield, "Orthodox Church Unholy Alliance with Putin," *Telegraph,* February 23, 2008.

40. Crosby, *Battlefield Chaplains,* 214–45.

41. Randall M. Miller, "Catholic Religion, Irish Ethnicity, and the Civil War," in *Religion and the American Civil War,* edited by Randall M. Miller, Harry S. Stout, and Charles Reagan Wilson (New York: Oxford University Press, 1998), 269.

42. Ibid., 274; Steven E. Woodworth, *While God Is Marching On: The Religious World of Civil War Soldiers* (Lawrence: University Press of Kansas, 2001), 123, 137.

43. Victor Dobbin and Stephen Deakin, "United Kingdom," in *Religion in the Military Worldwide,* edited by Ron E. Hassner (Cambridge, UK: Cambridge University Press, 2014), 74,

44. Marrin, *Last Crusade,* 215; Wilkinson, *Church of England,* plate 4. Most Western militaries have done away with such christening ceremonies, with the exception of the christening of ships, military and civilian, often accompanied by prayer.

45. Earl F. Stover, *Up from Handymen: The United States Army Chaplaincy 1865–1920* (Honolulu: University Press of the Pacific, 2004), 239; Mansfield, *Faith of the American Soldier,* 107.

46. Edward Madigan, *Faith under Fire: Anglican Army Chaplains and the Great War* (New York: Palgrave Macmillan, 2011), 100; Michael Snape, *The Royal Army Chaplains' Department 1796–1953: Clergy under Fire* (Woodbridge, UK: Boydell Press, 2008), 322, 338.

47. Dobbin and Deakin, "United Kingdom," 75.

48. Gardiner H. Shattuck, *A Shield and Hiding Place: The Religious Life of the Civil War Armies* (Macon, GA: Mercer University Press, 1987), 86.

49. Duff Crerar, *Padres in No Man's Land: Canadian Chaplains and the Great War* (Montreal: McGill-Queen's University Press, 1995), 142, citing National Archives of Canada, Series IIIc, Chaplain Service Records, Vol. 4675, "Extracts of Reports," Scott to McGreer, May 28, 1917.

50. Stephen H. Louden, *Chaplains in Conflict: The Role of Army Chaplains since 1914* (London: Avon Books, 1996), 77, citing Llewelyn Hughes, Unpublished Letter to DCG, August 5, 1943.

51. Miller, "Catholic Religion," 268; Crerar, *Padres in No Man's Land,* 142; Doris L. Bergen, "German Military Chaplains in the Second World War," in *The Sword of the Lord: Military Chaplains from the First to the Twenty-First Century,* edited by Doris L. Bergen (Notre Dame: University of Notre Dame Press, 2004), 180; Snape and Parker. "Keeping Faith and Coping," 401, 413; Dom Vincent Cavanagh, "With a Guards Brigade in Northern Norway," in *The Priest among the Soldiers,* edited by Martin Dempsey (London: Burns Oates, 1947), 13.

52. Christine R. Barker and Ines-Jacqueline Werkner, "Military Chaplaincy in International Operations: A Comparison of Two Different Traditions," *Journal of Contemporary Religion* 23, no. 1 (2008), 53.

53. Crerar, *Padres in No Man's Land,* 141–42.

54. Rafferty, "Catholic Chaplains," 44, citing Rudyard Kipling, *The Irish Guards in the Great War,* Vol. 1 (New York: Doubleday, 1923), 118.

55. Smyth, *In This Sign Conquer,* 257.

56. Gushwa, *Best and Worst of Times,* 185; Reverend Mgr. Joseph P. Stapleton, "In the Middle East," in *The Priest among the Soldiers,* edited by Martin Dempsey (London: Burns Oates, 1947), 34; Crosby, *Battlefield Chaplains,* 142; Honeywell, *Chaplains of the United States Army,* 274.

57. Martin L. Cook, "United States I," in *Religion in the Military Worldwide,* edited by Ron E. Hassner (Cambridge, UK: Cambridge University Press, 2014), 185, 187.

58. Parker C. Thompson, *From Its European Antecedents to 1791: The United States Army Chaplaincy* (Honolulu: University Press of the Pacific, 2004), 111, 171.

59. Woodworth, *While God is Marching On,* 74, 100, 245.

60. Harry S. Stout, *Upon the Altar of the Nation: A Moral History of the Civil* War (New York: Penguin, 2006), 90, 270, 391; James M. McPherson, "Afterword," in *Religion and the American Civil War,* edited by Randall M. Miller, Harry S. Stout, and Charles Reagan Wilson (New York: Oxford University Press, 1998), 409.

61. Hartmut Lehmann, "In the Service of Two Kings," in *The Sword of the Lord: Military Chaplains from the First to the Twenty-First Century,* edited by Doris L. Bergen (Notre Dame: University of Notre Dame Press, 2004), 132.

62. Vanessa Chambers, "'Defend Us from All Perils and Dangers of this Night': Coping with Bombing in Britain during the Second World War," in *Bombing, States and Peoples in Western Europe 1940–1945,* edited by Claudia Baldoli, Andrew Knapp, and Richard Overy (London: Continuum, 2011), 156.

63. Jenkins, *Great and Holy War,* 68.

64. Snape and Parker. "Keeping Faith and Coping," 401–3; Smyth, *In This Sign Conquer,* 216.

65. Gushwa, *Best and Worst of Times,* 146–47.

66. Honeywell, *Chaplains of the United States Army,* 242.

67. In O'Neill, "True Story."

68. Brinsfield, *Encouraging Faith, Supporting Soldiers,* 90.

69. See, for example, Mansfield, *Faith of the American Soldier,* 3–4.

70. Wilkinson, *Church of England,* 158; Snape, *God and the British Soldier,* 46–50, citing David S. Cairns, *The Army and Religion: An Enquiry and Its Bearing on the Religious Life of the Nation* (London: Macmillan, 1919), 7–8, 166–68; Elisha Atkins, "A Soldier's Second Thoughts," in *Religion of Soldier and Sailor,* edited by Willard L. Sperry (Cambridge, MA: Harvard University Press, 1945), 105–6.

71. Mansfield, *Faith of the American Soldier,* 103, 125.

72. Stouffer et al., *American Soldier, vol. 2,* 173–74, 185–86. The research was conducted by the Research Branch of the U.S. Army Information and Education Division and included 163 surveys involving 6,000 soldiers.

73. Smyth, *In This Sign Conquer,* 241–42, citing J. McLuskey.

74. Rafferty, "Catholic Chaplains," 45–46, citing *The Tablet,* October 3, 1914; Smyth, *In This Sign Conquer,* 224, citing John McKie Hunter. The singing of "Abide with Me" in the aftermath of the Battle of Arnhem was immortalized in the 1977

film *A Bridge Too Far* (screenplay by William Goodman, directed by Richard Atten-borough) and is attested to by participants. Snape, *God and the British Soldier*, 54.

75. Mansfield, *Faith of the American Soldier*, 170–75.

76. The Brigade Quartermasters website, http://www.brigadeqm.com/product-p/cam91.htm, accessed July 2004.

77. The psalm appears on the bandana in the New King James translation. All quotations are from Psalm 91.

78. Snape, *Royal Army Chaplains' Department 1796–1953*, 310, citing Imperial War Museum Sound, anonymous, 7698.

79. Becker, *War and Faith*, 63–64, citing *Lettres de Guerre a Notre-Dame Trouvees dans l'Oratoire du Parc de Noulette Pas de Calais*, July 4, 1915, Letter no. 17.

80. Conrad C. Crane, *Bombs, Cities, and Civilians: American Airpower Strategy in World War II* (Lawrence: University Press of Kansas, 1993), 51.

81. Becker, *War and Faith*, 97, citing Lucien Roure, "Superstitions du Front de Guerre," *Etudes* 153 (1917), 710–11.

82. In Crane, *Bombs, Cities, and Civilians*, 54.

83. In Crosby, *Battlefield Chaplains*, 45.

84. Dobbin and Deakin, "United Kingdom," 82, citing Chris Keeble, http://www.forachange.net/features/3266.html.

85. Dale R. Herspring, *Soldiers, Commissars and Chaplains* (Lanham, MD: Rowman & Littlefield, 2001), 41, citing Joseph T. O'Callahan, *I Was Chaplain on the Franklin* (New York: Macmillan, 1961), 54.

86. In Mansfield, *Faith of the American Soldier*, 61–62.

87. Dobbin and Deakin, "United Kingdom," 82, citing Stephen Garnett, *Salute the Soldier Poets* (London: Allen and Unwin, 1966).

88. Jon Meacham, *American Gospel: God, the Founding Fathers, and the Making of a Nation* (New York: Random House, 2007), p.28, citing "The Address of General Washington To The People of The United States on his Declining of the Presidency of the United States," September 19, 1796.

89. Dobbin and Deakin, "United Kingdom," 72, citing Rifle Brigade Standing Order 1801.

90. In Herman A. Norton, *Struggling for Recognition: The United States Army Chaplaincy: 1791–1865* (Honolulu: University Press of the Pacific, 2004), 48.

91. Snape, *God and the British Soldier*, 179, citing David Englander, "Discipline and Morale in the British Army, 1917–1918," in *State, Society and Mobilization in Europe during the First World War*, edited by John Horne (Cambridge: Cambridge University, 1997), 137and Imperial War Museum documents, M. Hardie.

92. In Gushwa, *Best and Worst of Times*, 186.

93. P. Middleton Brumwell, *The Army Chaplain: The Royal Army Chaplains' Department, the Duties of Chaplains and Morale* (London: Adam & Charles Black, 1943), 39, 51, 71.

94. Dobbin and Deakin, "United Kingdom," 80, citing *Chaplains' Handbook*, Character Training Series 22 (January 1989–December 1989), 1; U.S. Navy, *Religious Ministry in the Fleet*, NWP 1-05 (Newport, RI: Department of the Navy, August 2003), 3–2; and U.S. Army, *Religious Support*, FM 1-05 (Washington, DC: Department of the Army, April 2003), 3–16.

95. U.S. Marine Corps, *Religious Ministry in the United States Marine Corps,* MCW P 6-12, 2001, 4–5, www.combatindex.com/store/MCWP/Sample/.../MCWP_ 6-12.pdf.

96. Abdulaziz Aflakseir and Peter G. Coleman, "The Influence of Religious Coping on the Mental Health of Disabled Iranian War Veterans," *Mental Health, Religion and Culture* 12, no. 2 (2009): 175–90; Kent Drescher and David W. Foy, "Spirituality and Trauma Treatment: Suggestions for Including Spirituality as a Coping Resource," *National Center for PTSD Clinical Quarterly* 5, no. 1 (2005), 4–5; Zeev Kaplan, Michael A. Matar, Ram Kamin, Tamar Sadan, and Hagit Cohen, "Stress-Related Responses after 3 Years of Exposure to Terror in Israel: Are Ideological-Religious Factors Associated with Resilience?" *Journal of Clinical Psychiatry* 66, no. 9 (2005): 1146–54.

97. Judith A. Sigmund, "Spirituality and Trauma: The Role of Clergy in the Treatment of Posttraumatic Stress Disorder," *Journal of Religion and Health* 42, no. 3 (2003), 221–29; Kent D. Drescher, Gilbert Ramirez, Jeffrey J. Leoni, Jennifer M. Romesser, Jo Sornborger, and David W. Foy, "Spirituality and Trauma: Development of a Group Therapy Module," *Group* 28, no. 4 (2004): 71–87.

98. Tayebeh Zandipour, "The Role of Religious Beliefs and Thoughts of Holy Defence Veterans in Accepting the Difficulties of Imposed War," *Counselling Psychology Quarterly* 21, no. 1 (2008): 75–83.

99. Victor Florian and Mario Mikulincer, "The Impact of Death-Risk Experiences and Religiosity on the Fear of Personal Death: The Case of Israeli Soldiers in Lebanon," *OMEGA—Journal of Death and Dying* 26, no. 2 (1992): 101–11.

100. Aflakseir and Coleman, "Influence of Religious Coping"; Mevludin Hasanović and Izet Pajević, "Religious Moral Beliefs Inversely Related to Trauma Experiences Severity and Depression Severity among War Veterans in Bosnia and Herzegovina," *Journal of Religion and Health* 52, no. 3 (2013): 730–39.

101. Sanea Nad, Darko Marcinko, Bjanka Vuksan-Æusa, Miro Jakovljevic, and Gordana Jakovljevic, "Spiritual Well-Being, Intrinsic Religiosity, and Suicidal Behavior in Predominantly Catholic Croatian War Veterans with Chronic Posttraumatic Stress Disorder: A Case Control Study," *Journal of Nervous and Mental Disease* 196, no. 1 (2008): 79–83.

102. Joseph Sivak, Jody L. Swartz, and David X. Swenson, "PTSD and Chronic Suicidal Ideation: The Role of Counter Suicidal Cognition," *Traumatology* 5, no. 3 (1999): 1–6.

103. Ibid.

104. Joanna Bourke, *An Intimate History of Killing: Face to Face Killing in 20th Century Warfare* (New York: Basic Books, 2000), 283–84, citing Robert L. Garrard, "Combat Guilt Reactions," *North Carolina Medical Journal* 10, no. 9 (1949), 491.

105. Aflakseir and Coleman, "Influence of Religious Coping."

106. Howard Johnson and Andrew Thompson, "The Development and Maintenance of Post-Traumatic Stress Disorder (PTSD) in Civilian Adult Survivors of War Trauma and Torture: A Review," *Clinical Psychology Review* 28, no. 1 (2008): 36–47.

107. Neil J. Fernando and Ruwan M. Jayatunge, "Combat Related PTSD among the Sri Lankan Army Servicemen" (unpublished manuscript, Ministry of Health, Sri Lanka, July 2011), http://www.traumaticbraininjury.net/, accessed July 2014.

108. Jill Bormann, Lin Liu, Steven R. Thorp, and Ariel J. Lang, "Spiritual Well-being Mediates PTSD Change in Veterans with Military-Related PTSD," *International Journal of Behavioral Medicine* 19, no. 4 (2012): 496–502; Jill E. Bormann, Steven Thorp, Julie L. Wetherell, and Shahrokh Golshan, "A Spiritually Based Group Intervention for Combat Veterans with Posttraumatic Stress Disorder Feasibility Study," *Journal of Holistic Nursing* 26, no. 2 (2008): 109–16.

109. Julio F. P. Peres, Alexander Moreira-Almeida, Antonia Gladys Nasello, and Harold G. Koenig, "Spirituality and Resilience in Trauma Victims," *Journal of Religion and Health* 46, no. 3 (2007): 343–50.

110. J. Irene Harris, Christopher R. Erbes, Brian E. Engdahl, Paul Thuras, Nichole Murray-Swank, Dixie Grace, Henry Ogden, Raymond H. A. Olson, Ann Marie Winskowski, Russ Bacon, Catherine Malec, Kelsey Campion, and TuVan Le, "The Effectiveness of a Trauma Focused Spiritually Integrated Intervention for Veterans Exposed to Trauma," *Journal of Clinical Psychology* 67, no. 4 (2011): 425–38.

111. Kenneth Pargament, Harold G. Koenig, and Lisa M. Perez, "The Many Methods of Religious Coping: Development and Initial Validation of the RCOPE," *Journal of Clinical Psychology* 56, no. 4 (2000): 519–43.

112. Justin Orton, "Can Religious Coping, Religious Involvement, Spirituality, and Social Support Predict Trauma Symptoms at Six Months after Combat?" (PhD dissertation, George Fox University, 2011).

113. Kent D. Drescher and David W. Foy "When They Come Home: Posttraumatic Stress, Moral Injury, and Spiritual Consequences for Veterans," *Reflective Practice: Formation and Supervision in Ministry* 28 (2012): 85–102; Charlotte vanOryen Witvliet, Kelly A. Phipps, Michele E. Feldman, and Jean C. Beckham, "Posttraumatic Mental and Physical Health Correlates of Forgiveness and Religious Coping in Military Veterans," *Journal of Traumatic Stress* 17, no. 3 (2004): 269–73.

114. Honeywell, *Chaplains of the United States Army,* 341.

115. Albrecht Schuebel, *300 Jahre Evangelische Soldatenseelsorge* (Munich: Evangelischer Pressverband, 1964), 208.

116. Gushwa, *Best and Worst of Times,* 178.

117. On the significance of post-battle purification in medieval warfare and the implications of its absence in modern warfare, see Bernard J. Verkamp, *The Moral Treatment of Returning Warriors in Early Medieval and Modern Times* (Scranton: University of Scranton Press, 2006).

118. John E. Johnson, "The Faith and Practice of the Raw Recruit," in *Religion of Soldier and Sailor,* edited by Willard L. Sperry, 42–67 (Cambridge, MA: Harvard University Press, 1945); Atkins, "Soldier's Second Thoughts," 101–3, 109–10; Josef Perau, *Priester im Heere Hitlers: Erinnerungen 1940–1945* (Essen: Ludgerus, 1962), 89; George Hilton, "A Chaplain in Vietnam," in *Military Chaplains: From a Religious Military to a Military Religion,* edited by Harvey G. Cox (New York: American Report Press, 1972), 124.

119. Alan Fontana and Robert Rosenheck, "Trauma, Change in Strength of Religious Faith, and Mental Health Service Use among Veterans Treated for PTSD," *Journal of Nervous and Mental Disease* 192, no. 9 (2004): 579–84; Drescher and Foy, *When They Come Home.*

120. Sanea Mihaljević, Bjanka Vuksan-Ćusa, Darko Marčinko, Elvira Koić, Zorana Kušević, and Miro Jakovljević, "Spiritual Well-Being, Cortisol, and Suicidality in

Croatian War Veterans Suffering from PTSD," *Journal of Religion and Health* 50, no. 2 (2011): 464–73; Sherry Falsetti, Patricia A. Resick, and Joanne L. Davis, "Changes in Religious Beliefs Following Trauma," *Journal of Traumatic Stress* 16, no. 4 (2003): 391–98. As a rule, medical trauma tends to lead to religious seeking, more frequent prayer, and church attendance, whereas "event trauma" tends to have the opposite effect; Drescher et al., "Spirituality and Trauma."

121. Samuel J. Watson, "Religion and Combat Motivation in the Confederate Armies," *Journal of Military History* 58, no. 1 (1994), 1–2. For dissenting opinions, see Gerald F. Linderman, *Embattled Courage: The Experience of Combat in the American Civil War* (New York: Free Press, 1987); Bell I. Wiley, *The Life of Johnny Reb: The Common Soldier of the Confederacy* (Indianapolis: Bobbs-Merrill, 1943).

122. Shattuck, *Shield and Hiding Place,* 92, 99.

123. Kurt O. Berends, "Wholesome Reading Purifies and Elevates the Man: The Religious Military Press in the Confederacy," in *Religion and the American Civil War,* edited by Randall M. Miller, Harry S. Stout, and Charles Reagan Wilson (New York: Oxford University Press, 1998), 135; Woodworth, *While God Is Marching On,* 246, citing William W. Bennett, *A Narrative of the Great Revival in the Southern Armies during the Late Civil War between the States of the Federal Union* (Philadelphia: Claxton, Remsen, and Haffelfinger, 1877), 413–14, Gardiner H. Shattuck, "Revivals in the Camp," *Christian History* 11 (1992), 28–31.

124. Honeywell, *Chaplains of the United States Army,* 138.

125. Sidney Romero, *Religion in the Rebel Ranks* (Lanham, MD: University Press of America, 1983); James Robertson, *Soldiers Blue and Grey* (Columbia: University of South Carolina Press, 1998).

126. James M. McPherson, *For Cause and Comrades: Why Men Fought in the Civil War* (New York: Oxford University Press, 1997), 75–76.

127. Woodworth, *While God Is Marching On,* 190.

128. Watson, "Religion and Combat Motivation,"

129. McPherson, *For Cause and Comrades,* 72–73.

130. Woodworth, *While God Is Marching On,* 193; Watson, "Religion and Combat Motivation," 44.

131. Watson, "Religion and Combat Motivation," 43–53; McPherson, *For Cause and Comrades,* 64–65.

132. Woodworth, *While God Is Marching On,* 50–51, citing John McKee Diary, August 14, 1864, Civil War Miscellaneous Collection, USAMHI.

133. Woodworth, *While God Is Marching On,* 65–66, citing Mary Livermore, *My Story of the War* (Hartford: A. D. Worthington, 1890), 196–97.

134. Snape, *Royal Army Chaplains' Department 1796–1953,* 228, citing I. W. M. Documents, E. C. Crosse.

135. Crerar, *Padres in No Man's Land,* 129.

136. Martin Purdy, "Roman Catholic Army Chaplains during the First World War: Roles, Experiences and Dilemmas" (MA thesis, University of Central Lancashire, 2012), 43, citing Alfred O'Rahilly, *The Padre of Trench Street: Father William Doyle* (London: Longmans, Green and Company, 1920), 94.

137. Johnstone and Haggerty, *Cross on the Sword,* 109; Purdy, "Roman Catholic Army Chaplains," 2., citing Jane Leonard, *The Catholic Chaplaincy in Ireland and the First World War* (Dublin: Trinity History Workshop, 1986), 13; Becker, *War and Faith,* 47–59.

138. Rich Schweitzer, "The Cross and the Trenches: Religious Faith and Doubt among Some British Soldiers on the Western Front," *War and Society* 16, no. 2 (1998): 33–57.

139. Wilkinson, *Church of England,* 160–63; Rafferty, "Catholic Chaplains," 47.

140. Crerar, *Padres in No Man's Land,* 203.

141. Rafferty, "Catholic Chaplains," 47, citing Robert Graves, *Goodbye to All That* (London: Anchor, 1929).

142. Snape, *Royal Army Chaplains' Department 1796–1953,* 241, citing Philip Gibbs, *Realities of War* (London: Heinemann, 1920), 364.

143. Alan Wilkinson, "The Paradox of the Military Chaplain," *Theology* 84 (1981), 252.

144. Crerar, *Padres in No Man's Land,* 194–95, citing Will R. Bird, *And We Go On* (Toronto: Hunter-Rose, 1930), 337.

145. Gordon H. Zahn, *Chaplains in the RAF: A Study in Role Tension* (Manchester: Manchester University Press, 1969), 112; Wilkinson, "Paradox of the Military Chaplain," 252.

146. Snape, *Royal Army Chaplains' Department 1796–1953,* 253.

147. Becker, *War and Faith,* 169–70.

148. Stephen A. Garrett, *Ethics and Airpower in World War II: The British Bombing of German Cities* (New York: St. Martin's Press, 1993), 96.

149. Stanley High, "The War Boom in Religion," in *The Army Reader,* edited by Karl Detzer (Indianapolis: Bobbs-Merrill, 1943), 294–97.

150. Ibid.

151. William D. Cleary, "The Ministry of the Chaplain," in *Religion of Soldier and Sailor,* edited by Willard L. Sperry (Cambridge, MA: Harvard University Press, 1945), 78, 87. There were about 8 million servicemen enlisted in the army at the time, so these figures must reflect repeated attendance at weekly services.

152. Honeywell, *Chaplains of the United States Army,* 337.

153. Reverend John Coghlan, "Introduction," in *The Priest among the Soldiers,* edited by Martin Dempsey (London: Burns Oates, 1947), 3, 5; Schuebel, *300 Jahre Evangelische Soldatenseelsorge,* 47, 170.

154. Stouffer et al., *American Soldier, vol. 2,* 186–87, 612.

155. Brian Wansink and Craig S. Wansink, "Are There Atheists in Foxholes? Combat Intensity and Religious Behavior," *Journal of Religion and Health* 52, no. 3 (2013): 768–79.

156. William P. Mahedy, *Out of the Night: The Spiritual Journey of Vietnam Vets* (New York: Ballantine Books, 1986), esp. 125–66.

157. Bourke, *Intimate History of Killing,* 292–93, citing Robert Jay Lifton, "The Postwar World," *Journal of Social Issues* 31, no. 4 (1975), 186.

158. Drescher and Foy, *Spirituality and Trauma Treatment.*

159. Ibid.; Sigmund, "Spirituality and Trauma"; Stacy Smith, "Exploring the Interaction of Trauma and Spirituality," *Traumatology: An International Journal* 10, no. 4 (2004): 231–43.

160. Falsetti, Resick, and Davis, "Changes in Religious Beliefs Following Trauma."

161. Fontana and Rosenheck, "Trauma."

162. Drescher et al., "Spirituality and Trauma."

163. In Jeremy Sharon, "Religious Overtones in Letter from IDF Commander to His Soldiers Draws Criticism, Support," *Jerusalem Post*, July 14, 2014, http://www.jpost.com/Jewish-World/Jewish-News/Religious-overtones-in-letter-from-IDF-commander-to-his-soldiers-draws-criticism-support-362673; Coby Ben-Simhon, "The Holy War Being Waged within the Israeli Army," *Ha'aretz*, November 8, 2014, http://www.haaretz.com/news/diplomacy-defense/.premium-1.625020, accessed November 2014.

164. Brett Wilkins, "Troops Wearing 'Pork-Eating Crusader' Patches in Afghanistan," March 25, 2012, http://morallowground.com/2012/03/25/us-troops-wearing-pork-eating-crusader-patches-in-afghanistan; Matthew Cox, "Troops Still Embrace 'Infidel' Label," March 16, 2012, http://www.military.com; and Robert Johnson, "The Pork Eating Crusader Patch Is a Huge Hit with Troops In Afghanistan," *Business Insider*, March 16, 2012, http://www.businessinsider.com/this-whole-line-of-infidel-gear-cant-be-helping-international-relations-in-afghanistan-2012-3, accessed June 2014.

6. Religion on the Battlefield in Iraq, 2003–2009

1. "Last Words of a Terrorist," *Observer*, September 30, 2001, http://www.theguardian.com/world/2001/sep/30/terrorism.september113, accessed November 2014.

2. See Saskia Gieling, *Religion and War in Revolutionary Iran* (London: I. B. Tauris, 1999); Shahram Chubin and Charles Tripp, *Iran and Iraq at War* (Boulder: Westview Press, 1991); Scott D. Sagam, "Realist Perspectives on Ethical Norms and Weapons of Mass Destruction," in *Ethics and Weapons of Mass Destruction: Religious and Secular Perspectives,* edited by Sohail H. Hashmi and Steven P. Lee, 73–95 (New York: Cambridge University Press, 2004).

3. See Jose M. Sanchez, *The Spanish Civil War as a Religious Tragedy* (Notre Dame: University of Notre Dame Press, 1987), 11, 43–44; Bruce Lincoln, "Revolutionary Exhumations in Spain, July 1936," *Comparative Studies in Society and History* 27, no. 2 (1985): 241–60; Jose Luis Ledesma, "The Enemy Par Excellence: Anticlerical Violence in the Spanish Civil War (1936–39)," paper presented at the 9th Global Conference on Violence: Probing the Boundaries, Salzburg, Austria, March 12–14, 2010; Michael Sells, "Crosses of Blood: Sacred Space, Religion, and Violence in Bosnia-Hercegovina," *Sociology of Religion* 64, no. 3 (2003): 309–18; Jessi Taylor, "Unholy Coercion: The Complicity of the Serbian Orthodox Church in the Use of Rape as a War Tactic," (MA thesis, University of Ottawa, 2010); Philip Jenkins, *The Great and Holy War: How World War I Became a Religious Crusade* (New York: HarperCollins, 2014), 204, 307.

4. See, for example Assaf Moghadam, *The Globalization of Martyrdom: Al Qaeda, Salafi Jihad, and the Diffusion of Suicide Attacks* (Baltimore: Johns Hopkins University Press, 2008); Mohammed M. Hafez, *Suicide Bombers in Iraq: The Strategy and Ideology of Martyrdom* (Washington, DC: US Institute of Peace Press, 2007); Thomas Hegghammer, "Global Jihadism after the Iraq War," *Middle East Journal* 60, no. 1 (2006): 11–32; Mohammed M. Hafez, "Martyrdom Mythology in Iraq: How Jihadists Frame Suicide Terrorism in Videos and Biographies," *Terrorism and Political Violence*

19, no. 1 (2007): 95–115; Daniel Byman, "Fighting Salafi-Jihadist Insurgencies: How Much Does Religion Really Matter?" *Studies in Conflict and Terrorism* 36, no. 5 (2013): 353–71.

5. Thomas W. Lippman, "U.S. Claims Tacit Support from Arab Nations; Attack's Timing Propitious for Minimizing Negative Reactions in Region, Analysts Say," *Washington Post*, December 17, 1998, A30.

6. Ultimately, U.S.-Iraqi cease-fire talks began less than two weeks before the start of Ramadan. George Bush and Brent Scowcroft, *A World Transformed* (New York: Knopf, 1998), 385, 411; Richard M. Swain, *Lucky War: Third Army in Desert Storm* (Fort Leavenworth, KS: Diane Publishing, 1999), 71; Bruce Gottlieb, "Why Not Bomb on Ramadan?" *Slate Magazine*, December 18, 1998.

7. Charles M. Sennott, "Clinton Gets Little Sympathy in Iraq; The Clinton Impeachment," *Boston Globe*, December 20, 1998, A1; Barton Gellman, Dana Priest, and Bradley Graham, "Diplomacy and Doubts on the Road to War; U.S. Prepared to Bomb Iraq While Wondering If the Aftermath Would Be Worth It," *Washington Post*, March 1, 1998, A01.

8. Arianna Huffington, "Clinton Plays into Milosovic's Hand," *Chicago Sun-Times*, April 11, 1999, 31.

9. Bill Sammon, "No Pause in Bombing for Ramadan Month; Goal Is to 'Finish the Mission,' Rice Says," *Washington Times*, November 2, 2001, A4.

10. Secretary Donald Rumsfeld interview with Brett Baier, *Fox News*, U.S. Department of Defense, Office of the Assistant Secretary of Defense, August 19, 2002. See also Secretary Rumsfeld interview with Tom Bowman (*Baltimore Sun*), U.S. Department of Defense, Office of the Assistant Secretary of Defense, December 27, 2001.

11. Stephen Lynch, "Most Dangerous Game: What Went Wrong in the Hunt for Bin Laden," *New York Post,* October 5, 2008, 34.

12. Susan Sachs, "The Struggle for Iraq: The Occupation; U.S. Forces to Lift Night Curfew for Muslim Holy Month," *New York Times*, October 25, 2003, A8; David Ignatius, "Tikrit Tests Plan A," *Washington Post*, October 26, 2003, B07; David E. Sanger, "The Struggle for Iraq: Occupation; Iraq Paradox: Cracking Down While Promoting Freedom," *New York Times*, October 28, 2003, A10; Daniel Williams, "U.S. Grip Loosens in the Sunni Triangle; Tactical Shift In Iraq Leaves Power Vacuum," *Washington Post*, November 8, 2003, A16; Alex Berenson, "The Struggle for Iraq: Combat; U.S. Troops Raid Tikrit in Hunt for Guerrillas," *New York Times*, November 9, 2003, sec. 1, 15; Dexter Filkins, "A Region Inflamed: Strategy; Tough New Tactics by U.S. Tighten Grip on Iraq Towns," *New York Times*, December 7, 2003, sec. 1, 1.

13. Richard W. Stevenson and David Firestone, "The Struggle for Iraq: The White House; Bush Says Bombings Will Not Deter Him," *New York Times*, October 28, 2003, A12; Thom Shanker, "As Iraq Elections Near, Pentagon Extends Tours of Duty for about 6,500 U.S. Soldiers," *New York Times*, October 20, 2004, A8; Eric Schmitt and Thom Shanker, "Estimates by U.S. See More Rebels with More Funds," *New York Times*, October 22, 2004, A1; Richard A. Oppel Jr., "Rebel Attacks Kill 18 Iraqis; G.I.'s Injured," *New York Times*, October 24, 2004, sec. 1, 1; Eric Schmitt, "In Iraq, U.S. Officials Cite Obstacles to Victory," *New York Times*, October 31, 2004, sec. 1, 1; Bradley Graham and Walter Pincus, "U.S. Hopes to Divide Insur-

gency; Plan to Cut Extremism Involves Iraq's Sunnis," *Washington Post*, October 31, 2004, A1; Richard A. Oppel Jr., "In Wake of Falluja, Pace of Combat Intensifies in Ramadi," *New York Times*, November 14, 2004, sec. 1, 13; Jackie Spinner, "Danger, Boredom Converge at Checkpoint Near Baqubah; Soldiers Seek to Thwart Car Bombers, Distinguish 'Bad Guys' from Civilians," *Washington Post*, November 25, 2004, A30; Daniel Williams, "Explosions across Iraq Kill 3 GIs, at Least 15 Others; Car Bomb in Front of Mosul Police Station Claims 9," *Washington Post*, February 1, 2004, A20; Steve Fainaru, "Violence, Crash in Iraq Kill 6 Troops; 5 Baghdad Churches Targeted by Bombers," *Washington Post*, October 17, 2004, A1; Karl Vick, "Trouble Spots Dot Iraqi Landscape; Attacks Erupting Away from Fallujah," *Washington Post*, November 15, 2004, A1.

14. Edward Wong, "Rebels Dressed as Women Attack Iraqi Police Station," *New York Times*, November 5, 2005, A10; Amy Scott Tyson, "'06 Cuts In Iraq Troops Unlikely; General Points to Sectarian Violence in New Assessment," *Washington Post*, September 20, 2006, A1; Sudarsan Reghavan, "Since Threat, Attacks on U.S. Troops Have Risen," *Washington Post*, September 21, 2006, A19; Michael Luo, "After Burst of Violence, as Many as 60 Bodies Are Found in Baghdad," *New York Times*, September 29, 2006, A12; Reuters, "110 Bodies Found in Baghdad in Two Days," *Washington Post*, October 11, 2006, A12; Josh While and Thomas E. Ricks, "'Tough' Time in Iraq to Continue, Casey Says," *Washington Post*, October 12, 2006, A21; Joshua Partlow, "State Dept. Convoy Attacked in Baghdad, Sparking a Shootout; Security Guards Kill 9 Civilians, Iraqis Say," *Washington Post*, September 17, 2007, A14; Sudarsan Reghavan, "Blasts Kill at Least 30 across Iraq in Growing Campaign of Violence," *Washington Post*, September 27, 2007, A18.

15. This analysis relies on daily incident counts between March 20, 2003, and June 30, 2009, provided by Joseph H. Felter and Jacob N. Shapiro's Empirical Studies of Conflict Project (ESOC), https://esoc.princeton.edu/. The data were produced through a multiyear collaboration between ESOC and Iraq Body Count (IBC), https://www.iraqbodycount.org/, and are based on coding of press reports from multiple sources. Each incident is attributed to coalition forces, sectarian actors, or insurgents but without reporting the identity of the victims or perpetrators. The data have the disadvantage of registering only attacks in which civilians were killed and thus probably undercount the number of incidents, although there is no reason to assume that they do so in a consistently biased manner that overestimates or underestimates events during sacred dates in the calendar. For more details on IBC procedures, see http://www.iraqbodycount.org/. For other work with these data, see Luke N. Condra and Jacob N. Shapiro, "Who Takes the Blame? The Strategic Effects of Collateral Damage," *American Journal of Political Science* 56, no. 1 (2012): 167–87.

16. The slight rise in sectarian attacks during Ramadan is statistically insignificant at $p = 0.448$ for sectarian attacks and $p = 0.720$ for insurgent attacks, where statistical significance is defined at the standard $p < 0.05$ level. For this and all subsequent models, I assume a negative binomial distribution to model the number of incidents per day as an overdispersed event count skewed toward low values.

17. The findings on sectarian attacks (−24.41 percent) and the findings on insurgent attacks (−42.28 percent) are both significant at $p < 0.01$. This analysis controls for the effects of a one-day lag in the number of incidents, days since the beginning of the war, and fixed effects of years and months.

18. This finding (−30.63 percent) is significant at $p = 0.0133$. This model controls for the effects of a one-day lag in the number of incidents, days since the beginning of the war, and fixed effects of days of the week and years. The results for insurgent and coalition attacks are not significant. This may suggest that Muslim combatants regard Eid al-Fitr as an unsuitable occasion for attacks on fellow Muslims but an appropriate occasion for attacks on coalition forces. Alternatively, it may be that the movements involved in sectarian conflict and those involved in anti-coalition attacks are constrained by different interpretations of Islamic beliefs and practices regarding this sacred day. The available data do not suffice to adjudicate between these explanations.

19. Sectarian attacks declined by 24.38 percent (statistically significant at the $p = 0.0179$ level), and insurgent attacks declined by 69.4 percent (statistically significant at $p < 0.01$). This model also controls for the effects of a one-day lag in number of incidents, days since the beginning of the war, and fixed effects of days of the week and years. The results are robust to coding Eid al-Adha as a three-, four-, or five-day feast.

20. See Associated Press, "Angry Protests in Iraq Suggest Sunni Arab Shift to Militants," *New York Times*, January 2, 2007, 9; Thomas L. Friedman, "A Hanging and a Funeral," *New York Times*, January 3, 2007, 21; Hassan M. Fattah, "Hanging Images Make Hussein a Martyr to Many in Arab World," *New York Times*, January 6, 2007, 1.

21. I searched for incidents in the *New York Times*, the *Washington Post*, and the International Religious Freedom Report under "Abuses by Rebel or Foreign Forces or Terrorist Organizations." I counted only instances in which the targets were identified as Christian (or "Chaldean") and in which the date of the attack was specified.

22. This measure of the link between Christian sacred time and anti-Christian violence in Iraq is relatively conservative in that it excludes all Christian holy days aside from Sundays. In both 2008 and 2009, for example, several attacks coincided with Advent, the Roman Catholic Vigil of the Solemnity of Mary, and the Eastern Orthodox Nativity Fast. Nonetheless, we cannot conclude from these data that there is a statistically significant correlation between Sundays and anti-Christian violence in Iraq. After all, most Sundays in Iraq saw no attacks against Christians.

23. These attacks included the bombing of four churches in Baghdad and two churches in Mosul on August 1, 2004; attacks on four Orthodox, Catholic, and Anglican churches on January 29, 2006; the bombing of six churches and three convents in Baghdad and Mosul on January 6, 2008; and attacks on five Baghdad churches on July 12, 2009. See Somini Sengupta and Ian Fisher, "Bombs Explode near Churches in 2 Iraqi Cities," *New York Times*, August 2, 2004, A1; Pamela Constable, "Blasts Target Christian Churches in 2 Iraqi Cities; Attacks during Services Kill 11 in Baghdad, Mosul," *Washington Post*, August 2, 2004, A1; Robert F. Worth, "Bombings at Christian Sites Leave 3 Dead and 15 Hurt," *New York Times*, January 20, 2006, A12; Steven Lee Myers, "Churches and Envoy Attacked in Iraq," *New York Times*, July 13, 2009, A4; International Religious Freedom Reports for 2004, 2006, and 2008, http://www.state.gov/g/drl/rls/irf/, accessed March 2011.

24. On counterinsurgency and sacred space, see Ron E. Hassner, "Counterinsurgency and the Problem of Sacred Space," in *Treading on Sacred Ground,* edited by C. Christine Fair and Sumit Ganguly, 13–36 (Oxford University Press, 2008); Ron E. Hassner, "At the Horns of the Altar: Counterinsurgency and the Religious Roots of

the Sanctuary Practice," *Civil Wars* 10, no. 1 (2008): 22–39; Ron E. Hassner, "Islamic Just War Theory and the Challenge of Sacred Space in Iraq," *Journal of International Affairs* 61, no. 1 (2007): 131–52; Ron E. Hassner, "Fighting Insurgency on Sacred Ground," *Washington Quarterly* 29, no. 2 (2006): 149–66.

25. John F. Burns, "A Region Inflamed: Violence; At Least 143 Die in Attacks at Two Sacred Sites in Iraq," *New York Times*, March 3, 2004, A1; Dexter Filkins and Eric Schmitt, "A Region Inflamed: Security; Other Attacks Averted in Iraq, a General Says," *New York Times*, March 4, 2004, A1; Vali Nasr, "Iraq's Real Holy War," *New York Times*, March 6, 2004, A15.

26. "Iraq on the Brink," *New York Times*, March 1, 2006, A18; Volkhard Windfuhr and Bernhard Zand, "Religious Strife Is Pushing Iraq toward Civil War," *New York Times*, March 6, 2006, citing *Der Spiegel*, translated by Christopher Sultan; Jeffrey Gettleman, "Eighty-Five Bodies Found in Baghdad in Sectarian Strife," *New York Times*, March 15, 2006, A1; "Excerpts from the President's News Conference on the Iraq War and Iran," *New York Times*, March 22, 2006, A10.

27. Richard Oppel, "U.S. Apologizes for Baghdad Mosque Incident," *New York Times*, August 15, 2003, A12.

28. Jim Michaels, "Iraqi, U.S. Forces Target Insurgents in 7 Mosque Raids: Operations Increase in Sunni Stronghold," *USA Today*, October 13, 2004, A1; Edward Wong, "U.S. Raids in 2 Sunni Cities Anger Clerics and Residents," *New York Times*, October 13, 2004, A12.

29. "U.S. Troops Go Softly at Sacred Site," *Hobart Mercury*, April 5, 2003; "U.S. Soldiers Kneel to Calm Angry Crowd; Mighty American Army Tries to Win Over Iraqi Civilians," *Ottawa Citizen*, April 4, 2003, A6.

30. Dexter Filkins and Robert F. Worth, "U.S. Troops Set for Final Attack on Falluja Force," *New York Times*, November 13, 2004, A1; Thom Shanker and Eric Schmitt, "Falluja Data Said to Pressure Guerrillas," *New York Times*, December 3, 2004, A12. For the report, see http://www.defenselink.mil/news/Dec2004/d20041203entire.ppt, accessed March 2011.

31. Robert F. Worth, "Marines Find Vast Arms Cache in Falluja Leader's Mosque," *New York Times*, November 25, 2004, A22.

32. See Samantha Shapiro, "The War inside the Arab Newsroom," *New York Times*, January 2, 2005, sec. 6, 27.

33. John F. Burns, "U.S. Seeks Arrest of Shiite Cleric," *New York Times*, April 6, 2004, A1; Alex Berenson and John F. Burns, "8-Day Battle for Najaf: From Attack to Stalemate," *New York Times*, August 18, 2004, A1; Sabrina Tavernise, "Cleric Keeps Grip on Najaf Shrine, Even While Saying He'll Yield It," *New York Times*, August 22, 2004, sec. 1, 4.

34. Neil MacFarquhar and Steven R. Weisman, "Leaders at Talks in Egypt Urge Support for Political Resolution to the Turmoil in Iraq," *New York Times*, November 24, 2004, A14.

35. Edward Wong, "G.I.'s Report Killing 36 Insurgents around Kufa Mosque That Held Arms," *New York Times*, May 24, 2004, A11.

36. Colin H. Kahl, "In the Crossfire or the Crosshairs? Norms, Civilian Casualties, and the U.S. Conduct in Iraq," *International Security* 32, no. 1 (2007), 16–17.

37. U.S. Joint Forces Command, *Joint Fires and Targeting Handbook of the US Joint Forces Command,* Joint Warfighting Center (Suffolk, VA, October 2007), III-62,

http://www.globalsecurity.org/military/library/policy/dod/joint/joint-fires-targeting_hb.pdf.

38. Joint Chiefs of Staff, *Joint Targeting*, Joint Publication 3-60 (Washington, DC, January 31, 2013), A6.

39. Kahl, "In the Crossfire or the Crosshairs?"; Joint Chiefs of Staff, *Close Air Support*, Joint Publication 3-09.3 (Washington, DC, July 8, 2009); Joint Chiefs of Staff, *Joint Fire Support*, Joint Publication 3-09 (Washington, DC, June 30, 2010); Center for Law and Military Operations, *Legal Lessons Learned from Afghanistan and Iraq*, Vol. 1 (Charlottesville, VA: 2014).

40. Dexter Filkins and Robert F. Worth, "U.S.-Led Assault Marks Advances against Falluja," *New York Times*, November 10, 2004, A1; Dexter Filkins, "In Taking Falluja Mosque, Victory by the Inch," *New York Times*, November 10, 2004, A1.

41. Michael Kamber, "On a Mission in Sadr City, Waiting Silently for the Expected," *New York Times*, June 6, 2004, sec. 1, 14.

42. Richard A. Opel Jr., "In Wake of Falluja, Pace of Combat Intensifies in Ramadi," *New York Times*, November 14, 2004, A13.

43. William Tinning, "'If They Use the Mosque as a Military Machine, It's No Longer a House of Worship and We Strike,'" *Herald* (Glasgow), April 8, 2004, 6.

44. Nir Rosen, "Fallujah: Inside the Iraqi Resistance," *Asia Times*, July 15, 2004. See also Youssef M. Ibrahim, "Outside View: Muddy Boots in the Mosque," UPI, November 18, 2004.

45. In Michael Hoyt, "The Iraqi Inter-Religious Congress and the Baghdad Accords," in *Military Chaplains in Afghanistan, Iraq, and Beyond: Advisement and Leader Engagement in Highly Religious Environments*, edited by Eric Patterson (Lanham, MD: Rowman & Littlefield, 2014), 80.

46. Joint Chiefs of Staff, *Religious Affairs in Joint Operations*, JP 1-05 (Washington, DC, November 13, 2009).

47. See, for example U.S. Army, *Religious Support*, FM 1-05 (Washington, DC: Department of the Army, April 2003); U.S. Navy, *Religious Ministry in the Fleet*, NWP 1-05 (Newport, RI: Department of the Navy, August 2003); U.S. Marine Corps, *Religious Ministry Team Handbook*, MCRP 6-12A (Washington, DC: Department of the Navy, May 16, 2003); U.S. Marine Corps, *The Commander's Handbook for Religious Ministry Support*, MCRP 6-12C (Washington, DC: Department of the Navy, February 2, 2004).

48. U.S. Army, *Religious Support*, viii.

49. William Sean Lee, Christopher J. Burke, and Zonna M. Crayne, "Military Chaplains as Peace Builders: Embracing Indigenous Religions in Stability Operations," Air University, 2005, 21–23, http://oai.dtic.mil/oai/oai?verb=getRecord&metadataPrefix=html&identifier=ADA425869, citing Canada. National Defence, *Civilian-Military Cooperation in Peace, Emergencies, Crisis and War* (Ottawa: Queen's Printers, 1999); Ignatious F. Gqiba and Sybrand van Niekerk. "The Role and Influence of Chaplains in the South African National Defence Force" (unpublished paper, University of South Africa, Pretoria, 2003).

50. Dayne Nix, "Chaplains Advising Warfighters on Culture and Religion," in *Military Chaplains in Afghanistan, Iraq, and Beyond: Advisement and Leader Engagement in Highly Religious Environments*, edited by Eric Patterson (Lanham, MD: Rowman & Littlefield, 2014), 8.

51. Jon Cutler, "Peace Building through Religious Engagement in East Africa," in *Military Chaplains in Afghanistan, Iraq, and Beyond: Advisement and Leader Engagement in Highly Religious Environments,* edited by Eric Patterson, 113–28 (Lanham, MD: Rowman & Littlefield, 2014). See also Kim Philip Hansen, *Military Chaplains and Religious Diversity* (New York: Palgrave Macmillan, 2012); Steve K. Moore, *Military Chaplains as Agents of Peace: Religious Leader Engagement in Conflict and Post-Conflict Environments* (Lanham, MD: Lexington Books, 2014).

52. Hoyt, "Iraqi Inter-Religious Congress," 79, citing James Baker III and Lee H. Hamilton, *The Iraq Study Group Report,* 46.

53. Alex Thompson, "Religious Leader Engagement in Southern Afghanistan," *Joint Forces Quarterly* 63 (2011), 96; Lee, Burke, and Crayne, "Military Chaplains as Peace Builders," 3–4.

54. George Adams, "Chaplains as Liaisons with Religious Leaders," *Peace Works* no. 56 (2006), 5–6., United States Institute of Peace, www.usip.org/files/resources/PWmarch2006_2.pdf.

55. Adams, "Chaplains as Liaisons with Religious Leaders," 29.

56. Hoyt, "Iraqi Inter-Religious Congress."

57. Lee, Burke, and Crayne, "Military Chaplains as Peace Builders," 18; Adams, "Chaplains as Liaisons with Religious Leaders," 27; Thompson, "Religious Leader Engagement in Southern Afghanistan."

58. Hoyt, "Iraqi Inter-Religious Congress," 8.

59. Ibid., 13.

60. Chris Seiple, "Ready . . . or Not?: Equipping the U.S. Military Chaplain for Inter-Service Liaison," *Review of Faith in International Affairs* 7, no. 4 (2009): 43–49; Adams, "Chaplains as Liaisons with Religious Leaders"; Lee, Burke, and Crayne, "Military Chaplains as Peace Builders"; Douglas Johnston and Brian Cox, "Faith-Based Diplomacy and Preventive Engagement," in *Faith-Based Diplomacy,* edited by Douglas Johnston, 11–29 (Oxford: Oxford University Press, 2003). For a dissenting opinion on constitutional grounds, see Ed Waggoner, "Assessing the Role of Chaplains in the U.S. Armed Forces," paper presented at the annual meeting of the Southern Political Science Association, New Orleans, January 3, 2007.

61. Nix, "Chaplains Advising Warfighters," drawing on Douglas Johnston, "Religion, Culture and Globalization" (unpublished manuscript, FY01 PDTC Course Material, 2001).

62. Joint Chiefs of Staff, *Religious Affairs in Joint Operations,* JP 1-05 (Washington, DC, November 20, 2013), II-1.

63. U.S. Army, *Religious Support,* 3–5.

64. U.S. Marine Corps, *Religious Ministry in the United States Marine Corps,* MCWP 6-12, 2001, 4–5, www.combatindex.com/store/MCWP/Sample/.../MCWP_6-12.pdf.

65. Joint Chiefs of Staff, "Religious Affairs in Joint Operations," (2013), A-1, A-2.

66. Joint Chiefs of Staff, "Religious Affairs in Joint Operations," (2009), III-5.

67. Adams, "Chaplains as Liaisons with Religious Leaders," 16.

68. This section is based, in part, on Ron E. Hassner, "Religious Intelligence," *Terrorism and Political Violence* 23, no. 5 (2011): 684–710.

69. James Aho, *Religious Mythology and the Art of War: Comparative Religious Symbolism of Military Violence* (Westport: Greenwood Press, 1981); R. Scott Appleby, *The Ambivalence of the Sacred: Religion, Violence, and Reconciliation* (Lanham, MD: Rowman & Littlefield, 2000); Mark Juergensmeyer, *Terror in the Mind of God: The Global Rise of Religious Violence* (Berkeley: University of California Press, 2000).

70. Alexander De Juan and Andreas Hasenclever, "Framing Religious Conflicts—the Role of Elites in Religiously Charged Civil Wars," *Politische Vierteljahresschrift* 43 (2009): 178–205; Monica Duffy Toft, "Getting Religion? The Puzzling Case of Islam and Civil War," *International Security* 31, no. 4 (2007): 97–131; Jonathan Fox, "Religion and State Failure: An Examination of the Extent and Magnitude of Religious Conflict from 1950 to 1996," *International Political Science Review* 25, no. 1 (2004): 55–76.

71. Mircea Eliade, *Patterns in Comparative Religion* (New York: New American Library, 1974), 375.

72. Gerardus van der Leeuw, *Religion in Essence and Manifestation* (Princeton: Princeton University Press, 1986), 386; Barbara C. Sproul, "Sacred Time," in *Encyclopedia of Religion*, edited by Mircea Eliade, Vol. 12, 535–44 (New York: Macmillan, 1987); Mircea Eliade, *The Sacred and the Profane* (New York: 1959), 7.

73. Ron E. Hassner, *War on Sacred Grounds* (Ithaca: Cornell University Press, 2009); Joel P. Brereton, "Sacred Space," in *The Encyclopedia of Religion*, edited by Mircea Eliade, Vol. 12, 526–35 (New York: Macmillan, 1987); Clinton Bennett, "Islam," in *Sacred Place*, edited by Jean Holm, 88–114 (London: Pinter, 1994).

74. On religious ideas versus practice, see Bruce Lincoln, *Holy Terrors: Thinking about Religion after September 11* (Chicago: University of Chicago Press, 2003), 7–18, 73; Ernest Gellner, *Postmodernism, Reason and Religion* (London: Routledge, 1992), 9–22.

75. Robert H. Scales Jr, "Culture-Centric Warfare," *United States Naval Institute Proceedings* 130, no. 10 (2004): 32–36. See also Patrick Porter, "Good Anthropology, Bad History: The Cultural Turn in Studying War," *Parameters* 37, no. 2 (2007): 45–58; Max Boot, "The Struggle to Transform the Military," *Foreign Affairs* 84, no. 2 (2005): 103–18.

76. U.S. Army, *Counterinsurgency*. FM 3-24 (Washington, DC, December 15, 2006), esp. 1/15, 3/8.

77. Roberto J. Gonzales, "Towards Mercenary Anthropology? The New U.S. Army Counterinsurgency Manual FM 3-24 and the Military-Anthropology Complex," *Anthropology Today* 23, no. 3 (2007), 19. See also the reflections symposium articles on academics and military practitioners in *Perspectives on Politics* 8, no. 4 (December 2010): 1077–124.

78. Gonzales, "Towards Mercenary Anthropology?" 16. Hugh Gusterson goes a step further by describing the involvement of anthropologists in counterinsurgency campaigns as "prostituting ourselves as hired intelligence gatherers." "Anthropologists and War: A Response to David Kilcullen," *Anthropology Today* 23, no. 4 (2007), 23. See also Patricia Cohen, "Panel Criticizes Military's Use of Anthropologists," *New York Times*, December 4, 2009, C2.

79. Eli Kintisch, "Defense, NSF Team up on National Security Research," *Science* 321, no. 5886 (2008), 186; Patricia Cohen, "Pentagon to Consult Academics on Security," *New York Times*, June 18, 2008, 1.

80. Seiple, "Ready . . . or Not?"; Adams, "Chaplains as Liaisons with Religious Leaders."

81. Jacob Kipp, Lester Grau, Karl Prinslow, and Don Smith, "The Human Terrain System: A CORDS for the 21st Century," *Military Review* 86, no. 5 (2006): 8–15; Montgomery McFate and Janice Laurence, "Unveiling the Human Terrain System," in *Social Science Goes to War: the Human Terrain System in Iraq and Afghanistan*, edited by Montgomery McFate and Janice Laurence (London: Hurst/New York: Oxford University Press, 2015).

82. Kipp, Prinslow, and Smith, "The Human Terrain System," 13–15.

83. Several of these ideas were originally proposed in Montgomery McFate, "An Organizational Solution for DOD's Cultural Knowledge Needs," *Military Review* 85, no. 4 (2005): 18–21; Montgomery McFate, "The Military Utility of Understanding Adversary Culture," *Joint Forces Quarterly* 38, no. 3 (2005): 42–48.

84. McFate and Laurence, "Unveiling the Human Terrain System," 21.

85. Ibid., 36.

86. A thorough critique of HTS appears in Benn Connable, "All Our Eggs in a Broken Basket: How the Human Terrain System Is Undermining Sustainable Military Cultural Competence," *Military Review* 89, no. 2 (2009): 57–64.

87. McFate and Laurence, "Unveiling the Human Terrain System."

INDEX

Abbey of Monte Cassino in WWII, 20–26, 70, 172n65
Abizaid, John P., 139
Afghanistan
    chaplains liaison role, 151–52
    decision-making in, 7
Alexander, Howard, 21–23, 26
al-Faydi, Muhammad Bashar, 146
Allenby, Edmund, 55
Al Qaeda, 5
al-Sadr, Moktada, 147
al-Sistani, Ali, 147
American Commission for the Protection and Salvage of Artistic and Historic Monuments in War Areas. *See* Roberts Commission
anthropologists as advisors, 158–59, 214n78
Arab-Israeli War (1973), 30
    Sinai Peninsula invasion, Operation Badr, 41

Bachrach, David, 113
"Bädeker Blitz," 62
Basilica of Notre Dame de Brebieres, 56
Belgium, "Rape of Belgium," 59
Benedict XV, Pope, 38, 97
bin Laden, Osama, 26, 139
Brooks, Risa, 34
Bryce Committee (United Kingdom), 59
Bundy, Harvey H., 81–82

calendars. *See* sacred time
Casey, George W., 139
Catholicism
    altar stones and mass kits carried into battle, 116
    Catholic last rites, 11–14, 105
cause of war, 5–6
centrality of religion in conflict, ranking of, 155–56
chaplain field manuals (U.S.), 90, 98, 123–24
    Religious Affairs in Joint Operations, 149–50, 152

chaplain handbook (British), 90
chaplains
    acts of courage, 102–5
    advising commanders, 152–53
    battlefield spies, accusations, 159
    burial of dead, 92
    Catholic last rites, 11–14, 105
    combat motivation, 88, 89–91
    Council of Imams and Council of Bishops and, 151
    counselors, emotional and military, 93, 94
    discipline and religious practice, 91, 123
    fatalities in WWI, 11–13
    liaison role, 150–52
    morale of soldiers and, 105–9
    non-religious aspects of, 92
    Operation Desert Shield and camouflage covered bibles, 115
    Padre's Hour, 94
    physical presence on front lines, 11–13, 103–5, 130–31
    sermons, themes of, 94–96
    sex education instruction, 94
    treatment as POWs, 102, 106–7
    vulnerability on battlefield, 101–3
    See also sacred leaders
Chartres Cathedral, 83–84
Christmas
    Operación Navidad, Columbia, 38–39
    truce of 1914, 38
Churchill, Winston, 61, 63, 65, 112
Columbia, Operación Navidad, 38–39
Corby, William, 103, 116
Coventry Cathedral, 61
Crimean War, British chaplain deaths, 170n46
Crusades, inspiration in Antioch, 110
Currey, Cecil, 47

Davidson, Irving, 93
Davidson, Randall, 97
Davis, Jefferson, 118
Dayan, Moshe, 48

Diamare, Gregorio, 21
Doolittle, Jimmy, 66

Eban, Abba, 45
Eden, Anthony, 62
Egypt, 30
  Sinai Peninsula invasion, Operation
    Badr, 41
Eisenhower, General Dwight, 23, 57, 64, 69
Elazar, David, 49
Eliade, Mircea, 29
England
  aerial bombing of churches, 60–61
  Coventry Cathedral and retribution, 61
  decline in organized religion post WWI,
    129
  exploitation, 16–18
  sacred space, 57–59, 181n24
  sacred time, 19, 41
  sacred time in reliously motivated
    conflicts, 142

Falkenhayn, Erich von, 55
Florence, and Roberts Commission work,
    78–80
Foundation for Relief and Reconciliation
    in the Middle East, 151
France
  Rheims Cathedral, shelling of, 60
  "the Miracle of the Marne," 112

Gamasy, Mohammed Abdel Ghani El-, 47, 50
Geneva Convention (1864), Additional
    Protocols (1977), 102
Germany
  days of prayer, 118–19
  Lübeck, 62
Giap, Vo Nguyen, 43, 47
Gleig, George, 90
Goldstein, Baruch, 41
Graves, Robert, 130
Gwynne, Llewellyn H., 97, 100, 108

Haig, Douglas, 90, 100, 108
Hajime Sugiyama, 42
Harris, Arthur, 59
Hilldring, John H., 81
Hirohito, Emperor, 42
Hitler, Adolph, 70, 71, 72
holy days. See sacred time
holy sites. See sacred space
Horowitz, Elliott, 41
Hoyt, Michael, 151, 152
Human Terrain System, 159–60

Hunter, John McKie, 106
Huntington, Samuel, 3–5, 26, 165n6
Hussein, King (Jordan), 55

India
  Indo-Pakistani wars, religious-identity
    element, 136
  Operation Blue Star (Sikh Golden
    Temple complex), 45–46
  Sikh *granthis* and Guru Granth Sahib, 115
inhibition
  sacred space, 19, 144
  sacred time, 30, 36–39
Iran, Fordow uranium enrichment facility,
    63
Iran-Iraq War
  Operation Ramadan, 41, 176n43
  religious-identity element, 136
Iraq
  decision-making in, 7
  insurgents and Christian sabbath, 35
  Iraq war, Muslim forces' role, 148
  Iraq War, role of religion, 137
  Iraq war, U.S. forces in, 147–49
  Muslim or non-Muslim assaults, 144–46
  "no strike" list (NSL), 148
  Sabbath attacks on Christians, 142,
    210n22, 210n23
Iraq Interreligious Congress (IIRC), 151
Ireland, Easter Rising of 1916, 39–40,
    175n38
Irish Brigade, 169n38
Islam
  Ashura massacre, 145
  Eid al-Adha and Eid al-Fitr, reduction in
    attacks, 141, 210nn18-19
  Eid al-Fitr, 44
  global terrorism, and, 8
  instruction manual of terrorists, 136
  "Pork Eating Crusader" on European
    and U.S Soldiers, 133
  Shi'a, Ashura and martyrdom of
    Hussein, 40
  violence reduction on Fridays, 139–41,
    209n15, 209n17
  See also Ramadan
Israel, 50
  accusations of "Holy War," 132–33
  Operation Cast Lead and vision of
    Rachel, 111
  Operation Defensive Shield, 45
  Operation Opera, Shavuot, 173n8
  Passover Massacre (Hamas), 45
  Sabbath attacks by, 35, 173n8

Six Day War, 95
Yom Kippur War, 30, 40, 45, 47–51, 176n39
See also Judaism
Italy
damage to cultural monuments, 60
Pisa, 58, 81, 181n23
See also Abbey of Monte Cassino in
WWII; Florence; Rome

Janabi, Abdullah, 146–47
Japan, 115–16
Jerusalem, 55
Johnson, Kermit, 100
Judaism
King Ptolemy I, conquers Jerusalem, 42
Maccabees and Sabbath battle, 42
Purim, 34, 41

Keeble, Chris, 122
Kennedy, G. A. Studdert, 105
Kesselring, Albert, 21, 72
Kilcullen, David, 158
Kipling, Rudyard, 118
Kippenberger, Howard, 21
Kluck, Alexander von, 111
Korea, POW camps, 196n147

Lateran Treaty of 1929, 66
Layton, Rear Admiral Edwin T., 43
leadership, sacred time and, 30, 33–36
Lee, Robert E., 36
Leonard, Stewart, 84
Lincoln, Abraham, 36, 118–19
local population
awareness of religious practices, 19
chaplains liaison role, 151, 152–53
combatants use of sacred space, and, 144
cooperation of, 77
desecration of religious sites, and, 75–76
Najaf, Shrine of Ali standoff, 146–47
salience of religious observance, 156
Logue, Cardinal Michael, 12
Loveland, Anne, 94
Luftwaffe, aerial bombing and churches, 56

Marshall, George C., 62, 64, 123
McClellan, George B., 37
McFate, Montgomery, 158
McLeish, Archibald, 82
medieval warfare and religion, 113–14
mental health. *See* sacred rituals: mental
health and resilience
military discipline, impact of, 15, 18, 35
military effectiveness, rituals, impact of, 35

military operations
control of religion, 20
effects of religious practices, 7, 27–28
use of religion in, 15, 18–19, 157
Milosevic, Slobodan, 39, 138
Monte Cassino. *See* Abbey of Monte
Cassino in WWII
Montgomery, Bernard Law, 90, 108, 118
"monuments men." *See* Roberts Commission
mosques, 62–63
Abdul Aziz al-Samarrai mosque, 149
Al-Basrah mosque dome, 62
ammunition storage in, 146–47
"no strike" list (NSL), 148
Ramadi coalition attack, 146
Shi'a and Sunni fighting, 145–46
use by insurgents, 147
motivation
prominence in conflict, and, 154
sacred leaders and, 88, 89–91, 93–94
sacred time and, 30, 39–41
Mussolini, Benito, 71

Naismith, James, 92
New Zealand, Flagstaff War, Maori
uprising, 42
Nimitz, Chester W., 109
9/11, 3, 5
instruction manual of terrorists, 136

O'Callahan, Joseph, 122
Omar, Abdullah Abu, 146
O'Neill, James H., 110–11
Osami Nagano, 42

Pakistan, Kargil War, Operation Badr, 41
Patton, George, 110–11, 119
peace-making, influence on, 8
Pershing, John Jay, 108
Petraeus, David, 149
Plumer, Herbert, 108
Portal, Sir Charles, 58, 64
Powell, Colin, 147
prayer
Congressional order of prayer, 118
days of prayer, 118–19
effect of prayers before Battle of El
Alamein, 118
miracles and, 110–12
prayer "against firearms," 122
proclamations of day of prayer, 118–19
public prayer ceremonies, 118–19
soldiers' private and group prayer, 119–22,
201n74

Proctor, Redfield, 90
prominence of religion in a conflict, 154–55
protective charms, during modern warfare,
    114–15
provocation
    German Propaganda Ministry, 60
    sacred leaders and, 88
    sacred space, 59–62
    sacred space and, 143
    sacred time and, 30, 44–45

Ramadan, 34, 35
    and attacks by the West, 138
    Battle of Badr, 40–41, 50, 179n100
    Iraqi insurgency (2003), 139
    Operation Ramadan, 41
    violence during, 209n16
    Yom Kippur War and, 50
religion
    as a cause of war, 3–6
    definition of, 8–10, 168n24, 168n33
    force multiplier or divider, 1–2, 17, 20,
        30–31, 53, 135, 156
    nature of war, and, 1, 7–8
    See also exploitation; inhibition;
        motivation; provocation
religiosity, effects of war on, 126–32
religious conflicts, explicit, 135–37
religious environment
    compliance and desecration, 15–18
    military training and, 18
religious identity, role of, 4–5, 144
religious intelligence, 153–60
religious leaders. See sacred leaders
religious practices, 6, 8, 10–11, 168n34
Riesebrodt, Martin, 9–10
Roberts Commission, 54, 72–78, 181n24,
    186n104
    architectural treasures of France, 82–83
    conduct of war, and, 78–82
    countering Axis propaganda, 77
    impact, 78–84
    mission and procedures, 72–74
    priorities of, 74–77, 186n113
Rome
    American attitude toward monuments, 71
    bombing of, 25–26, 62–69
    British debate on bombing, 70–71
    German attitude towards, 71, 72
    Lateran Treaty of 1929, 66
    liberation, 69–72
    Roberts Commission work, and, 78–79
Roosevelt, Franklin D., 24, 44, 64–65, 68,
    70, 71

Rosecrans, William, 36
Royal Air Force (RAF)
    aerial bombing and churches, 60
    chaplain survey, 99
Russia
    Orthodox blessing of military equipment,
        116
    Orthodox priests and blessed icon, 115

Sabbath
    Civil War, restrictions on fighting,
        36–37
    Flagstaff War, Maori uprising, 42
    Israel Air Force actions on, 35
    King Ptolemy I, conquers Jerusalem, 42
    Maccabees and, 42
    Native American attacks on colonial
        settlers, 176n50
    Pearl Harbor attack, 42–43, 44, 177n71
Sachs, Paul, 73
sacred authority, 2
    See also chaplains; sacred leaders
sacred leaders
    attempts to constrain war, 97–101
    counseling, 93–94
    effectiveness, 105–9
    instructing, 94–95
    Iraq counterinsurgency, 149–53
    motivating, 89–97
    preaching, 95–97
    sources of distraction, 91–92
    sources of morality, discipline, and
        morale, 91–97
    vulnerability and provocation, 101–5
    See also chaplains; sermons, themes of
sacred relics, 115–16
    blessing of soldiers, 116–17
    Orthodox blessing of military equipment,
        116
sacred rituals, 11, 110–34
    blessing of equipment, 200n44
    Catholic last rites, 11–14, 105
    compulsory attendance at chapel services,
        117
    loss of faith, 127, 130, 205n120
    mental health and resilience, 123–26,
        131–32
    "Psalm 91 Camo Bandana," 121, 202n77
    religiosity in wartime, 126–27
    services prior to battle, 118
    suicidality and, 124–25
    unanswered questions, 132–34
    See also prayer; protective charms; sacred
        relics

sacred space, 7, 52–54
  churches during WWI and WWII, 55–61, 85–86
  exploitation, 57–59
  force multiplying effect of, 53, 63, 143
  Geneva Convention (1977) Protocols, 180n1
  Hague Convention, Article 27, 53
  in Iraq counterinsurgency, 144–49
  motivation, 55–57
  provocation, 59–63
  tactical advantage by insurgents, 143–44
  See also Abbey of Monte Cassino in WWII; Jerusalem; mosques; Roberts Commission; Rome; World War II
sacred space, symbols of
  L'Ange ou Sourir, 60
  "Leaning Virgin" of Albert, 56
sacred time
  conflict initiation, 36
  constraints in counterinsurgencies, 138
  "Crispin Effect," 176n40
  decline in Sabbath observance, 37
  definition, 31–33, 173n3
  exploitation, 41–44
  force-multiplying effects, 33–35
  importance ranking by practitioners, 32–33
  inhibition, 36–39
  intentional timing, 46, 178n81
  in Iraq counterinsurgency, 139–42
  martial symbols and, 34
  motivation, 39–41
  provocation, 44–46
  role in modern warfare, 51
  sensitive dates, impact of, 7, 141
  understanding of other, 50–51
  war initiation, 30
Sadat, Anwar el-, 47
Schwarzkopf, Norman, 95–96
Scott, Frederick George, 93, 97
Serbia
  Orthodox Easter, 138
  Vidovdan, defeat by Ottomans, 39
sermons, themes of
  divine protection, 95–96
  influence of military leaders, 100–101
  religious justification of military objectives, 96–97, 100
Shazly, Saad al, 48
Sikhism, Operation Blue Star (Sikh Golden Temple complex), 45–46
Sinclair, Archibald, 64
Somervell, Brehon, 108

South Africa, reconciliation role of chaplains, 150
Sri Lanka, reincarnation and coping with combat trauma, 125
Steele, John W., 99
Stimson, Henry L., 64, 119
Stout, George, 76
Strenski, Ivan, 9
Stumm, Baron Gustav Braun von, 62
Sulzberger, Cyrus L., 22

terrorists and terrorism, 5–6
Therese of Lisieux, Saint, 111
Thwaites, Sir William, 100
Tittmann, Harold H., 68

United States
  Afghanistan war and Ramadan, 138–39
  Battle of Okinawa, 46
  Congressional order of prayer, 118
  First Gulf War, 138, 208n6
  Operation Desert Fox, 138
  Operation Desert Storm, 95–96
  Pearl Harbor attack, 42–43, 44
  Second Gulf War, liaison role of chaplains, 150–51
  "Shield of Strength," 115
  Tet Offensive, 43–44, 45, 47
  See also Iraq; World War I; World War II
"Uriah's Law," 103
U.S. Civil War
  Gettysburg chaplain bravery, 103
  Irish Brigade deaths, 169n38
  proclamations of days of prayer, 118–19
  religiosity in, 127–29
  Sabbath restrictions on fighting, 36–37
Ushakov, Fyodor, 115

Vatican, 64–66, 68
  Pacem in Terris (1963) and Gaudium et Spes (1965), 97
  See also Abbey of Monte Cassino in WWII; Rome
Vietnam War
  decrease in religiosity, 131–32
  Tet Nguyen Dan holiday, 43–44, 45, 47, 178n83

Walzer, Michael, 166n8
Washington, George, 123
Wellington, Duke of, 108
Westmoreland, General William, 43
Winter, Ofer, 132

World War I
  British chaplain deaths, 11–14, 169nn35–37,
    170n45
  British chaplains and front lines, 170n39
  Catholic University library and church
    (Leuven), 59
  Christmas truce of 1914, 38
  death penalty for cowardice abolished, 89
  feast of St. Vitus and Serbian defeat, 39, 40
  impact on religion, 130
  Jerusalem in, 55
  "Leaning Virgin" of Albert, 56
  "the Miracle of the Marne," 112
  missionary role, hope for, 129
  Muslim chaplains employed by Germans,
    106
  Passchendaele offensive, 96, 97
  prayer "against firearms," 122
  Rheims Cathedral, shelling of, 60
  St. Martin's Cathedral (Ypres), 53
World War II
  Allied policy toward historic and religious
    buildings, 23, 54, 71, 74–77, 80–83
  Allied policy toward Japanese and
    non-Western shrines, 75–76

  Battle of Okinawa, 46
  bombing, accuracy of, 187n137
  Cathedral of Saint Paul (London),
    56–57
  church spires as visual guides, 58
  crew of *Enola Gay* blessed, 116
  effect of prayers before Battle of El
    Alamein, 118
  impact on religion, 131, 206n151
  Lindemann Memorandum on dehousing
    and morale, 58–59
  "monuments men" during liberation, 82
  Pearl Harbor attack, 42–43, 44
  Royal Welch Fusiliers' prayer, 121
  See also Abbey of Monte Cassino in
    WWII; Italy; Rome

Yom Kippur War. *See* Israel: Yom
  Kippur War
Yugoslavia, 3
  ethnic cleansing campaign on
    Eid al-Fitr, 44
  mediation role of chaplains, 150

Zabelka, George, 116